LITERARY

STUDIES

A NORTON GUIDE

M. A. R. Habib (D.Phil. Oxford) has taught both literature and composition for over twenty-five years in various schools and cultures, at both undergraduate and graduate levels. In addition to serving as director of the writing and undergraduate literature programs at Rutgers University, Professor Habib is the author of ten books, including *Literary Criticism from Plato to the Present: An Introduction* (2011) and *Hegel and the Foundations of Literary Theory* (2019).

LITERARY
STUDIES

A NORTON GUIDE

M. A. R. HABIB

RUTGERS UNIVERSITY

GULF UNIVERSITY FOR SCIENCE AND
TECHNOLOGY, KUWAIT

W. W. NORTON   NEW YORK   LONDON

W. W. Norton & Company has been independent since its founding in 1923, when William Warder Norton and Mary D. Herter Norton first published lectures delivered at the People's Institute, the adult education division of New York City's Cooper Union. The firm soon expanded its program beyond the Institute, publishing books by celebrated academics from America and abroad. By midcentury, the two major pillars of Norton's publishing program—trade books and college texts—were firmly established. In the 1950s, the Norton family transferred control of the company to its employees, and today—with a staff of five hundred and hundreds of trade, college, and professional titles published each year—W. W. Norton & Company stands as the largest and oldest publishing house owned wholly by its employees.

Composition by Westchester Publishing Services
Manufacturing by LSC Communications, Crawfordsville
Book design by Marisa Nakasone
Production manager: Elizabeth Marotta

Library of Congress Cataloging-in-Publication Data
Names: Habib, Rafey, author.
Title: Literary studies : a Norton guide / M.A.R. Habib.
Description: New York : W.W. Norton & Company, [2020] | Includes bibliographical
    references and index.
Identifiers: LCCN 2019031026 | ISBN 9780393937954 (paperback) |
    ISBN 9780393427165 (epub)
Subjects: LCSH: Literature—Study and teaching. | Literature—History and criticism.
Classification: LCC PN59 .H26 2020 | DDC 807—dc23
LC record available at https://lccn.loc.gov/2019031026

ISBN: 978-0-393-93795-4 (pbk.)

W. W. Norton & Company, Inc., 500 Fifth Avenue, New York, NY 10110
wwnorton.com

W. W. Norton & Company Ltd., 15 Carlisle Street, London W1D 3BS

1 2 3 4 5 6 7 8 9 0

CONTENTS

PART THREE   Elements of Literature

PART FOUR   Historical Periods

PART FIVE   Literary Criticism and Theory

PART SIX　Writing about Literature

PREFACE

The aim of this book is to serve as a guide that students will find easy to use. During my time as director of the Writing Program and director of undergraduate studies at Rutgers University, I experimented with many guides and handbooks. Some were well written and full of useful information. But nearly all suffered from the same problem: students were reluctant to read them.

The main reason seemed to be that these books went into too much detail and were too long. Nowadays, students struggle to manage their time; most simply don't have the luxury of doing *extra* reading before turning to their actual assignments. Many students have told me that they find handbooks and guides to be too wordy.

Over the past few years, I have tested various chapters of this guide with almost two hundred students. I have done my best to accommodate their criticisms and suggestions. I have also shown many parts of the book to university colleagues and high school teachers, and I have learned enormously from their insights. The result, I hope, is a book that is readable, enjoyable, and easy to use. Here are some of the features that I believe will make the book helpful:

- **User-friendliness.** Every section of the book is designed to be skimmed, to be taken in at a glance. Even the sections on deconstruction and postcolonial criticism are only about three pages long. They give the students only the essential information—which students can always build on, should they so wish, by consulting more specialized studies. Even in the more substantial historical sections, students need to refer only to the relevant sections. A student working on Alexander Pope, for example, can go right to the "neoclassicism" section.

- **Overview of literary studies.** The *Guide* gives a clear overview of the field, its rapidly changing nature, and what students can do with their knowledge of literary studies in their professional lives.

- **Rubric for reading and writing.** The *Guide* offers students a rubric for reading and analyzing any literary text, which they can modify or adapt as they see fit.

- **A simple guide to documentation and research.** Again, most students don't want to sift through dozens of pages of instructions. What they need to know regarding documentation and research are a few basics. They can always turn to detailed guides if they need more specialized information.

Given how much the fields of English and literary studies have changed over the past decade or so, it's important that any guide to these fields be up-to-date not only in the material it includes but also in its approach. Over the past several years, I have been deeply involved in the sometimes arduous process of instituting curricular changes, at both departmental and university-wide levels. Again, I have learned a great deal from both my colleagues and the administrators involved in these endeavors, not to mention my students. As a result of my research and numerous conversations, I have tried to produce a book that is consonant with contemporary discourses in a number of ways:

- **Figures of speech.** The chapter on figures of speech offers definitions of terms that students are expected to learn. It also explains these figures as functions of "ordinary" language use. In the process, it shows students how to use these literary devices to analyze literary texts across a range of historical periods.

- **Contemporary genres.** It's necessary for students to situate their study of literature in the world of multimedia that surrounds them, and to be able to apply and extend their skills of literary analysis to all kinds of "texts." Students are often asked in litera-ture programs to discuss films and even video games. Hence, this book's discussion of genre extends to electronic and digital genres, offering basic guidance on how to analyze a television program, a film, and a video game.

- **World literature and global studies.** Students need to be aware of these rapidly growing fields for both their academic and their pro-fessional lives. The *Guide* includes a chapter on analyzing world literature as well as a section on global studies.

- **Historical periods.** Most students (including many graduate stu-dents) have little knowledge of history or what the features are of, say, classicism and Romanticism. The chapters in this section sketch the main characteristics of various historical eras and offer sample analyses of texts from them. I have included brief sections on Plato and Aristotle because it may be helpful for students of lit-erature to know something about the foundations of Western thought—which are later impugned by much theory.

These are some of the aims of the *Guide*. I hope that students using this book will emerge not only with improved reading and writing skills and greater knowledge of literary techniques and terms, but also with a deepened ability to think and to contextualize, as well as a sense of his-tory and of the process of globalization. All these skills are valued today not only in education but also in the workplace, by employers of all types. I hope that this book will help students to see the rich potential of the humanities and to begin realizing that potential in their own lives.

I owe a debt of gratitude to many students and colleagues, but I will espe-cially thank here Angela Miller, Sarah Skochko, Advait Ubhayakar, Wil-liam Fitzgerald, Travis Dubose, Barbara Lee, Joe Barbarese, Lisa Zeidner, Terry Eagleton, Ron Bush, Fredric Jameson, the late Frank Kermode, and the chief librarian at Rutgers, Julie Still. I am profoundly grateful to them for their time, insight, and expertise. I should like to add a note of thanks to the editors at Norton, Marian Johnson and Alice Falk, for their meticulous reading and emendation of my manuscript, and also to Edwin Jeng and Alice Gribbin, who were very helpful. Finally, I must acknowledge any errors or oversights as entirely my own.

M. A. R. HABIB

PART ONE

LITERARY STUDIES

CHAPTER 1

SO WHAT CAN I DO WITH A DEGREE IN ENGLISH?

In April 2014, a man handed a bank teller a note demanding money, typed in perfect English. The man went on to rob four banks in the Denver metro area within one week. One of the reasons for his "success" was that he communicated clearly. The bank personnel knew exactly what he wanted and were able to cooperate in a prompt and effective manner. An FBI spokesman, Dave Joly, actually praised the robber's notes, saying: "Spelling, punctuation, sentence structure—everything is really done well." Joly pointed out that bank robbers' notes were often so poorly written that tellers could not understand them.[1] Clearly, as this story demonstrates, training in English can be put to all kinds of uses and may be essential to success, even in such unorthodox "professions" as bank robbing.

Fortunately, you have access to many more respectable professions. The skills and training you acquire in the study of literature are fundamental for gaining *any* kind of knowledge, in any field. Those skills—critical reading, contextualization, assessment of various perspectives, the cultivation of an ethical and intellectual identity—will affect every

---

[1] Mark Berman, "Meet the Colorado Bank Robber Dubbed the 'Good Grammar Bandit,'" *Washington Post*, April 8, 2014.

aspect of your life, personal, professional, and civic. I recently spoke with a hiring manager in the field of business and information technology (IT). He told me that the main qualities he looks for in new graduates are the ability to think critically and independently and the ability to display initiative in any situation. These qualities are fostered by training in literary study.

To better understand where a degree in English can take you, let's read a few anecdotes and then consider some harder evidence for why we should be optimistic about literary studies as a major.

From 2008 to 2014 Jane Mendillo was the head of Harvard University's endowment. Her total compensation for her final eighteen months was $13.8 million. She had obtained a BA in English literature from Yale before earning an MBA from the Yale School of Management. From 2012 until December 2017, John Skipper was president of ESPN. He has a BA in English from the University of North Carolina and a master's degree in English literature from Columbia. He does not have an MBA. As these and countless other examples show, the world of business is wide open to English majors.

The presentation skills we learn in literary studies are essential for many fields. For example, in a 2014 article, Mary Elizabeth Williams quotes the journalist Celeste Headlee as saying that her liberal arts education "taught me how to stand in front of a crowd with poise and articulate my thoughts clearly, in a way that others can understand. I can't tell you how many smart people can't influence others because they're nervous, inarticulate, or just plain boring." And former Etsy CEO Chad Dickerson, who described himself as a "proud English major," affirmed that to be successful in modern society "requires a broader understanding of humanity and people."[2]

Moreover, in a study published in 2013, 93 percent of employers surveyed stated that "a candidate's demonstrated capacity to think critically, communicate clearly, and solve complex problems is more important than their undergraduate major." Ninety percent valued "intercultural skills" and "the capacity for continued learning." Among the education practices praised by employers were those "that require students to (a) conduct

---

[2] Mary Elizabeth Williams, "Hooray for 'Worthless' Education!," *Salon*, March 27, 2014.

research and use evidence-based analysis; (b) gain in-depth knowledge in the major and analytic, problem solving, and communication skills; and (c) apply their learning in real-world settings." College students in all majors, according to 80 percent of those surveyed, "should acquire broad knowledge in the liberal arts and sciences." Indeed, 74 percent said that they "would recommend this kind of education to a young person they know as the best way to prepare for success in today's global economy."[3] These findings were confirmed in 2015 in an updated version of this report. Employers continued to value the liberal arts (78%), writing skills (82%), and critical thinking/analytic reasoning (81%).[4]

Employers recognize that breadth of knowledge and depth and variety of skills are more important than narrow specialization. In a 2013 article, Bryan Goldberg remarks that the old adage "a jack-of-all-trades is a master of none" must be discarded, because we live in an era when "experts" are on their way out. "Apple thrived," says Goldberg, "because its CEO was a jack-of-all-trades who stood atop a mountain of experts. And he knew when to listen to each one, and when to stop listening to each one." The twenty-first century, Goldberg concludes, "belongs to the jack-of-all-trades, and the VCs [venture capitalists] and Wall Streeters who put their confidence in the esteemed 'experts' are going to get very badly burned."[5]

Another interesting anecdote is offered by Michael S. Malone, whose friend Santosh Jayaram, "the quintessential Silicon Valley high-tech entrepreneur," said, "English majors are exactly the people I'm looking for." To start up a new company today, "you must spend a year searching for that one undeveloped niche that you can capture. And you must also use that time to find angel or venture investment, establish strategic partners, convince talented people to take the risk and join your firm, explain your

---

[3] "It Takes More Than a Major: Employer Priorities for College Learning and Student Success: An Online Survey among Employers Conducted on Behalf of the Association of American Colleges and Universities," Hart Research Associates, April 10, 2013, pp. 1, 2.

[4] "Falling Short? College Learning and Career Success: Selected Findings from Online Surveys of Employers and College Students Conducted on Behalf of the Association of American Colleges & Universities," Hart Research Associates, January 20, 2015, pp. 3, 4.

[5] Bryan Goldberg, "You Don't Want Experts. You Want Jacks-of-All-Trades," *Pando.com*, March 22, 2013, pando.com/2013/03/22/you-dont-want-experts-you-want-jacks-of-all-trades/.

product to code writers and designers, and most of all, begin to market to prospective major customers. And you have to do all of that without an actual product."

How do we do all this? Jayaram writes, "'You tell stories.' Stories . . . about your product and how it will be used that are so vivid that your potential stakeholders imagine it already exists and is already part of their daily lives." Malone also relates an anecdote about Steve Jobs, who explained why his company is so special: "It's in Apple's DNA that technology alone is not enough—it's technology married with liberal arts, married with the humanities, that yields us the result that makes our heart sing."

Malone concludes that although this is going to be a century of technology, "the edge will go to those institutions that can effectively employ imagination, metaphor, and most of all, storytelling." Such "twenty-first-century storytelling" will use multimedia and must "draw upon the myths and archetypes of the ancient world, on ethics, and upon a deep understanding of human nature and even religious faith."[6]

What all these anecdotes and statistics point to is that while a degree in English or the liberal arts may not prepare you for a specific job, it will give you a foundation or basis for a wide range of careers. No job (unless it involves teaching) is going to ask you to analyze a Shakespeare sonnet; but many jobs will ask you to analyze a report, to read it closely, to assess its strengths and weaknesses. Some jobs will require you to write creatively and persuasively and concisely, with a keen awareness of your audience. Many positions will demand the ability to look at problems from several angles, to consider various perspectives and multiple contexts. And, whatever profession you choose, you will find it crucial not only to present your ideas clearly but also to be able to relate to a variety of people, to discuss a broad spectrum of issues, and to display initiative. For the highest-level positions, you will need a broad vision, one that considers the entirety of a situation and its component parts, as well as the differing personalities and attributes of the people involved, and you will need to be able to develop effective strategies. If you become a politician

[6] Michael S. Malone, "How to Avoid a Bonfire of the Humanities," *Wall Street Journal*, October 24, 2012.

or a policy maker or a lobbyist, or a journalist or corporate executive, you will need *all* of these skills.

Now, let's get a little more specific. Exactly what kinds of careers can one pursue with a degree in English? We can organize numerous jobs under a few main headings: marketing, government, media, and education.

Marketing comprises many different fields. Areas that have attracted English majors include search-engine marketing and mail-based marketing. Both involve helping companies to market their products, but the former uses digital media while the latter relies on letters, flyers, and brochures. Content marketing involves research, and many marketing companies employ digital copywriters and technical writers. Other aspects of marketing include sales, investor relations, corporate blogging, and advertising. All these jobs require analytical and creative skills, as well as the ability to write concisely and clearly. All these fields offer internships.

Government-related jobs include working in public relations, policy analysis, lobbying, and communications. In these fields, you may write news releases, explain government policy to the public, design newsletters and brochures, plan events, write proposals, and give presentations. To do these things, you'll need research skills and the ability to write quickly and accurately. Plus, you'll need to be able to interact effectively with a wide variety of people from different professions. A good way to get started might be to get an internship at a local government office working for a U.S. representative or senator or to volunteer in a political campaign.

The media comprise a vast and growing field, covering all kinds of journalism, online writing, and editing. The combination of an English degree with a qualification in IT or media studies would be a distinct advantage for anyone looking to work in a media job. You might also consider working in social media. Private companies, sports teams, and government agencies hire people to develop social media strategies so that they can engage in the most effective way with their client base.

Education is a world of enormous opportunity, whether you decide to go into teaching or administration. As long as you care about learning and ideas—and people—you can be a passionate teacher. If you are thinking of entering education, you can use your experience in literary studies to improve not only your critical reading and writing skills but also your ability to give effective presentations, lead discussions, and communicate effectively with people from diverse backgrounds.

Whichever field you decide to explore, research it thoroughly. If you make a decision ahead of graduation, you can find out exactly what you need to do, whether it's serving an internship with a company or taking additional courses—perhaps a minor or a second major—in a particular specialty. Seek advice: not only from a career counselor at college but also from people already in the field. In a sense, it doesn't matter which field you choose—or even if you change your mind a few times. Earning a degree in English or the humanities is only a preliminary step, a laying down of vital skills: critical reading, close analysis, vivid writing, effective presenting, and balanced assessment of various perspectives, situations, and audiences. You may find yourself putting these skills to use in a field that hasn't even been invented yet. Above all, you need *passion*—a passion for reading and writing, for being involved, for expressing yourself, and for making a difference in the world—in your own way.

CHAPTER 2

THE NATURE AND SCOPE OF LITERARY STUDIES

THE MEANING OF "LITERARY STUDIES"

What people study in English classes has changed over the past few decades. Largely a creation of the later nineteenth and early twentieth centuries, the Department of English arose partly in response to the professional need of English professors to carve out their own domain. What was important to them was to look at literature *as* literature: in other words, to focus on the literary and aesthetic qualities of the text rather than delve into the author's biography or historical or social circumstances. Those inquiries, the professors felt, would lead away from literature into other disciplines such as psychology, sociology, and history.

The earliest curriculums included mostly courses in English literature, with a handful in American literature. There was an emphasis on Shakespeare, perhaps a class in Chaucer or medieval literature, and courses in Romantic, Victorian, and modern literature, and sometimes linguistics. Alongside literature, composition was also taught—but separately, usually with little or no connection with the literature curriculum. Literature was taught by tenured or tenure-track professors, while composition was taught mainly by adjunct professors and teaching assistants. This is what many English departments looked like as recently as twenty years ago.

But things have changed. Today, if you walk into an English department, you'll find people who teach graphic novels and cartoons; professionals who train students in the uses of digital media and game theory; novelists and poets who conduct workshops in creative writing; academics who teach courses that explore sexuality, gender, and queer theory. You'll meet educators who will help you analyze film and media, as well as the theories behind them. You will find experts who can teach you how to write for diverse professional purposes. There may be a variety of courses in journalism and popular culture, and even courses that have a "civic engagement" or service learning component, which require students to get experience in local community and business settings. You'll be pleasantly surprised to see courses that examine the notions of childhood, privilege, immigration, and exile, as well as translation studies. And of course you will still find professors of literature—who will help you understand literary texts in relation to economic conditions, women's struggles, the history of imperialism, and the rapid globalization of our world. Indeed, the "literature" they teach is from all parts of the world, offering access to many of the world's diverse cultures.

All these teachers have at least two things in common. First, they are all in different ways dealing with important aspects of our lives, ranging from ethnicity and gender to moral and professional decision making. They help you understand your history, your relationship with the past and with other cultures, as well as with the forces shaping the world as we know it. In short, they will help you understand who you are. Second, all these teachers are committed to improving students' reading and writing skills, oral communication and digital presentation skills, and ability to think critically and contextually.

You'll also see that what counts nowadays as a "text" is broad, including not just works of literature but TV news, sitcoms, ads, political speeches, newspaper articles, magazines, comics, and posts on various social media. The skills that we bring to the analysis of a Shakespeare sonnet can also be used in analyzing all these other kinds of "texts." You might, one day, need to analyze a letter from a landlord or an advertisement for a car or a contract from a potential employer. A literary education can give you the tools to do so.

LITERARY STUDIES TODAY

Life is what *all* literature is about. If literature can't somehow be related to crucial dimensions of life, there would be little point in studying it. Many of the debates in English departments over the past few decades reflect this deep-seated desire to study literature in a way that strengthens its connections to the rapidly changing larger world.

One of the fiercest debates has centered on the "canon," or the accepted tradition of literary texts. Conservatives have tended to view the Western canon as a repository of the finest literature produced by European and North American cultures. They see this literature—stretching from Homer and Virgil through Chaucer, Shakespeare, Milton, and the Romantics to T. S. Eliot and James Joyce—as embodying the highest traits and values of Western civilization, or what the nineteenth-century critic Matthew Arnold called "the best which has been thought and said." Others have seen the traditional canon as limited, as expressing the elitist perspectives of "dead white males." Many progressive critics have pointed out the exclusion of ethnic minorities, of women, and of gay and lesbian writers, and have challenged the claim of this tradition to represent "universal" values. Why should students living in inner cities read Shakespeare? they ask. What can *Hamlet* or *Twelfth Night* offer them? Wouldn't they be better off reading Alice Walker or James Baldwin or any number of other writers who present different visions of life? From their perspective the Western tradition is not only racist and sexist but also Eurocentric, always privileging a European (or American) view of the world, always overlooking the diversity offered by the literatures of other cultures.

Since these "canon wars" and "culture wars" erupted in the 1980s and 1990s, things have changed. Curricula now include programs in gender studies, race theory, and cultural studies, incorporating texts from around the globe. Fortunately, Shakespeare is still taught, for he has a lot to teach us about character, emotion, and the clash of varying worldviews. But the "master canon" of the past has by and large given way to a series of mini-canons, each with its own rationale and range of perspectives. How to integrate all this variety into a single overarching vision—and whether it is desirable to do so—still challenges us, but we have undoubtedly made progress toward greater pluralism and diversity, without sacrificing the classics of literature.

Another fundamental question in English departments is, What is the function of criticism? After all, what professors of literature really teach is not "literature" as such but the *criticism* of literature. The word "criticism" comes from a Greek verb that means "to judge." But what does it mean to "judge" a work of literature? Should criticism *describe* what literature does, focusing on its techniques and how its themes develop? Should criticism *evaluate* literature and tell us which works are truly great? Or should it merely *interpret* and explain those works? From the 1940s until the early 1960s, the most popular kind of criticism in America was "practical criticism," popularized by the so-called New Critics: this criticism focused on the text itself, the "words on the page," and tried to offer a detailed account of how the literary work functions as an independent verbal and aesthetic structure, employing irony, ambiguity, paradox, and metaphor.

THE RISE OF THEORY

New Criticism has since given way to much broader concerns and to various theoretical perspectives. Literature is now treated as one type of "discourse" among other cultural discourses, which include media, popular culture, politics, and religion. In these larger contexts, we look at literature in relation to notions of identity, language, gender, race, and the development of democracy and capitalism. Criticism here returns to its broader function of helping to train future citizens, nurturing in them a literary and cultural sensibility that might enhance their broader participation in the public sphere of ethical and political debates.

A closely related dispute concerns the nature of literature itself. Do we appreciate it mainly for its beauty and technical perfection? In other words, is it primarily an aesthetic object? Or is it also important for the moral lessons it imparts and the kinds of knowledge it conveys? For over two thousand years, literature was thought to have two essential tasks— to *delight*, by means of its aesthetic qualities, and to *teach*, both morally and intellectually—which it accomplished mainly through representation, or mimesis (imitation). Literature represented nature, both internal (human) and external, the latter including not just the visible physical world but the entire hierarchy of the cosmos, in which human beings had a predetermined place. Later, literature came to be regarded, notably by the Romantics, as a form of self-expression and self-discovery. In modern times, many critics think of literature not as representative but as "performative," engaging in a linguistic performance that is not necessarily tied to the outside world or even to the internal world of the human psyche.

Again, recent theories engage with these views in complicated ways. For example, the (Romantic) notion of the author as the source of the text and its meaning has been widely challenged. Modern theorists and linguists see the author not as creating anything new but as simply occupying a certain "position" within language, mixing and assembling idioms that are already there. The "reader," too, is not necessarily a homogeneous prefabricated entity but likewise a "position," created by interacting with this text and other texts—as was famously argued by the French critic Roland Barthes in his essay "The Death of the Author" (1968).

Many modern theories are rooted in the acknowledgment that language does not represent reality or the world. There is no one-to-one correspondence between language and the world outside—for example, between the word "table" and an actual table. Rather, the table in the world is seen *through* the concept of a table: it is the *creation* of a human community, of a collective and historical human subjectivity. The same is true even of supposedly natural objects. For example, when we talk about a "tree," we are designating an object that is already invested with meanings that humans have put into the concept. A tree has associations with life, with growth, with age, with shade, with religious conceptions, and with an entire system called "nature." In general, then, language is not somehow separate from some independent reality but instead *contributes to* the creation of that reality, whether we are talking about the reality of the external world or the reality of the human self.

WORLD LITERATURE

Much recent theory has devoted itself to a fascinating debate concerning "world literature." This term refers not to the so-called world masterpieces from Plato to T. S. Eliot, which have been taught in survey courses for years, but rather to an *approach*: viewing literary texts in a global setting. Perhaps we might look at a modernist American text not in relation to the American tradition but in its connections with modernism in other cultures. How do these versions of modernism differ from each other in their worldviews and literary styles? What social and historical factors underlie those differences? Was there any influence between them? For example, modernism in America and Britain was in large part a reaction against the literary realism of the nineteenth century and was heavily influenced by symbolism; but in Arab and Indian traditions, classical literature was already very stylized and symbolic, so "modernism" in those traditions entailed a shift away from symbolism toward realism.

In examining world literature, we consider the transmission of texts between different cultures; we look at how a text is received and read differently in different places. An important part of this process is the study of translation, which has generated heated debates. For example, should African writers write in their native languages, from which their works can then be translated, or in English, which would enable them to directly reach a larger, worldwide audience? Some believe that translation betrays the ethic of the originating culture and yields a work of inferior literary quality. Robert Frost famously said that poetry is "what gets lost in translation." Others hold that certain literatures gain in translation because translation makes them available across many cultures; moreover, because the translation of a work is necessarily also an interpretation, it can help us see aspects of the work that were relatively hidden. Translation studies is a rapidly growing field.

TEACHING LITERATURE

In recent decades, the literature classroom has undergone fundamental changes. Most notably, the old model of transmitting information to passive recipients is gone. When I was an undergraduate in England, learning was formally divided into "passive" and "active" modes. Passive learning occurred when a professor lectured on a broad topic, such as neoclassical poetry; active engagement occurred when we met in tutorial groups with our professor to discuss particular aspects of that topic, such as a poem by Alexander Pope. There is a certain logic to this arrangement: while the lecture provided the broad framework, details and questions could be addressed in the tutorial. In the United States this model still survives in large lecture courses in which aspects of the professor's lecture are discussed in recitation sessions run by teaching assistants.

But what if the lecturer is not interesting or clear? What if the logic of the presentation doesn't make sense to a student? The average attention span is around twenty minutes, and many students will lose interest and focus during a long lecture. More importantly, when we give a lecture—with or without tools such as PowerPoint—we assume that knowledge is something cut-and-dried, fixed and static, that can be simply passed on to our students. Most literature classrooms today are more interactive environments. We know now that students learn best when they are *active* in their learning, and they often learn best from one another. Reading a book on our own is only the first step in acquiring knowledge. Until we think about what we read by writing about it, until we talk about it with others, until we see with their help what the limitations of our ideas are, we have not really engaged with the text, and we have not actively engaged in the process of knowing. Knowledge is not a static thing or entity, but a dynamic *process*, which in its very essence involves interaction with people. Knowledge is dialogic: we acquire it by joining a conversation and finding our own voice within that conversation.

THE PROCESS OF KNOWLEDGE

Some instructors, including myself, begin class by having one or two students give a presentation on a text; it's their job to guide the class through a discussion of that text, identifying and exploring central themes and questions. I often sit at the back of the room for the entire period, and with a particularly good class I can barely get a word in. Teachers find that this format engages the students in a lively discussion and that students take responsibility for their own learning. Yes, instructors can tell them the conventional interpretation of a poem. But each class should be a process of *discovery*—for professors as well as for students; every time I teach a given poem, I leave with a different understanding of it. This process, of course, is not neat; students don't leave with a fixed understanding of what a poem means. In fact, at times we are forced to acknowledge that we still don't understand some elements of a text, even after an hour's discussion. I tell my students that this is okay. The process of knowledge is messy. The process of discovery is not linear and predictable.

However, that process is far more valuable to students than simply parroting an easy interpretation. They have engaged in a conversation, forcing themselves to think deeply and critically and genuinely, instead of pretending to agree with the teacher. In doing this, they have discovered—each of them—what they think of the text. They discover something about themselves in the text; they see themselves in the text; they begin to clarify their own thought processes. More fundamentally, they begin to find their own voice, their own intellectual and ethical identity, within a dialogue that extends beyond the classroom into the larger public conversation, where such issues are fiercely contested.

The value of this process is inestimable. Students begin to acquire a framework for making both intellectual and moral judgments; they see that judgments are historically and culturally conditioned, that there are differing value systems; and their thinking is broadened beyond the mechanized reflexes of thought that suffice in much of daily life. They learn not just to repeat information but to question knowledge, to examine it critically; they learn to look at an issue from diverse angles; and they begin to be aware of a range of perspectives.

Most importantly, these are skills that students will acquire for themselves—not from the instructor—if they are placed into an appropriately supportive atmosphere. And they will have these skills for the rest of their lives, able to apply them whether they are talking in a job interview, negotiating with their landlord or tenants, discussing a situation with a boss or employees, giving an important presentation at work, or even interacting with friends or family members. Once this understanding of "knowledge" takes hold of us, we realize that we have something to say on any issue. If we don't know much about an issue, we realize that we must ask questions. Studying literature helps us to realize that we have a position in the world, a position determined largely by our ability to participate in the world's conversation, by our ability to find our own voice—the mark of our own identity—and to know our position within the larger system of language.

PART TWO

READING
LITERATURE

CHAPTER 3

BASIC READING

The prospect of reading literary texts—and writing about them—can be intimidating as well as exciting. But it's worth remembering that reading and writing are skills that improve with practice; and, as you grow more familiar with and adept at analyzing literature, you'll begin to see how rewarding reading can be. Reading is a process of discovering not only the world but ourselves. No matter what our position in the world is, and no matter how much our narratives change over time, reading and writing are central to our lives. Reading can help us develop a better understanding of our personal narratives, of how we intersect with the larger social fabric, of what our goals might be and how to achieve them. Indeed, it will give us a better understanding of almost every aspect of the world around us, including our domestic and romantic lives and the important moral, economic, and political decisions that we must often make.

WHAT DOES "READING" MEAN?

There are many kinds of reading: we don't read a bus ticket in the same way that we read a Shakespeare play. And we don't read a lunch menu in the same way that we read a note or text message from a friend with whom we've had an argument. To start with the most obvious difference, we are looking for different things in each case: with a bus ticket, we don't care who wrote it—we just want to know that the information about our destination is correct. Our main concern in reading a lunch menu is to find a few items that suit our appetite. When we receive an important note or text, we do of course care intensely about who sent it, how to interpret its every word, and how we might formulate a response. Reading a Shakespeare play draws on a whole different set of concerns. We have to grapple with the general conventions of playwriting, with the challenging language of early modern England, and with the details of character and plot that are specific to the play in question. Plus we have to take into account the author: who was Shakespeare and what do we know about him—and how important is this information to our reading of *Macbeth* or *The Tempest*?

This example makes clear that the kind of reading done in college is intense and detailed. But you'll find it more enjoyable and rewarding if you approach it in a particular way—doing what we can call "academic" reading. What's important to understand about reading for academic purposes is that it's a dynamic process. It involves continued interaction with the text, not passively sitting back and just "receiving" what is written. Each text is initially an "object" in the world, outside of us. We need to internalize it, to make it our own, to make it part of the lens through which we see the world. If I just sit in my room and casually take in the words of a novel or essay, without thinking about them, without trying to understand them, without working out my opinion of them, I have not really "read" the text.

PRELIMINARY STRATEGIES

In order to get the most out of your reading, try some preliminary strategies.

> **Understand *why* you are reading this text (aside from the fact that it's on the syllabus). What are you looking for?**
>
> What is your purpose in reading this text? What are you trying to accomplish? Do you want to summarize it? Are you trying to evaluate

its argument? its structure? its representation of a specific topic such as gender, race, or class? Or are you attempting to grasp its rhetorical qualities and *how* it conveys its message? Once you know your purpose, you'll know what to look for.

Annotate!

Annotating is an indispensable part of the reading process. In order to really engage with a text, you need to make it "yours" by marking it up—underlining or highlighting, and making notes in the margins—thereby creating a kind of personal commentary on it and a personal dialogue with it. Then, when you come back to the text, you don't have to reread the whole thing; you can just glance at what you underlined or highlighted and can easily make notes. For example, whether you are looking for a text's views about religion or trying to summarize its basic argument, highlighting all parts of the text that strike you as important will help you when it comes to writing.

Ask questions about things in the text that you don't understand or that you find controversial.

Many texts are difficult on first (or second) reading, and that's okay; to make texts *less* difficult, identify what you don't understand about them, such as a reference (to a work or thinker or event). After doing a little research and finding some relevant information, reread these parts of the text carefully and see if they are less baffling.

Look up words you don't know.

Though I've been teaching for many years, I still come across words whose meanings I am not sure of, and I make a point of looking them up. Any good desk dictionary, such as *Merriam-Webster's Collegiate*, will provide not only the meaning but also the etymology or origins of a word in a contemporary text (for older texts, the *Oxford English Dictionary* may be necessary). Looking up words helps us improve our vocabulary overall and our ability to express ourselves more accurately and effectively. Plus it helps you get more comfortable in the world of the text you're reading.

Reread the text.

This time, you'll read the text with a sense of its overall structure and how each element contributes to that structure. Do later parts of the text or the ending make you think again about the meanings of earlier passages? Did you miss anything in your initial round of underlining and note-taking? Remember that reading is not a linear process, done just once. Rather, it's a recursive process, as we keep *returning* to a text to arrive at a fresh or increased understanding of it. I often teach texts that I have studied for many years; and I always leave class with a slightly (sometimes drastically) modified understanding of its meaning and significance. I learn a lot from my students because they offer perspectives that are new to me.

Discuss the text with someone else.

It's always good to find out what other people think, how they might disagree with you, and how you might want to modify your views in response. Perhaps they saw something that you missed, or vice versa. It's only when you enter a *conversation* about the text that you begin to understand its full range of significance—a conversation that includes not only other students and the professor but also other teachers, critics, and writers. Sometimes these conversations have been going on for centuries: take Shakespeare—opinions differ widely on the sources of Shakespeare's greatness, on the complex nature of his most challenging characters—Hamlet and Iago, for example—and on the accuracy of the way he represents places he never saw, such as Venice, Cyprus, and Egypt. A large part of the process of being educated is knowing how to find our own voice within, and contribute to, these larger conversations.

PRELIMINARY READING EXERCISE

W. B. Yeats, "When You Are Old" (1893)

Let's apply these strategies to a poem by the Irish poet W. B. Yeats, written when he was young.

When you are old and gray and full of sleep,
   And nodding by the fire, take down this book,
   And slowly read, and dream of the soft look
Your eyes had once, and of their shadows deep;

5   How many loved your moments of glad grace,
   And loved your beauty with love false or true,
   But one man loved the pilgrim soul in you,
And loved the sorrows of your changing face,

And bending down beside the glowing bars,
10   Murmur, a little sadly, how Love fled
   And paced upon the mountains overhead
And hid his face amid a crowd of stars.

Before doing anything else, read the poem aloud to yourself or to someone else. Enjoy the words and their sound, their rhythm. Believe it or not, this is one of the main steps toward understanding the poem. You can also listen to someone else recite it, a friend or on YouTube, and let the poetry work on you. Can you imagine sending or receiving this poem as a Valentine's gift?

Now move on to the first step: what's your **purpose** in reading this poem? What are you looking for? The possibilities are numerous. Your professor might ask you to look for elements of Romanticism in the poem or for biographical elements. Perhaps you will be writing a feminist analysis or comparing this poem to other texts on the subject of love. But no matter what you are looking for, your analysis will be stronger if you can identify the major theme and the stylistic devices used to develop it. In other words, work to understand what the text is saying and how it says it.

To gain this understanding, annotate the text and start asking questions that will help you understand the poem on a basic level.

Preliminary questions: Things I don't understand about Yeats's poem

What does "this book" refer to in line 2? The book of life? experience?

What is meant by "glad grace" in line 5? Elegance? happiness? success?

In stanza 2, what is the difference between "beauty" (loved by the "many") and "the pilgrim soul" (loved by "one man")? Is the former superficial and external, while the latter indicates an inner spiritual journey?

In stanza 3, what is the significance of "bending down"? That the woman is now humbled?

What is the significance of Love hiding his face among "a crowd of stars"? That Love hides from waking reality and drowns himself in sleep?

Once you've answered these questions—at least to some degree—you should have a basic sense of what the poem is saying and can proceed to the next stage of reading, which we can call "critical reading."

CHAPTER 4

CRITICAL READING

W e are now ready to move from *basic* or *preliminary* reading to *critical* reading. The word "critical" implies the making of some kind of judgment or assessment, a response that doesn't just accept a text at face value but analyzes it in some detail. To "analyze" something literally means to break it down. So we need to break down the text into its various components and see how they are put together.

THEME–FORM–CONTEXT FRAMEWORK

Reading a text critically entails addressing a number of elements, such as the theme and style, the circumstances or context in which the text was written, and its purpose and audience. With most texts, we can start by identifying the **theme**. It's worth noting the distinction between theme and **subject matter**, or what the text is about. For example, we might say that James Joyce's story "The Dead" (1914) is about Irish middle-class life or a middle-class man and his wife. But the theme will be something like "death" or "love" or "the inauthenticity of middle-class life." Joseph Conrad's *Heart of Darkness* (1899) is about a voyage up the river Congo; but its theme might be something like "imperial exploitation" or "the breakdown of European values."

Once we've identified the theme(s), we can use a simple pattern or framework for posing further questions. To be sure, there is no formula for analyzing literature, but certain flexible paradigms or frameworks can be useful. The simplest might be **theme–form–context**, which we can break down as follows:

THEME: What is the central idea or argument of the text?

FORM: How does the text express this theme or themes?

CONTEXT:

Rhetorical Situation	**Who** is speaking or narrating the text, and to **whom? Why** did the author write it?
Underlying Assumptions	What is the **worldview** of the text, its basic values and assumptions? **When** and **where** was it written?
Reader/Theory	What is **my** interest in this text? What approach will I take in analyzing it?

We can use this framework to analyze any kind of text, whether a poem by Yeats, an ad on television, a political speech, or even the threat of eviction from a landlord. All questions about the text can be organized under this framework, which we can modify (and expand) according to the type of text we're looking at and the approach we want to take. And the elements don't have to be analyzed in a fixed order. With some texts, we might want to focus on the form; with others, starting with context might be more useful. And with still others, the theme will be most important. But any analysis of a literary text will usually involve some interplay among these three elements.

Here's a longer and more complete version of the theme–form–context framework, which involves the use of ever-wider critical "frames." We begin with the textual frame, focusing on the "text itself." Then we broaden our frame of analysis to include the text's relationship to its author, its rhetorical situation, and its historical and intellectual contexts.

THEME

What **is the central idea?**

What is the basic theme or central idea or argument?

How is the theme developed? Logically, emotionally, through point of view?

Does a central conflict or opposition structure the text?

Does the text convey a moral or lesson?

FORM

How **does the text express the central idea?**

What genre is the text? Lyric, sonnet, epic, tragedy, comedy, fiction?

What literary devices does the text use? Meter, rhyme, symbolism, metaphor, personification, irony, plot, point of view, characterization?

Textual Frame

CONTEXT

Rhetorical situation

Who is the speaker of the text? The author or a persona?

Who is being addressed? A specific person? The general reader?

What may have motivated the author to create the text?

Can we relate the text to an event or circumstance in the author's life?

Rhetorical Frame

Underlying assumptions

What is the worldview of the text, its basic values and assumptions?

When and where was it written?

What is the literary, intellectual, religious, social background of the text?

Literary/ Intellectual/ Historical Frame

Is it classical, medieval, Renaissance, Romantic, modern, postmodern?

How does the text connect to other texts?

What is my interest in this text? What approach will I take in analyzing it?

What do I most relate to in this text?

Does it appeal to my emotions, intellect, or moral sense?

Does it throw light on any aspect of my world and my situation in the world?

Does it help me understand something about myself and my relations with others?

On the basis of my interest, what is my theoretical approach going to be? Liberal humanist, deconstructive, feminist, Marxist, postcolonial, something else?

Reader/ Theoretical Frame

A good starting point for you as a reader is to find a *point of entry* into the text and the larger conversation about it. Try to find *your* perspective, where you stand. This means deciding what strikes you as most important or valuable about the work. You can develop some basic patterns or templates for analyzing the text on the basis of your answers to the questions above. But there is one thing to be clear about: you don't need to answer *all* these questions about every text you read; nor do you need to organize your responses in any particular order. You can choose the questions that interest you the most and start with them. For example, you might want to focus on a poem's style or form. Or your primary concern might be to show how a poem is Romantic or modern, or to relate it to the author's biography, or to analyze its treatment of gender and class. What matters is that your analysis be coherent and use evidence from the text.

CRITICAL READING EXERCISE

W. B. Yeats, "When You Are Old" (1893)

Let's start to analyze Yeats's poem with the help of this framework. Our purpose right now is simply to write a good paragraph. I'll begin by saying that what appeals to me about this poem is its evocation of the sense of loss and the sadness of being able to value something only when it is too late. So my point of entry into the poem is the theme of loss and how it is conveyed. With this in mind, I might make the following notes to answer the *framework* questions about the theme and how it is developed:

The *theme* of this poem is

- the loss of love, and the struggle to communicate that loss.

- how we don't recognize genuine love until it's too late.

To *develop* this theme, the poet

- uses a three-part structure: (1) the poet asks the woman to imagine herself in her old age, (2) he encourages her to reflect on the uniqueness of his love, and (3) he suggests that she will realize, sadly, how genuine love "fled" from her.

- uses a central image, the woman's "pilgrim soul."

This theme is reinforced by several aspects of the poem's *style*:

- It is divided into three quatrains (four-line stanzas), each fulfilling a specific function.

- It uses the rhyme scheme *abba cddc effe*, a kind of "envelope" rhyme (one set of rhymes is "enclosed" within another) called an Italian quatrain.

- The poem repeats the word "and," which makes the verse move slowly, makes it more meditative. It also creates the impression of something accumulating over time, perhaps the sense of loss or regret.

- It personifies "Love," which is described as fleeing and pacing and hiding.

From here it will be easy to write a paragraph, since its template could be

> The theme of this poem is . . . . , which is developed in these ways: a . . . , b . . . , c . . . .

The paragraph might look something like this:

> Yeats's "When You Are Old" is essentially about the sense of loss that the poet feels at having been rejected by a woman, and his attempt to make her feel this as her own loss. The theme of loss is developed in three parts. First, he asks the woman to imagine herself when she is old—when she will remember how she was when she was young. Then he points out to her that he was the only one who loved her genuinely, not only in her moments of "glad grace" but also when she was undergoing sorrow and hardship. Finally, he asks her to admit that she doesn't have real love in her life, that genuine love "fled" with him.

We might now add another paragraph, this time about the poem's *style*. The template here could be

> This theme is reinforced by the following aspects of the poem's style: e . . . , f . . . , g . . . .

Our next paragraph might look like this:

> A number of stylistic elements help develop this theme. To begin, the poem is divided into three quatrains, each fulfilling a specific function. Moreover, the poem uses the rhyme scheme *abba cddc effe*, which is a kind of "envelope" rhyme, whereby one set of rhymes is "enclosed" within another. This type of quatrain is called an Italian quatrain, and the progression of the quatrains through different sets of rhymes gives us the sense that the progression of time is irreversible and the loss of love absolute. But the use of different rhymes in each quatrain also isolates each quatrain from the others, enabling the poet to pause, interrupting his own address to the woman with a general observation in the middle quatrain about the uniquely genuine nature of his love. Finally,

the most prominent literary technique is the personification of love, which reinforces the suggestion that the woman has lost not just this man but love itself.

Now we have two paragraphs, one on the poem's theme and the other on the poem's form.

CRITICAL READING EXERCISE

Matthew Arnold, "The Study of Poetry" (1880)

Here's a famous passage from the nineteenth-century British writer Matthew Arnold, originally published in 1879 and then included in his essay "The Study of Poetry" (1880):

> The future of poetry is immense, because in poetry, where it is worthy of its high destinies, our race, as time goes on, will find an ever surer and surer stay. There is not a creed which is not shaken, not an accredited dogma which is not shown to be questionable, not a received tradition which does not threaten to dissolve. Our religion has materialized itself in the fact, in the supposed fact; it has attached its emotion to the fact, and now the fact is failing it. But for poetry the idea is everything; the rest is a world of illusion, of divine illusion. Poetry attaches its emotion to the idea; the idea *is* the fact. The strongest part of our religion today is its unconscious poetry.

Admittedly, this passage is difficult; but taking an organized approach to it will make it easier to understand. Before using our framework to analyze it, let's ask some questions.

Preliminary questions

To whom does "our race" refer in the second line? Presumably not just the English—perhaps the human race in general?

What is meant by "stay" in the third line? A dictionary will tell us that one meaning is "support," which seems to be relevant here.

What is meant by "religion has materialized itself in the fact"? To answer this, we need to ask, **What is the significance of "fact" here?** Perhaps it represents the world of science, of observation, of material reality. So, does the author mean that religion now expresses itself in a scientific way, or perhaps that science has replaced religion? Probably the latter, since this was written in the late nineteenth century, when Western religion was being challenged from many directions.

What does "idea" represent? Clearly, it represents the opposite of science and materialism; and since it is associated with poetry, perhaps it represents spirituality, or an attempt to transcend a crude materialistic way of thinking.

But what, then, is meant by "the idea is the fact"? Perhaps, that for poetry the *real* fact, the most basic reality, is the idea itself; and that the idea is more important than the physical world, which is the province of science.

Now, we are ready to use our theme–form–context framework.

Under **theme** we can ask the questions we asked before:

What is the basic theme or central idea or argument?
How is the theme developed? Logically, emotionally, or through point of view?
Does a central conflict or opposition structure the text?
Does the text convey a moral or a lesson?

We might come up with answers such as these:

The central idea or argument of this passage is

 – that humankind will increasingly depend upon poetry for its spiritual sustenance.

Matthew Arnold supports this idea by pointing out

- that by the time of the era in which he writes, all systems of belief and all traditions have been undermined.

- that the new "religion" of the age is science, which deals with a world (the material world) that is ultimately illusory.

- that poetry can deal with the true reality, perhaps humankind's spiritual nature.

- that poetry will replace religion in terms of providing spiritual meaning and fulfillment.

Now we can ask questions about the **form** or **style** of the passage. What genre is the text? What literary devices does it use? Our answers might look like this:

Some stylistic characteristics of this text include

- the use of repetition: "surer," "not," "fact," "illusion."

- the opposition of fact vs. idea, religion vs. poetry.

- the equation of religion and science.

Now we are ready to write two paragraphs about the passage, one about its content and the other about its form. We will need to add transition words between the points we have just listed. Here's a draft paragraph about the content:

In this passage, Matthew Arnold claims that humankind will increasingly depend upon poetry for its spiritual sustenance. He points out that by the time of his own era, all systems of belief and all traditions have been undermined by science. Indeed, he argues that the new "religion" of his age is science. Science merely deals with the physical world, a world of "fact," which is what is most real for human beings. But what is actually real, he suggests, is the idea, by which he means spirituality. It is poetry, he suggests, that expresses this idea, which satisfies humankind's spiritual nature. Poetry, therefore, is destined to replace the function of religion. It will be poetry, not religion, which expresses the human quest for meaning and fulfillment.

And here's a draft paragraph about the form:

> What characterizes Arnold's style is repetition. He talks about how humankind will find a "surer and surer" support in poetry; here he uses repetition for emphasis. But his later repetition, when he speaks of "fact . . . the supposed fact," is meant to question the validity of what counts as "fact." When he repeats "illusion, of divine illusion," he is stressing that it is religion which is responsible for our illusory vision of life. Indeed, the whole passage is centered on the opposition of "fact" and "idea," only to conclude that they are the same thing.

This is of course an incomplete interpretation, and many other types of reading are possible; but it is a basic explanation of a difficult passage. If we wanted to take this reading to the next level, we could challenge what Arnold says: surely his prediction about the importance of poetry has not come true; poetry has become increasingly marginalized. Why did Arnold make such grand claims for poetry? Perhaps, like many humanities professors today, he was defending it from attack by scientists and businessmen who considered poetry to be of no practical use in the world—and who considered practicality to be the central aim of all human endeavor. Or we could place the passage in its Victorian context and show that it is typical of its age in talking about the loss of faith and in suggesting that literature or poetry will somehow replace religion. We could also point out that Arnold sometimes does not make himself clear: what does he mean, for example, by "divine illusion" or "unconscious poetry"?

CRITICAL READING EXERCISE

Frances Burney, "A Mastectomy" (1812)

Frances Burney, a British writer, produced a number of novels and plays that were praised by some of the most eminent authors of her time; she also wrote many letters and journals, which might fall under the broad genre of "life writing." In her late fifties, when she was living with her husband in France, she was told that she had breast cancer and would need radical surgery, a mastectomy, which would be performed without anesthesia. In a harrowing letter to her sister, she describes her ordeal:

> M. Dubois . . . stammered and could not go on. No one else attempted to speak, but I was softened myself, when I saw even M. Dubois grow agitated, while Dr. Larrey kept always aloof, yet a glance showed me he was pale as ashes. I knew not, positively, then, the immediate danger, but everything convinced me danger was hovering about me, and that this experiment could alone save me from its jaws. I mounted, therefore, unbidden, the bedstead—and M. Dubois placed me upon the mattress, and spread a cambric handkerchief upon my face. It was transparent, however, and I saw, through it, that the bedstead was instantly surrounded by the seven men and my nurse. I refused to be held; but when, bright through the cambric, I saw the glitter of polished steel—I closed my eyes. I would not trust to convulsive fear the sight of the terrible incision.

After examining this passage, we can ask our preliminary questions and then apply our theme–form–context framework.

Preliminary questions

Who are M. Dubois and Dr. Larrey? Who are the seven men? Elsewhere in the letter, we learn that M. Dubois is the chief physician and that the seven men are five other doctors and two students.

What is the meaning of "experiment"? In this context, can we infer that "experiment" means "operation" or "surgery"?

What is the "danger"? At first, it may seem that this word refers to the operation. But if we scrutinize the entire sentence, we can see that it's precisely the surgery that will save the narrator from the "jaws" of this danger. So, could "danger" refer to the probability that she would die of the cancer if it was left untreated?

Questions about form

What genre is the text?

- This is a letter from Burney to her sister. It relates details about the author's life; it would thus seem to fall under the genre of "life writing," which includes autobiography, journals, and letters.

What literary devices does it use?

- By focusing on the writer's emotional and mental state, the passage describes an intensely subjective experience. On the other hand, it also features careful observation of both people and external objects.

- We can't help noticing **personification**, as "danger" is treated as an active agency, "hovering about" the narrator, who fears its "jaws." We might also regard this as a **metaphor**, as "danger" assumes the shape of a predatory animal.

- The image—horrifying in this context—of "the glitter of polished steel" can be seen as a **metonym**, in which the steel represents not only the surgeon's knife but the entire ordeal the narrator is facing.

- Above all, the narrator evokes an atmosphere in which she is trapped and surrounded (by seven men). Despite being in a vulnerable position, she still exhibits calmness and defiance: "I refused to be held."

Questions about context

Why was this text written? Who is the audience?

- This letter is addressed to the narrator's sister in England. In another passage, Burney explains that she wants her family to learn about her ordeal from her own pen so that she can give them a full account and reassure them as to her "perfect recovery" (she is writing to them a year after the operation).

- Although this is a "private" letter, many of its characteristics indicate (as is true of many memoirs and autobiographies) an expectation that it might be read more widely. The piece is carefully crafted and, as we've seen, uses a number of literary devices.

Moving from notes to thesis

From these notes, we can make some general observations about life writing. Notice that although the author is relating her own experience, she doesn't do it in a straightforward way. Rather, she uses literary devices and rhetorical strategies. Moreover, she is conscious of her audience— not just her sister and family but a larger public that might "overhear" what she is saying. These considerations might raise questions about the line between autobiography and fiction. Is autobiography a kind of fiction? Indeed, is the human "self" a fiction, something we create in language? Burney's style is both deeply personal and intensely observational. Does this genre challenge conventional distinctions between "subjective" and "objective"?

These questions suggest many possible approaches to a thesis. We could formulate an argument about the nature of life writing; or perhaps about how a woman writer appears to challenge male conventions of objectivity (Arnold's passage above does not even use the word "I"). Another option is a thesis arguing that a private letter might actually presume a public audience.

PART THREE

ELEMENTS OF LITERATURE

CHAPTER 5

GENRE, PART I

The word **genre** refers to the general "class" or "type" to which a literary text belongs. The most conventional scheme of genres, as passed down (with considerable modification) in a long tradition from Plato and Aristotle to the present, consists of drama (tragedy and comedy), epic, romance, lyric poetry, fiction (novel, short story), and nonfiction prose (essay, letters, life writing, and memoir). Within each of these there are subgenres (such as historical novel, mock-epic, and realist drama), as well as mixtures of genres (such as tragicomedy and epic romance).

For over two thousand years, Aristotle's hierarchy of genres prevailed: tragedy was ranked higher than epic and lyric poetry, and comedy was viewed as the lowest genre. But at various times, especially since the Renaissance, this hierarchy has been challenged. For example, the Romantics tended to favor lyric poetry. And since the later nineteenth century, the very concept of genre has been questioned. Much modern theory, rejecting the notions of fixed identity, as well as claims to universality, stresses the idea of "intertextuality," or the interdependence of literary texts. It therefore tends to see genre, like everything else, as a social construction or institutional convention.

During the nineteenth century, a number of journalistic genres became the "mass media"—newspapers, magazines, specialized journals, advertising brochures—each with subgenres such as editorials, news features, and interviews. The twentieth century added genres related to film (Westerns, thrillers, horror films, among others) and television (news, soap operas, documentaries, dramas, comedies), as well as numerous digital genres.

This chapter will offer a brief overview of the main literary genres and guidelines on how we might analyze them, focusing on lyric poetry, drama, and fiction. Chapter 6 will consider digital and electronic media.

COMMON ELEMENTS

Some features are common to nearly all literary genres.

- **Plot** refers to the arrangement of events or incidents in a story, which is *not* the same as the chronological sequence of events. For example, Shakespeare's *Hamlet* begins with two guards on the battlements of a castle talking together and then seeing a ghost. But we would describe the plot as something like "Prince Hamlet seeks revenge for his murdered father against his usurping uncle Claudius." Often a conflict—between characters or between a character and her environment or within a character—drives the plot. Here, the conflict is not only between Hamlet and Claudius but also within Hamlet himself. Homer's *Iliad* is driven by the conflict between Agamemnon and Achilles, as well as by the war between the Trojans and the Greeks.

- **Action** refers to what the major characters do, the purposes and motives behind what they do, and the consequences of it.

- **Character,** according to Aristotle, is concerned primarily with a person's moral traits, but most of us probably have a slightly broader view, as we talk of someone's character as honest or hardworking or spiteful. The main character in a story is the **protagonist**, who is often in conflict with an **antagonist**. In fiction and drama, these might be called the **hero/heroine** and **villain**, though most characters are not so clear-cut. Sometimes minor characters serve as a **foil**, or contrast, to the main characters, bringing their good or bad qualities into sharper relief. Various genres depict character in different ways. Fiction might use detailed description and give us direct insight into a person's mind. Drama relies on performance, which includes action, gesture, speech, facial expression, and intonation.

- **Setting** refers to the scene (place and time) of the action. It can be used to create a mood or atmosphere and can influence how we interpret actions and events. Charles Dickens's description of Coketown early in *Hard Times* (1854) tells us a great deal about the kinds of characters we can expect and the kinds of lives they lead. The setting of Samuel Beckett's *Waiting for Godot* (1952) is so sparse that it conveys almost nothing about the characters or the action. This meagerness is perhaps meant to emphasize the emptiness of human life or the passage of time.

POETRY

Conventionally, poetry has been divided into three types, though the boundaries between them are not always clear.

- **Narrative poetry** is usually long and tells a story. It often shares elements with fiction, such as plot, character, and setting. A prominent form of narrative poetry is the **epic**.

- **Lyric poetry** is the kind of poetry you are probably most familiar with. A lyric poem is usually short, expresses personal thoughts and feelings, and represents the words of a single speaker or **persona**.

- **Dramatic poetry** includes plays written in verse (such as those of Shakespeare) as well as poems that consist of dialogues or monologues. Two examples are Robert Browning's dramatic monologue "My Last Duchess" (1842) and Edgar Allan Poe's "The Raven" (1845); both contain elements of narrative as well as dramatic poetry.

The Epic

An epic is a long narrative poem that recounts the deeds of heroes. Following are some characteristics of the epic:

- It expresses the **worldview** of a people or nation, its history, its myths, its religion, and its culture—in other words, its way of life.

- It tends to use **elevated language**, as appropriate to its lofty subject matter.

- It begins with an **invocation** to a goddess, asking for inspiration; for example, the *Iliad* starts with "Sing, goddess, of the wrath of Achilles."

- Its action starts *in medias res* (literally, "in the middle of things"). The *Iliad* starts in the middle of an argument between Achilles and Agamemnon.

- It uses many **similes** (Athena "rose from the gray sea like a mist"). It uses **stock themes**, such as the arming of the hero; and it may repeat passages word for word.

- It uses **epithets** (such as "swift-footed Achilles" or "gray-eyed Athena") and descriptive **formulas** (such as "when early-born rosy-fingered dawn appeared").

There are many different kinds of epics (on how to analyze them, see chapter 9). For example, Milton's *Paradise Lost* (1674) is a religious epic. Pope's *The Rape of the Lock* (1715) is a mock-epic; it produces humor by satirizing a trivial subject using epic conventions. Although the Marxist thinker György Lukács called the epic an ancient form that expressed the vision of an entire people, he went on to say that such a collective vision is not possible in the fragmented and individualistic modern world, which is more attuned to the novel. Hence he characterized the novel as the "epic of a world abandoned by God."

The Lyric

As mentioned above, lyric is probably the type of poetry with which you are most familiar. It's usually on the short side (from a few lines to a few hundred lines) and expresses emotion—often by a voice in the first person. Narrative, or the telling of a story, and the presentation of a world-view are not the goals of a lyric poem. The word "lyric" comes from the Ancient Greek word "lyre," a stringed instrument, and we typically think of lyrics as the words that accompany a song. As such, the intensely musical nature of much lyric poetry shouldn't surprise you. Think back on Yeats's poem to his lost love, "When You Are Old," which we analyzed in chapter 3. It is personal, carefully crafted, and in some intangible way like a song sung to the past. Interestingly, despite the connection with music and song, lyric poems aren't always gentle and quiet and don't always take beauty, or love, or sadness as their themes—as we shall see below, when we turn to William Blake's "The Tyger."

ANALYZING A LYRIC POEM

William Blake, "The Tyger" (1794)

"The Tyger" is one of the best-known poems by the Romantic poet William Blake.

> Tyger! Tyger! burning bright
> In the forests of the night,
> What immortal hand or eye
> Could frame thy fearful symmetry?
>
> 5 In what distant deeps or skies
> Burnt the fire of thine eyes?
> On what wings dare he aspire?
> What the hand dare seize the fire?
>
> And what shoulder, & what art,
> 10 Could twist the sinews of thy heart?

And when thy heart began to beat,
What dread hand? & what dread feet?

What the hammer? what the chain?
In what furnace was thy brain?
15 What the anvil? what dread grasp
Dare its deadly terrors clasp?

When the stars threw down their spears
And water'd heaven with their tears,
Did he smile his work to see?
20 Did he who made the Lamb make thee?

Tyger! Tyger! burning bright,
In the forests of the night,
What immortal hand or eye
Dare frame thy fearful symmetry?

Let's try applying the theme–form–context framework to this poem.

Theme

Our first task is to work out, on a basic level, what the poem's language means and what its central idea might be, probably reading it more than once to get a sense of its structure. If you make a brief note of what you think is happening in each stanza, along with questions, you will get some idea of how the poem develops. Make sure you look up the meanings of unfamiliar words. Our early notes on the poem might look something like this:

Stanza 1: image of tiger in a forest. What does "immortal hand" refer to?

Stanza 2: talks about where the tiger might have been created. What do the "wings" and "hand" refer to?

Stanza 3: refers to qualities of the tiger's creator.

Stanza 4: image of tiger being created in the workshop of a blacksmith.

Stanza 5: comparison of tiger and lamb, and how creator felt about having made both of them.

Stanza 6: same as first, with only one word changed ("Could" becomes "Dare").

So we have movement from (a) wondering who or what could have created a tiger through (b) imagining that the creator is a cosmic blacksmith to (c) wondering if the creator felt satisfied at having created such opposites as the tiger and the lamb.

Form

Now that we have a basic sense of how the poem is divided up and how it develops, let's try to figure out how the poem achieves its powerful effect. Once again, let's ask questions.

Stanza 1: Why is "tyger" repeated? And why followed by an exclamation mark? How can a tiger "burn bright"? What does that mean? And why is the plural "forests" used? Is there any physical description of the tiger? Is the "persona" or speaker of the poem talking about a specific tiger, or perhaps the concept of a tiger, used as a powerful symbol? Does "immortal" refer to God? If so, why does the third line refer to his "hand or eye," to his physical attributes? What is the effect and purpose of referring to a spiritual being in physical terms? In the last line, why does the speaker use the word "symmetry"? We know that the tiger is "fearful." Does he want to say that it is also beautiful or aesthetically perfect? Is this a contradiction (an oxymoron)?

Stanzas 2–4: The image of God as a blacksmith is continued for three stanzas. Is this a simile, an analogy, or a metaphor? Is God *like* a blacksmith, or is he in fact a divine blacksmith? Is the work of creation mechanical and mundane? The word "dread" is used three times to describe the creator's qualities: why?

Stanza 5: Is the question about the creator meant to be sarcastic or ironic (be sure you know the difference between "irony" and "sarcasm")? Is it an implicit criticism of the creator?

Stanza 6. Why does the last stanza repeat the first? What is the purpose of repeating a chorus or refrain? Why is "Could" changed to "Dare"?

Meter and rhythm: The basic rhythm of English is iambic (an unstressed syllable followed by a stressed syllable: e.g., "de-feat"). If you try to scan the poem, you'll notice that much of it is not iambic but trochaic (a stressed syllable followed by an unstressed syllable: "Burnt the" or "What the"). But the first line can be seen as beginning with two spondees (a spondee has two stressed syllables). What is the effect of this?

Context

Here we take up aspects of the poem's rhetorical situation, its historical context, and its relation to other texts.

The entire poem is a series of unanswered questions. What might this tell us about the state of religious belief when Blake wrote this poem?

How does the poem's force or meaning change if we see these questions as coming from a child or as asked in a voice assuming the persona of a child?

In its simplicity and tetrameter form (four metrical feet), the poem evokes a children's nursery rhyme. Why?

Moving from notes to thesis

Now we are ready to bring all our ideas about "The Tyger" together and ask: What is the **theme** of this poem and how is it developed? (There may of course be more than one theme.) It's worth remembering that the theme is not necessarily the same as the subject. This poem seems to be about a tiger; that is its *topic* or *subject*. As we can see, its *themes* are a little deeper: perhaps the nature of creation or the nature of God.

We are also now in a position to ask: What are the most important **formal** or stylistic features of this poem? And how do they contribute to the poem's development? In other words, we are now trying to see how content and form work together in the poem. Once we've answered those questions, we are actually well into the writing process. Indeed, critical reading and writing are not separate enterprises. We don't *first* read a text and *then* write about it—the two processes overlap considerably. So if you've asked yourself the relevant questions about Blake's "The Tyger," and thought deeply about the answers, you've already done much of the work needed to write about this poem. (For further guidance on how to write about this poem, see chapter 17.)

DRAMA

Aristotle divided drama into five components: plot, character, the thought process of the actors, the language used by the actors, music or song, and spectacle (or staging). In part because of the influence of Aristotle's views, the plot of a play is conventionally seen as moving through five stages.

- **Exposition** introduces the characters and the situation in which they find themselves. For example, Sophocles' *Antigone* (ca. 441 B.C.E.) begins with a dialogue between one of the main characters, Antigone, and her sister, Ismene. In it, we learn about their disastrous family history—the fall of their father, Oedipus, and the subsequent war between their brothers, Eteocles and Polyneices, in which both were killed. Because Eteocles refused to give up the rule of Thebes, as they had previously agreed, Polyneices led foreign troops against his own city; thus the new king, Creon, has forbidden the honorable burying of Polyneices' corpse.

- **Rising action** is initiated by an **inciting event**, which leads to a **conflict**. In this case, the conflict is provoked by Antigone's resolve that she will bury her brother, in defiance of Creon's edict.

- **Climax** or **turning point** is the moment at which the conflict reaches its highest intensity. In *Antigone*, the climax is somewhat drawn out. First, we have an impassioned and bitter argument between Creon and Antigone, ending with Creon's condemnation of Antigone (lines 485–577).* But we then have an equally impassioned argument between Creon and his son Haemon, who is engaged to Antigone (lines 680–818).

*Line references to and quotations from the play are from the translation by David Grene.

- **Falling action** brings a release of the tension created by the conflict and its **denouement** or **resolution**. Creon eventually realizes that he is in the wrong and agrees with the chorus that he should free Antigone (lines 1170–72).

- The **conclusion** is the actual ending scene. Creon's change of heart has come too late: he has lost almost his entire family, as Antigone, Haemon, and Creon's wife, Eurydice, have all committed suicide.

While these terms help divide the plot into its various stages, they should not be treated as hard-and-fast distinctions. For example, we could argue that the "climax" of *Antigone* occurs in stages—or even that the ending of the play is more "climactic" and intense than the actual conflict. Let's draw on our theme–form–context framework in analyzing the play. We can begin by determining some of the main themes of *Antigone* and then identifying one or two passages in which those themes are presented clearly. We can then consider how their treatment in the play is specific to the genre of drama.

ANALYZING DRAMA

Sophocles, *Antigone* (ca. 441 B.C.E.)

Themes

We know that the conflict between Creon and Antigone is not simply personal. Each of them embodies or represents certain values and loyalties. Recognizing that will help us identify some of the play's larger themes.

- **The tension between divine law and human law.** In general, Antigone seems to speak for divine law, which she associates with the rights of the family, while Creon represents human law as embodied in the state. Antigone claims that the divine laws are not merely for "today or yesterday; / they live forever" (lines 500–501) and that the god of death "demands these rites" of burial for both brothers (line 570).

- **The tension between woman and man.** Antigone is often viewed as a conflict between male and female characters. Creon stresses this many times: "When I am alive no woman shall rule" (line 577), and "we cannot give victory to a woman" (line 729). Some critics have seen Antigone as a heroine who defies the king in defending "God's ordinances, unwritten and secure" (line 499) and thus the rights of her family.

- **The connection between character and fate.** Perhaps Creon's downfall—like that of Oedipus in *Oedipus the King*—stems from his own character. Although he cares about his people, he is extremely impulsive, as we see in his interactions with his son Haemon and the prophet Tiresias. Creon greets the prophet by saying, "Never in the past have I turned from your advice" (line 1039), yet within a few lines he is accusing him of being a fraud: "the whole breed of prophets certainly loves money" (line 1110). Moreover, as king, Creon clearly shows himself to be an autocrat who "must be obeyed" even when his commands are unjust (line 718).

Performative situation

The themes mentioned above could also be treated in an epic or in fiction. What is specific to the way they are presented in drama? To answer this question, let's consider the historical context of the play and some essential features of ancient Greek drama.

- **Context.** *Antigone* was written in the late fifth century B.C.E. during a time of intellectual revolution. Rationalist and skeptical philosophies were beginning to challenge older beliefs about the gods. Is this skepticism something we see in Creon? At several points in the play, and at its end, the chorus reminds us that there should be "no irreverence towards the gods" or "haughtiness" (lines 1410–11).

- **The chorus.** The chorus in *Antigone*, as in most Greek tragedy, is a part of the dramatic situation, guiding the audience's interpretation. The chorus contextualizes the action, explaining how Antigone came from the "accursed" family of Oedipus (lines 639–53). It also makes generalizations about human beings, talking about their strengths and limitations. Perhaps more importantly, it tries to engage the conscience of the actors, giving them advice and reminding them to revere the gods and to listen to others (lines 1162–63, 1409–10). Finally, the chorus provides a kind of assessment of the major characters, as when it mentions the "savage spirit" Antigone has inherited from her father (lines 515–16) and her headstrong nature (lines 875, 920).

- **Dialogue.** To see how performance might affect our understanding of the play, let's focus on one scene: the sentry has seized Antigone, and after bringing her before Creon he describes in detail how he found Polyneices' body buried (lines 447–84). When the sentry's account is finished, Creon addresses Antigone:

> CREON: You there, that turn your eyes upon the ground,
>   do you confess or deny what you have done?
>
> ANTIGONE: Yes, I confess; I will not deny my deed.
>
> . . . .
>
> CREON: And did you dare to disobey that law?
>
> ANTIGONE: Yes, it was not Zeus that made the proclamation.
>
> *(lines 485–94)*

How are we to read Antigone's defiance? As an expression of her headstrong nature, as the chorus suggests? Or as showing deference to a greater power than humankind—the gods?

- **Gesture and audience.** What are we to make of the fact that Antigone is staring at the ground? Her defiance might have shocked an ancient Greek audience, and perhaps her respectful gesture—which contradicts her words—is intended to appease them. Or perhaps her gesture indicates her allegiance to the "gods below." A great deal depends on how an actor performs this scene. Try to attend a live performance of the play or view one or two different performances on YouTube. How do you (audience) receive Antigone's gesture (staring at the ground)?

In analyzing drama, we should consider theme–form–context, but we also need to pay attention to the performative situation—the chorus, the dialogue, the actors' gestures, and the likely audience response—in order to grasp a play's overall impact and write about it effectively.

FICTION

We can find plot, dialogue, and action in both epic and drama—and in fiction. But here are some of the elements unique to fiction: (a) multiple levels of narration, (b) the delving into a character's mind to elaborate points of view, and (c) detailed descriptions of people, objects, and events. Let's consider each of these in turn.

Narrator. Critics use the term "implied author" to designate the perspective that controls the entire narrative framework of a text. And we usually understand that the story is told by some kind of "narrator" or storyteller (and not by the author herself). The most common are the following:

- The **omniscient** or **unlimited narrator**, who can tell us the inner thoughts and feelings of all the characters.

- The **limited narrator**, who tells the story from a single point of view (often that of one of the characters).

- The **objective narrator**, who simply describes the actions of characters, without revealing their subjective psychological states.

- The **unreliable narrator**, who provides an account that we or the other characters know to be false or inaccurate.

Point of view. A story can be told from many points of view. A narrator usually tells the story in the third person ("she did this") or the first person ("I recall"). But in many modern novels and stories, the point of view shifts. For example, in Virginia Woolf's *Mrs. Dalloway* (1925), the omniscient third-person narrator takes us through the consciousnesses of many characters.

In one scene, we are exposed to Septimus's imaginings as he sits in Regent's Park in London, with his wife, Rezia, walking toward him. The narrator interrupts his stream of thought with a parenthesis—"(he was talking to himself again—it was awful, awful!)"—which clearly represents Rezia's view of her husband. Thus, within one paragraph, we have the thought processes of two characters, one enclosed within the other.

Setting. The setting of a story serves a number of functions. To begin, it establishes the uniqueness of a situation, locating it in a specific time and place. In fiction as in life, actions and events are tied to particular circumstances. So the setting can drive a plot and motivate the actions of characters. It can also create the atmosphere and emotional background of a story, as well as add to the story's sense of realism (by using detailed descriptions of people and objects) or its symbolism.

ANALYZING FICTION

Charles Dickens, *Hard Times* (1854)

Dickens's novel is often read as a critique of industrialism and the commercial, fact-based mentality that accompanies it. Let's analyze a paragraph from *Hard Times* in terms of fiction's typical elements.

> It was a town of red brick, or of brick that would have been red if the smoke and ashes had allowed it; but as matters stood, it was a town of unnatural red and black like the painted face of a savage. It was a town of machinery and tall chimneys, out of which interminable serpents of smoke trailed themselves for ever and ever, and never got uncoiled. It had a black canal in it, and a river that ran purple with ill-smelling dye, and vast piles of buildings full of windows where there was a rattling and a trembling all day long, and where the piston of the steam-engine worked monotonously up and down, like the head of an elephant in a state of melancholy madness. It contained several large streets all very like one another, and many small streets still more like one another, inhabited by people equally like one another, who all went in and out at

the same hours, with the same sound upon the same pavements, to do the same work, and to whom every day was the same as yesterday and to-morrow, and every year the counterpart of the last and the next.

This passage displays many of the characteristics of the novel as a whole, and we can see in it the operation of setting, narration, and point of view.

- **Setting.** The detailed description of Coketown is the passage's most obvious feature. It conveys Coketown's symbolic status as a typical modern industrial town, which is "sacred to fact," full of the noise of machinery, characterized in its activity and physical layout by sameness and repetition, choked with smoke and fumes, and, all in all, a black blot on the landscape. A number of literary devices here evoke an atmosphere of gloom and empty routine: we have similes (with "savage" and "elephant"), a metaphor ("serpents of smoke"), and images of the pollution of nature (the black canal and dyed river). But above all, the passage itself seems to imitate the town's monotony by repeating certain words (for example, "same hours," "same sounds," "same work").

- **Narration.** Is the narrator of this novel "omniscient"? It's hard to tell from the paragraph we just read, but while not offering any explicit judgment, the narrator goes to great lengths to direct the reader's response by using details and descriptions to evoke the conditions of this industrialized way of life: we can't help being appalled.

- **Point of view.** Although the story is not told from the point of view of any particular character, can we tell where the narrator's sympathies lie? The passage above uses repetition and hyperbole to get its point across. Later in the same chapter we are told that this society is devoted solely to "fact" and profit making: "Fact, fact, fact, everywhere," and what was not "purchaseable in the cheapest market and saleable in the dearest" simply did not exist. Clearly, the narrator is critical of this way of life, but is he blaming the working people, or is he viewing them as victims? Other parts of the novel suggest that the narrator's sympathies lie with the working class.

He portrays the relationships within this class as based on mutual trust, respect, and support.

Once again, we can use our theme–form–context framework to analyze this novel, or even a part of it. We could explore the theme of industrialism as an overwhelming negative force. We could examine the portrayal of the working class or compare it with the depiction of middle-class life. Or an entire paper could be devoted to techniques of narration, examining the points of view established in this novel.

At the beginning of this chapter we saw that elements such as plot, character, action, and setting were common to a number of literary genres. We noted that the flexible framework of theme–form–context could be used in the analysis of all genres. In the next chapter we'll see how these categories might be used in examining electronic and digital genres.

CHAPTER 6

GENRE, PART II

W hen we look at the world, much of what we "see" is shaped by the ideas and conventions of our culture. For example, we have pre-conceptions as to what constitutes "beauty" or "goodness," as well as what kinds of values we should strive for and what kinds of lives we should live. Films can have a profound impact on how we view people and events. When *Born on the Fourth of July*, starring Tom Cruise, came out in 1989, it diverged from earlier, more jingoistic movies about the Vietnam War by bringing us painfully close to the violence of battle and the killings of innocent civilians, and by showing the extraordinary costs for both the protagonist, who becomes an antiwar activist, and his family. By zeroing in on the personal toll war takes, the film shifted some viewers' vision: war is not only about what happens during the conflict but perhaps even more about what happens after.

Movies are sometimes our only source of "knowledge" about other parts of the world or other cultures. Television is an even more pervasive influence. Watched daily by most people, it shapes how we view others and ourselves. Television and film have given rise to numerous genres—such as soap opera, sitcom, documentary—some of which we will examine below, before moving on to social media and video games.

FILM: ANALYZING *GLADIATOR*

Film uses many of the techniques employed by drama, such as voice, gesture, and action. But film involves additional elements, many related to the use of the camera, such as close-ups of facial expressions and sequences of frames, deep focus, long shots, and montage. *Gladiator* (2000), directed by Ridley Scott, provides a particularly rich "text" for the analysis of how film works, of why directors and screenwriters make the choices they do, and of what impact those choices have on us, the viewers.

One late scene embodies the themes of the entire movie. It begins with a wide shot of crowds on several levels of the Coliseum rapturously and defiantly chanting "Maximus." We then get an eye-level shot of the senators, sitting on a balcony and talking. The camera now takes us to an image of Maximus himself, in chains. Ensuing shots show, first, a group of gladiators watching the proceedings and then the senator, Gracchus. Finally, we are shown Commodus and Maximus facing each other. Let's begin by analyzing elements of the movie's **form**, as seen in this scene, and then its **themes** and **context**.

- **Reading the sequence of shots.** What does this series of shots "mean"? Why are they put together in this way? By this point in the movie, we realize that the general population and the senators are on the same side—against Commodus, the irrational tyrant.

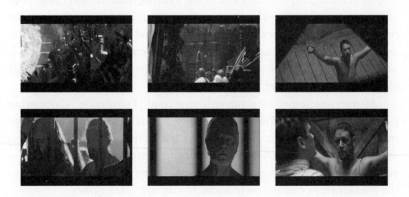

Maximus is their hero, the only one who can stand up to the emperor. The gladiators and Gracchus are shown because they are part of the plot to oust the corrupt ruler.

- **Dialogue.** When Commodus faces Maximus, he addresses him in the third person, calling him "the general who became a slave, the slave who became a gladiator, the gladiator who defied an emperor; a striking story . . . and now the people want to know how the story ends. Only a famous death will do." Perhaps Commodus is stepping back momentarily from the role of character to the role of narrator: he summarizes the plot and expresses not only the expectations of the crowd but *our* expectations as the movie's audience. In this way, the movie foregrounds its own dramatic character. We might say that though Commodus speaks these words, they appeal to our modern populist and democratic sentiments, and even to the idea of the American dream, in which an ordinary person can rise to high political or economic status.

- **Themes.** The shot of Commodus facing Maximus embodies perhaps the central conflict of the movie: tyranny versus freedom, corruption versus justice, the one versus the many. But these are conflicts *within* the empire. A larger conflict, that of the empire itself against the "barbarians"—here represented by the Germans, against whom the Romans fight at the beginning of the movie— may also be in play. Another theme could be the development of character: for example, Maximus becomes disillusioned with the notion of empire. Early in the movie he says, "Much of the world is dark; Rome is the light." How does his opinion change—and how does he change—as he sees what Rome is capable of?

- **Context.** Even a small amount of research reveals that the movie is historically inaccurate. Maximus was not a historical figure; his character is invented. Marcus Aurelius, a second-century emperor, did name his son Commodus as his successor, but Commodus was killed by a wrestler in an assassination plot. And of course, no emperor wanted to restore the Roman Republic, which was governed largely by the Senate. Nor did Marcus Aurelius ban gladiatorial games. In these respects, we might relate *Gladiator* to earlier movies such as *The Fall of the Roman Empire* (1964). Both have a love interest and both feature protagonists who never actually existed. We could compare not only the cinematography but the distortions of history: Is there a pattern here, a pattern characteristic of Hollywood?

- **Overall interpretation.** What commentary does this movie make about the world today? about American life? Why all these historical distortions? What was Ridley Scott's motivation in making this film? To educate people? to give us a lens through which we can view modern conflicts? to entertain? to make money? We could easily see the Roman Empire as a metaphor for the United States. The Germans are the Other—they look savage, they speak a strange language, and they are portrayed only from the outside. So the film might be delivering the message that, yes, there is corruption within the empire, but the ills can be remedied, and the ideal of empire itself can be justified.

Drawing on the notes above, we could analyze *Gladiator* in many different ways. We could talk about its relation to history and the motives behind its distortions of fact. Or we could analyze one of its basic themes—such as the conflict between emperor and people—showing how the movie uses certain techniques to express it. And of course we could analyze the movie's relation to its audience and its own ideological function. The important thing is that the analysis pay attention to the characteristics specific to the medium of film. We can analyze any movie by isolating a significant theme and showing how it is treated in a particular scene, looking at the camera work and dialogue, examining the portrayal of character, and considering the overall context. And it's worth noting that with a little research into the conventions specific to other genres of film, such as drama, documentary, and animation, we can analyze them as texts as well.

TELEVISION: ANALYZING
THE BIG BANG THEORY

Interpreting the texts of television is one of the most important acts of "reading" that we can undertake today. Television is a large part of many people's daily lives, not only giving us news from across the globe but also providing us with comic relief; showing us what we can buy, what we can eat, and how we should diet and exercise; and displaying and shaping the powerful stereotypes that many of us try to conform to or avoid. Indeed, some people argue that it is primarily through television that many people see reality. Television uses many of the same techniques as film but adds other elements, such as being offered in series of individual episodes, the pervasiveness of advertising, and the control of most broadcasting by a handful of corporations. Not surprisingly, literary training provides a good foundation for the "reading" of television. Let's see how we can adapt and apply what we've learned to analyzing a few scenes from the comedy series *The Big Bang Theory,* which ran on CBS from 2007 to 2019.

The main male characters (Sheldon, Leonard, Raj, and Howard) on this show are science nerds, with interests in comic books and Star Wars, a love of superhero memorabilia, a lack of success with relationships, and general social ineptitude. The women in the show are presented as having more social and emotional awareness, with Penny playing the part of the "normal" blonde (without a college degree) and Bernadette and Amy the successful scientists. We could analyze *The Big Bang Theory* from many perspectives, but since it's a comedy, let's look at its humor. Consider the following scenes from "The Thespian Catalyst," in which Sheldon, thinking he has given a "triumphant" lecture to a group of graduate students, learns from his roommates that it was in fact a disaster.

The Thespian Catalyst*

Scene: A lecture hall.

SHELDON: Good evening. I'm your guest lecturer, Dr. Sheldon Cooper. . . . I agreed to speak to you this evening, because I was told that you're the best and the brightest of this university's doctoral candidates. . . . Of course, that's like saying you are the most important electron in a hydrogen atom. 'Cause, we see, there's only one electron in a hydrogen atom. Best and brightest, my sweet patootie. All right, let's begin. . . . Who here is familiar with the concept of topological insulators?

(Several students raise their hands.)

SHELDON: Don't kid yourselves.

Scene: The apartment.

LEONARD: I found another tweet from a student at Sheldon's lecture. "Dr. Cooper has taken a relatively boring subject and managed to make it completely insufferable. Plus, he looks like a giant insect."

HOWARD: . . . Listen to this one. "Does Einstein's theory explain why time flies when you're having fun, but when you're listening to Dr. Cooper, it falls out of the sky, dead?"

. . . .

Enter Sheldon.

HOWARD: So, how'd the lecture go?
SHELDON: In a word, triumphant.
LEONARD: Really? Triumphant?

---

* Written by Chuck Lorre, Bill Prady, Steven Molaro, Maria Ferrari, Lee Aronsohn, and Jim Reynolds, season 4, episode 14, CBS, 3 Feb. 2013.

SHELDON: Oh, yes, you should have seen those young people. Thirsty for knowledge, drinking in my wisdom. I may have changed a few lives today.

PENNY: Oh, please let me tell him. . . .
SHELDON: Tell me what? . . .

(Raj reads out the tweets.)

SHELDON: Oh, tweets about my lecture. . . . That's downright cruel. Plus, insects have six legs. Yeah, I'm not familiar with the acronym KMN.
LEONARD: Oh, uh, from the context, we think it means "kill me now."

The creation of humor in *The Big Bang Theory*

There are many sources of humor in this show, and a number of them are present in the scenes above. Let's focus on just a few.

- **Character.** Sheldon exhibits repetitive and obsessive behavior and is perhaps too direct in social communication. He has a tendency to take everything literally and to apply strict logic even to delicate emotional matters. Thus he talks to students without taking into account their feelings or realizing the need for genuine interaction.

- **Situational irony.** What generates the humor? Perhaps it is the juxtaposition of the two scenes, each of which offers a different perspective on how Sheldon's lecture was received. The irony lies in the discrepancy between perspectives: Sheldon's narrow perspective, which assumes that his lecture was "triumphant," and the broader perspective of the other characters (and the audience), which takes note of Sheldon's limitations. This irony is reinforced by the amusing tweets.

- **The laugh track.** How much of these scenes do we actually find funny, and how much of our response is guided by the laugh track (the separately recorded sounds of a studio audience)? To what extent does the laugh track legitimize the stereotypes projected by the show, stereotypes that involve not just women and scientists but also India (in the character of Raj) and the third world?

On the basis of these notes, we could ask several questions about *The Big Bang Theory*. What image of American life does it project? What values does it propagate? Does it perpetuate stereotypes about scientists and students, or does it undermine them? Does it counter the culture of anti-intellectualism by showing us nerds who are both intelligent and human-ized? Or does it portray these characters as infantile, as hopelessly obsessed with a life of cartoons, card games, and gadgetry? These are all important questions since this show, watched by more than fifteen mil-lion, had the potential to influence its audience's lives. Other TV genres, such as game shows, documentaries, music videos, and talk shows, raise equally interesting questions.

DIGITAL GENRES

Electronic and digital media play a powerful part in life today, making it crucial for us to understand how to analyze these genres, especially since they sometimes influence our thinking about literature. For example, when we encounter a traditional literary text in an online format, we read it dif-ferently than we do a print version. In fact, an entire new field—digital humanities—is devoted to exploring how traditional humanities disci-plines are being changed by their expression in digital forms. Here are some of the topics being studied by scholars in this still-emerging field.

- **Reading and writing.** How have reading and writing changed in the digital era? Hypertext presents a nonlinear transmission of information. In hyper-reading, we filter, skim, and scan a text, occu-pying at once a "reading mode" and a "navigating mode." Digital text is an interactive medium, as the reader selects her own path through the text and its hyperlinks.

- **Displacement of print culture by multimedia.** Print now exists in a larger world of multimedia configurations. What is the function of "text" today, and how does it relate to the auditory and the visual? A combination of media—text, audio, graphics—is now typically used for all kinds of purposes, including educational, commercial, and political. The nature of the "digital" is inherently malleable, and scholars are researching the kinds of changes that occur when information moves from one medium to another. For example, one's response to a *New York Times* article accessed from the paper's homepage is different from one's response to the same article accessed by clicking through to it from Facebook after seeing a friend's comments on it.

- **The production and dissemination of knowledge.** How have digital tools and media changed the ways in which knowledge is produced and disseminated? At one time, digital technology was viewed as merely an instrument, useful for categorizing, accessing, and storing information. But now we see that it changes our modes of investigation, making them more collaborative and interactive. It enables us to visualize results and to create models of interpretation and explanation, as well as to assess the impact of audience responses on the development of products for mass consumption.

- **Ethical and political implications of digital technology.** How can intellectual and ethical standards be maintained? What can we do about websites that deliberately communicate false information? What is the impact of advertising and corporate interests on how websites are made? What is the potential of digital technology to reshape politics? All of these issues are being widely debated.

- **Use of digital media in education.** Many students now access literature through mobile apps or through ebooks. They have become used to electronic note-taking, interactive media, and self-conducted quizzes. In high schools and colleges, digital technology provides embedded assessments, tools that enable students to collaborate, and activity-based approaches to learning. Resources abound, such as searchable digital versions of Shakespeare's plays and sites containing interactive maps for the teaching of history.

Among the many digital genres or forms of social media are home pages, blogs, emails, Twitter, Facebook, Instagram, Snapchat, and YouTube.

All of the issues identified above are engaged by each of these genres, which share a number of characteristics.

- **The medium is the message.** This famous saying from the communications theorist Marshall McLuhan might be an overstatement—but it is certainly true that the definition of a digital genre must take account of its medium, which plays a role in how web-mediated genres are made to appear and how they can be used.

- **Shared communities.** Each type of social media creates and is sustained by a "discourse community," which has a set of shared assumptions, expectations, and communicative goals. For example, YouTube users tend to form communities around particular interests, such as musical or political preferences, or around certain educational aims, such as language learning.

- **Conventions.** Each platform has its own set of conventions. For example, Instagram consists almost entirely of photos and videos with captions, while Facebook accommodates not only the visual but also sometimes a great deal of text. The primary feature of Snapchat, a popular social media app among teenagers, is that the photos and videos disappear once they're viewed, the idea being that such messaging captures life in the moment, as something transitory. Twitter, where one can post a maximum of 280 characters (expanded from 140), is a kind of micro-blog that can be used for social messaging, marketing, news reporting, or political campaigning. Another interesting app is Pinterest, which allows users to curate collections of images and videos on specific topics.

- **Rhetorical strategies.** Aristotle divided the rhetorical modes of persuasion into *logos* (an appeal to reason and logic), *pathos* (an appeal to an audience's emotions), and *ethos* (an appeal to ethical considerations). The different platforms and mediums draw on these modes in varying combinations.

FACEBOOK AND OTHER SOCIAL MEDIA PLATFORMS

As of the beginning of 2019, Facebook was the largest social networking platform in the world, with 2.38 billion monthly active users. Facebook acquired Instagram in 2012. Given the huge global impact of Facebook, Twitter, Instagram, and Snapchat, they are phenomena that we need to understand, not simply use. Once again, we may find our literary training helpful.

Let's start by identifying some of the **themes** typically occurring in the newsfeeds of these platforms; then we can look at the **rhetorical strategies** behind them, as well as the **context**.

- **Themes.** We might categorize posts into six basic types:

  - **Personal pictures.** These are mostly holiday or vacation pictures, pictures of people's children or pets, and pictures of food.

  - **Pictures with a message.** One person posted a picture of *The Trojan War*, a book by Olivia Coolidge that her child is currently reading. Another posted a picture of a snail on her shoulder, commenting that snails are therapeutic.

  - **Pictures of text, often indicating a search for spirituality or meaning.** One person posted a picture of the words "Pray for the world"; another, "I've decided to be happy because it's good for health."

  - **Statements of personal experience.** One person called his radiation treatment for cancer "painful." Another described in detail her move to a distant town to do graduate work. Yet another remembered her father on the anniversary of his death.

  - **Political opinions.** Thousands of people have posted statements criticizing or supporting politicians and movements.

  - **Advertising.** On Facebook, we are inundated by ads for the kinds of items we may have searched for on sites such as Amazon.com.

- **Rhetoric.** What is the rhetorical situation of these posts? Why are people creating them, and how are they trying to affect their audience? Without psychologizing too much, we can detect a number of basic motivations.

  - **Please like my post.** It's natural to seek the approval of "friends." And a guaranteed way to get approval is to share an appealing picture of our cute child or a place we happen to be visiting. We are here appealing to *pathos*.

  - **I'm a profound person.** We want people to know that we are thinking beings who engage with the world in caring and intelligent ways. We are now appealing to *ethos*.

  - **I'm going through some unusual experiences.** We like to share genuine news about ourselves, especially if we are at a point of upheaval or transformation in our lives.

  - **This is me.** Some people like to state their preferences, whether these are political or reflect their taste in music and clothes. They are here employing *logos*.

  - **I want to be supportive.** It's not possible to dislike a post on Facebook or Instagram or Snapchat. We can like a post or be sad or angry. There seems to be a tacit understanding that usually—except with political disagreements—people will be supportive and will respond with hyperbolic praise such as "amazingly beautiful."

  - **I'm talking to a sympathetic audience.** As on most other social networking platforms, on Facebook we create our own community of "friends," which could be composed of actual friends, family members, colleagues, and people from our local community. Because this community comes together voluntarily, the people in it are likely to be sympathetic toward one another. This means that we can indulge in certain liberties with the language we use, the jokes we make, and the affiliations we presume.

- **Context.** Since being founded as a private platform at Harvard in 2004 and going public in 2006, Facebook has expanded beyond its initial aim—that of helping people stay in touch with friends—in many ways. This is also true of the other platforms, which generally share the following features:

- They furnish a participatory platform for various kinds of online communities: political, educational, recreational.

- They provide a forum for the advertising of community events.

- They are used by organizations within educational institutions to promote their functions and establish communities around specific interests.

- They constitute an important means of communication. Surveys have shown that while teachers and professors communicate mostly via email, most students interact with one another through social networks, whose informality they prefer.

- Perhaps most importantly, they offer a stage for the representation of self, and for a multimodal construction of autobiography. Prior to Facebook and other platforms, the only avenues open to us were formal ones such as writing books or memoirs. Otherwise, the narratives we constructed about ourselves remained implicit in our life decisions. Social media platforms offer an array of media through which we can construct a narrative of our lives—which we narrate to ourselves as much as to the "audience" that we have constructed through our choice of "friends."

Many dimensions of social media platforms can be fruitfully analyzed. We could look at the kinds of language people use, or the kinds of material they post. We could consider the most common rhetorical techniques and the significance of the audience we create. Has social media, at least for some people, replaced the need to socialize in person? Are platforms such as Instagram and Twitter a symptom of our tendency to inhabit a largely virtual reality where we relate to others primarily in a digital mode? Are they just another means for corporations and advertisers to categorize us as consumers, with an ever-more intimate and perhaps intrusive knowledge of our likes and interests? In any analysis of social media we need to take account of the conventions of the different spaces, their discourse community or audience, their rhetorical strategies, and their larger historical contexts. Finally, do Facebook, Instagram, Twitter, and Snapchat each constitute a genre or are they instead a medium, a platform for other genres?

VIDEO GAMES: ANALYZING *SUPER MARIO BROS.*

There is no doubt that gaming has had an enormous impact on American culture. Since video games first gained widespread commercial success with *Pong* in 1972,† the number of gamers has risen sharply and their demographics have broadened to include not just young people but adults and even the elderly. A 2007 poll showed that more people in Canada could identify the character Mario from *Super Mario Bros.* than Stephen Harper, who was then prime minister. In 2015 the PEW Research Center stated that 49 percent of Americans—about 150 million people—play video games.

Gaming has become part of our mainstream culture, influencing it on many levels. Live-action film adaptations of video games have proliferated since *Super Mario Bros.* (1993), as have machinima, or animated films based on characters in video games, such as the numerous *Pokémon* movies. With both federal and state support, gaming has begun to transform education, making it more visual, collaborative, and interactive. Gaming technology is even used by the military in creating simulations—virtual training for real situations. Gaming is becoming an art form in its own right and, like film and television, it is influencing individuals' perception of reality.

There are numerous subgenres of video games, such as platformer, shooter, strategy, simulation, fighting, racing, and role-playing. Each has conventions regarding behavior, goals, setting, and language. Let's look at some of these features using the *Mario* game franchise, which was launched by the Japanese company Nintendo in the 1980s.

---

* A game called *Spacewar!*, created by MIT students, was made public in 1962; it was very popular among programmers but was never released commercially.

Mario, an Italian plumber, is perhaps the most famous video game character of all time, and more than two hundred games feature him. In some of Mario's most iconic appearances, the plot centers on his quest to save Princess Peach from Bowser, a weaponized turtle. Here are a few aspects of *Super Mario Bros.*, an early and important game in the franchise.

- **Themes.** The basic theme is rescue. The evil King Bowser urges his turtles to attack the peaceful inhabitants of the Mushroom Kingdom, kidnapping their king's daughter, Princess Toadstool. Mario and his brother, Luigi, set out to rescue the princess and release the Mushroom Kingdom from a spell that has turned its inhabitants into inanimate objects. The game has eight levels, or "worlds," each with its own setting. The ultimate fight against Bowser or his proxies always takes place in a fortress or castle.

- **Player participation.** This game allows up to two players, one playing Mario and the other Luigi. Essentially, they have the same task: to fight the turtle forces and rescue the princess. In other words, the player takes the role of the hero and combats the villain. The skills required include fast reactions, anticipation, and dexterity with the controls, which determine how high and far the characters can jump or run.

- **Motivation.** This game appeals to people for a number of reasons.
  - ○ **Identification.** Many people can identify with Mario, who is both an "ordinary" person and a hero.
  - ○ **An alternative self.** We can inhabit an imaginary world, where instead of merely reading about or watching the adventures of others, we ourselves can have thrilling experiences. Much of our identity is actually a "fiction" created by us and other people. So, in a sense, the way in which we fantasize about ourselves is an integral part of who we are. And in the Mario games, we can have many diverse selves.
  - ○ **Fantasy world.** The world of this game does more than offer an escape from our everyday lives: it takes us into a world that is full of charm and surprise, possibly recalling worlds we knew in childhood through television or movies or literature.
  - ○ **Morality.** The characters are engaged in a well-defined struggle between good and evil—something we don't often get in real life, where moral and ethical choices are rarely easy.
- **Audience.** The *Mario* games have won a large and varied audience.
  - ○ Since they have been popular for decades, they appeal to both older and younger generations of gamers.
  - ○ New games in the franchise have been released on every Nintendo console from the Nintendo Entertainment System (1985) to the new Nintendo Switch (2017).
- **Connection with other genres:** The theme of the "damsel in distress" has a long tradition, including in
  - ○ **Literature.** We might see Helen, whose "rescue" by the Greeks in the Trojan War is recounted in Homer's *Iliad*, as the most famous ancient example. This theme also appears in works as different as the Middle Eastern and Indian *Thousand and One Nights*, Samuel Richardson's *Clarissa* (1748), and Edgar Rice Burroughs's *Tarzan of the Apes* (1912).
  - ○ **Children's stories.** Famous examples are "Snow White" and "Sleeping Beauty."

- ○ **Movies.** *King Kong* (1933), *The Searchers* (1956), *Superman* (1978), and many others.

Clearly, we could analyze *Super Mario Bros.* in several ways. We could focus on player motivation: Why do people spend hours playing these games? Or we could write about the connection between this genre and other genres: How do the conventions of this game differ from those of movies like *Superman*? We could write about the ways in which women are portrayed in these games, and the significance of the "damsel in distress" theme. Finally, we could analyze the general effect of such games on our culture: How do they benefit us, and could they harm us?

LUDOLOGY

Those who specialize in ludology—the study of games—explore how games can encode ideologies and control the experiences of players. Because certain modes of interaction—such as violence—are already part of a game's rules, much of the "freedom" experienced by a player is illusory. Researchers approach ludology from a number of perspectives. Humanities scholars might look at the creation of meaning, the portrayal of race and gender, and the kinds of story or narrative or plot expressed in games. Social scientists explore games as cultural systems, investigating their effects on individuals and society. Design researchers examine audiovisual techniques and elements of simulation, such as the use of controls in games.

Yet the distinction between these approaches is not always sharp; any one of them, for example, could consider the aesthetics of video games or their interaction with audiences or their relation to reality. Indeed, a heated "ludology vs. narratology" debate has been raging, as narratologists have argued that games are essentially a form of narrative, while ludologists have focused more on the rules and design of a game than on its representational elements. The need to better understand games will increase as digital technology becomes more sophisticated, and we must take seriously the potential of gaming to affect education and the ways in which we interact with the world.

As noted earlier, the skills we use to analyze digital genres, film, and television are continuous with the skills we use to analyze poetry and fiction. It could be argued that rhetorical strategies and figurative language, in different ways, underlie all of these genres.

CHAPTER 7

LITERARY LANGUAGE AND FORM: FIGURES OF SPEECH

"Figures of speech" are devices or techniques that are used to enhance the effects of language. The Roman rhetorician Quintilian (35–ca. 100 C.E.) defined a figure as "a form of speech artfully varied from common usage." Each literary figure represents a specific kind of variation on or departure from ordinary speech.

A FEW REFLECTIONS

Keep in mind that the literary devices and figures discussed below don't represent some kind of external addition to, or embellishment of, an "ordinary" language that is purely "literal." There's no language in which every word has a clear and indisputable meaning. As you read in chapter 2, there is no one-to-one correspondence between words and objects in the "real" world—for example, between the word "table" and the physical object with a flat surface and four legs. Both the word and the object it denotes are cultural *constructs*; we see the object *through* the concept. So even what we call ordinary language plays a role in our perception of reality.

The implications of this are profound. When, for example, we use the phrase "a white man" or "a black man," are we literally talking about a man who is white or one who is black? Of course not. These descriptions are cultural constructs; they are loaded with connotations that vary according to time and place.

So if language is not "literal," if there is no transparent connection between words and things in the real world, then how do we characterize language? Language is a shared system; it embodies a consensus, which develops over time, as to what certain words or phrases mean. It might be viewed as an internally coherent system, a system of signs, in which the meanings of "black" and "white" are opposed *within* the system but have no necessary or natural connection with the outside world. Some theorists, such as the French thinker Jacques Derrida, view language as intrinsically metaphorical, always displacing or explaining one term by another term in an infinite signifying chain that never reaches any real object. If, for example, we want to define "love," we might use terms such as "self-sacrifice" or "devotion," but we will then have to explain those terms, and so on and so on.

Derrida and other theorists view certain rhetorical figures such as irony, metaphor, and metonymy as *foundational*, integral to both the system of language and the process of thinking. What we call "ordinary" language is actually full of metaphors and other figures of speech—which often shape it from within.

METAPHOR

A **metaphor** is an implied comparison between two apparently unlike entities: "Juliet is the sun." An explicit comparison—"Juliet is *like* the sun"—is not a metaphor but a **simile**. A metaphor is sometimes defined as the *displacing* or substituting of one term for another. Juliet is seen in terms of the sun, perhaps to express her dazzling beauty.

Why do we use metaphor, and why is it so powerful? If we just say "Juliet is dazzlingly beautiful," we are describing Juliet in terms of an abstract quality, beauty; nothing about that concept helps us picture her. The metaphor "Juliet is the sun" forces us to picture the sun in all its beauty and to relate that image to Juliet.

A metaphor appeals to our senses and our imagination, creating a vivid impression. It is a way of thinking that enables us to see unanticipated connections. It also enables us to express things that might otherwise be inexpressible. When we say "God is the Light," we are using knowable features of our world to describe what in its essence is unknowable.

To see how metaphor operates, consider Shakespeare's Sonnet 18 (1609):

> Shall I compare thee to a summer's day?
> Thou art more lovely and more temperate:
> Rough winds do shake the darling buds of May,
> And summer's lease hath all too short a date;
> 5   Sometime too hot the eye of heaven shines,
> And often is his gold complexion dimmed;
> And every fair from fair sometime declines,
> By chance or nature's changing course untrimmed.
> But thy eternal summer shall not fade,
> 10   Nor lose possession of that fair thou ow'st;
> Nor shall death brag thou wander'st in his shade,
> When in eternal lines to time thou grow'st:
>   So long as men can breathe, or eyes can see,
>   So long lives this, and this gives life to thee.

The first line of the poem is not a metaphor but a simile, since it explicitly *compares* the poet's beloved to a summer's day. In the first part of the sonnet (the first eight lines, or octave), the poet offers a number of reasons why his beloved fares better in this comparison: the summer is sometimes windy, hot, or cloudy ("dimmed"); and, perhaps most importantly, summer is too short—like every beautiful ("fair") thing, it "declines" and loses its beauty. It is only in line 9—the beginning of the second part of the sonnet (the last six lines, or sestet)—that the metaphor is made real: "thy eternal summer shall not fade." There is another kind of "summer" in the poet's beloved, and it is this which is being compared to the actual season. This other summer, this summer that exists within the beloved, will not fade or diminish in beauty or die.

In the last three lines, the poet declares that what will preserve the beloved's beauty and other qualities are the "eternal lines" of *his* poem, this sonnet. In a sense, then, the poem is really not about the beloved but about itself—its own power to preserve youth and beauty. Hence we need to redefine our metaphor: the "eternal summer" of the beloved is the poem itself. This sonnet shows how figures of speech can merge into each other. What began as a simile becomes in retrospect a metaphor, and the true metaphorical direction or meaning reveals itself only at the end.

SIMILE

A **simile**, as noted above, is a comparison between two things, using "like" or "as." This simple technique can be very powerful. Consider the opening line from a 1796 poem by the Scottish writer Robert Burns: "O my Luve's like a red, red rose." Of course, no one is really like a red rose—but that may add to the line's charm. The poet doesn't tell us anything about his beloved; but we know what a rose is like, and the verse forces us to think of her in terms of the rose's bright color (emphasized by repetition) and perhaps also its delicateness or beauty. Another powerful simile occurs in Samuel Taylor Coleridge's *The Rime of the Ancient Mariner* (1798), where the narrator describes how he and his shipmates find themselves marooned motionless on a frozen sea:

> Day after day, day after day,
> We stuck, nor breath nor motion;
> As idle as a painted ship
> Upon a painted ocean.

(2.115–18)

The simile in the last two lines captures the utter stillness of both the ship and the sea by comparing them to a painting—in which all the elements are frozen in the moment of their portrayal.

METONYMY

Metonymy occurs when a word or phrase is substituted for another with which it is closely associated in some way other than resemblance: "White House" refers to the U.S. presidency or an entire presidential administration. The "Crown" might refer to a monarch or to a monarchy in general.

Metonymy allows one to write or speak concisely. "France declared war" is more compact than "The government of France declared war." But more importantly, metonymy enables us both to describe something by merely hinting at one or two of its characteristics and to develop a complex symbolism. For example, the title of Joseph Conrad's *Heart of Darkness* (1899) is itself metonymic: the "darkness" on one level could refer to Africa, but it could also signify the corruption of the European imperialistic enterprise and, on yet another level, the human propensity for evil.

Let's look at a striking passage from Conrad's novella in which Marlow, the narrator, describes the journey of the Europeans up Africa's Congo River:

> We penetrated deeper and deeper into the heart of darkness. It was very quiet there. At night sometimes the roll of drums behind the curtain of trees would run up the river and remain sustained faintly, as if hovering in the air high over our heads, till the first break of day. Whether it meant war, peace, or prayer we could not tell.

Clearly, "the drums" in this passage have a metonymic significance—shorthand perhaps for an unfamiliar culture, strangeness, the forest, the unknown. But remarkably, this significance works in two metonymic directions: it signifies not only what is "out there," the forest and the alien surroundings, but also the inner state of the Europeans, a state of geographical and cultural anxiety and lostness. Here again, we see how a great writer doesn't use a literary figure mechanically but complicates it by creating a new context for it, thereby not merely embellishing language but shaping the very process of thought.

SYNECDOCHE

In **synecdoche**, a part is used to represent the whole: for example, "hands" can refer to "workers," or "stage" can refer to the entire enterprise of theater and acting. In metonymy, in contrast, the word or phrase is simply associated with what it represents; it is not part of it. But the distinction between metonymy and synecdoche is sometimes a matter of interpretation.

Like metonymy, synecdoche can be used to achieve conciseness and vividness. When Conrad's narrator Marlow talks about an African boatman in terms of "a bloodshot widening of his eyes and a flash of sharp teeth," the image could be regarded as a synecdoche for the entire notion of "savagery" (Marlow is describing a cannibal). While the characterization is vivid, it has also been regarded as racist. Would a European ever be described as having "sharp teeth"?

We see, once again, how literary figures inform our everyday views, in ways that can be dangerous if unexamined. The words "freedom," "democracy," and "terror" are often used either as metonymies or as synecdoches. They acquire their status as figures largely from their linguistic context, from the words that surround them, as well as from the larger context of assumptions and prejudices in which they operate. Literary figures achieve their significance in relation to other entities, not in isolation.

IRONY

Irony has a number of meanings. For rhetoricians, it is a figure of speech in which the meaning undermines or opposes the actual words used. Hence, there is a contradiction between the form of a statement and its content. Thus sarcasm is sometimes called **verbal irony**. For example, we might say "Great job!" to someone who has messed up.

Dramatic irony occurs in a play or fictional text when the audience knows more than a given character about what is going on. For example, near the end of Shakespeare's *Romeo and Juliet*, the audience knows that Juliet is merely drugged, not dead; but Romeo does not, and he kills himself when he finds her seemingly lifeless body.

Socratic irony occurs in almost all of Plato's dialogues. The main speaker, Socrates, feigns ignorance and questions others to reveal the problems with their ideas and to elicit the truth about a topic. For example, in the *Republic*, Socrates questions several people regarding their definition of justice, continuing until they admit that those definitions are incoherent or incomplete or even self-contradictory. In the process, Socrates arrives at, and they are led to accept, his own conception of justice.

At the end of the eighteenth century, irony acquired a broader meaning, becoming an entire way of looking at the world. We call this **romantic irony**.

At its core is a capacity to view the world from irreconcilable perspectives, or with detached skepticism, and a tendency to reject any unity except that provided by the subject himself.

A powerful example of Romantic irony occurs in the first part of the drama *Faust* (1808) by the German writer Johann Wolfgang von Goethe. Faust, the play's protagonist, is a scholar with an immense thirst for knowledge and experience. When his lover Margarete asks whether he believes in God, his answer is profoundly ironic in the Romantic sense.

> FAUST: Who, my dear,
> Can say, I believe in God?
> Ask any priest or learned scholar
> And what you get by way of answer
> Sounds like mockery of a fool.
> MARGARETE: So you don't believe in God.
> FAUST: Don't misunderstand me, lovely girl.
> Who dares name him,
> Does affirm him,
> Dares say he believes?
> Who, feeling doubt,
> Ventures to say right out,
> I don't believe?
> The All-embracing,
> All-sustaining,
> Sustains and embraces
> Himself and you and me.
> . . . .
> Happiness! Heart! Love! Call it God!—
> I know no name for it, nor look
> For one. Feeling is all,
> Names noise and smoke,
> Dimming the heavenly fire.
>
> *(1.3135–51, 3164–68, trans. Martin Greenberg)*

Romantic irony here operates on several levels. To begin, Faust adopts a skeptical attitude toward the conventional explanations of priests or philosophers. A second level of irony occurs in his presentation of various perspectives of belief and doubt. A third level is that the operations of the universe are held to be mysterious and beyond human comprehension. Finally, Romantic irony lies in Faust's acknowledgment of the human inability to understand or "name" the divine, and his assertion that God is to us no more than a feeling.

Modernist irony developed from Romantic irony, becoming even more skeptical and self-doubting as it both rejected prevailing values and institutions and at the same time remained involved with them. Modernist irony is thus more nihilistic, despairing over the possibility of transcending or changing the current state of affairs. This kind of irony can be found in T. S. Eliot's *The Waste Land* (1922) and in the plays of Samuel Beckett, which present the world as fragmented and unable to be harmonized into any kind of totality or meaning.

In Eliot's "The Love Song of J. Alfred Prufrock" (1915), the speaker, Prufrock, rejects the upper-middle-class values that surround him, seeing them as judgmental and rigid. For example, he imagines himself at a social gathering where guests will point out his defects:

> (They will say: "How his hair is growing thin!")
> My morning coat, my collar mounting firmly to the chin,
> My necktie rich and modest, but asserted by a simple pin—
> (They will say: "But how his arms and legs are thin!")

> *(lines 41–44)*

The irony here is that, as his self-description shows, the speaker himself is a part and product of that same culture. In fact, those conventions reveal themselves in his mode of dress, which is prim and proper. In professing his own elegance or taste, he is being just as judgmental as his (imaginary) accusers.

Indeed, the irony in this poem runs even deeper, expressing the fragmented condition of a world where no sense of unity or purpose can be found. Prufrock acknowledges that *his* indecisiveness is insignificant, unlike Hamlet's (which had major consequences for the kingdom of Denmark). He is imprisoned in a world of trivial decisions ("Do I dare to eat a peach?"), meaningless gestures ("Shall I part my hair behind?"), and social alienation ("I do not think that they will sing to me"). The entire substance of the poem, and whatever conversation it contains, exists only in Prufrock's mind. At the end of the poem he makes it clear that the "we" and "I" that started the poem have journeyed only through his mind: for when actual human voices interrupt and "wake" them, they will "drown." In this larger sense, then, the poem embodies an inability to understand the world or to find one's place in it, a rejection of any unifying schemes beyond what human subjectivity itself can impose.

HYPERBOLE

Hyperbole is the use of exaggeration to create emphasis, amusement, or emotional intensity. We use hyperbole a great deal in everyday speech, whether we are happy ("It was the best pizza ever"), critical ("He is the professor from hell"), or flattering ("You have the most beautiful eyes I've ever seen"). There is an element of irony in all these cases, since words are being used to convey something other than their literal meaning. Hyperbole can also take the form of simile, as in "Your face is like a softly glowing moon," or of metaphor, as in "Juliet is the sun."

Marvell's poem "To His Coy Mistress" (1681), one of the most famous seduction poems in all literature, offers excellent examples of hyperbole. The speaker states that if he and his prospective mistress had time, he would spend a "hundred years" gazing on her forehead and "two hundred" adoring each breast. But since they don't have this luxury, he urges, they should make love now:

> Let us roll all our strength and all
> Our sweetness up into one ball,
> And tear our pleasures with rough strife
> Through the iron gates of life.
>
> *(lines 41–44)*

These lines are a transparent metaphor for sexual intercourse: here it is the use of the metaphor that constitutes the hyperbole, whereby the poet exaggerates both the force of the sexual act and the resistance to it ("iron gates"). This is another illustration of the interdependence of figures of speech.

Hyperbole in love poetry is by no means restricted to men extolling the exaggerated virtues of women. A number of women in the sixteenth century wrote bold and sometimes defiant poems about men. In Louise Labé's Sonnet 10 (1555), hyperbole takes a rather different tone from Marvell's:

> When I see your blond head in its laurel crown
> and hear your melancholy lutestrings sing
> with a sound that would seduce almost anything,
> even rocks or trees; when I hear of your renown,
> 5   all the ten thousand ornaments that surround
> your virtue, endowing you more than a king
> so the highest praise grows dim with your sparkling—
> then my heart cries, in a secret passion of her own.
> Since all your graces are well-loved and known,
> 10   since everyone's esteem for you has grown
> so strong—shouldn't these graces help you start
> to love? To all the virtues that make you great
> adding knowledge of my own pitiable state,
> so that my love can softly enflame your heart?
>
> *(trans. Annie Finch)*

Much love poetry by men parades its technical virtuosity and its ability to immortalize a woman's beauty. Labé doesn't make such grandiose claims. Rather, her hyperbole—presenting the man as a diamond or stone that outshines any praise and is ornamented more than a king (with virtues)— becomes the premise of a logical argument. This is also true of Marvell's poem, but whereas the logic there is directed toward seduction, it here calls for an extension of the virtues or "graces" already possessed by the man: to those virtues should be added the ability to love. The poet is calling for reciprocity, not subjection. It seems, though, that in both cases hyperbole necessarily entails an absence of realistic details. Just as love poetry written by men rarely presents a composite picture of the woman who is being addressed, so the man in Labé's poem is shrouded in fancy descriptions.

OXYMORON

An **oxymoron** occurs when we put together two normally contradictory or incongruous words or ideas. Common examples include "bittersweet" or "deafening silence" or "strangely familiar" or "global village." As these show, this figure of speech frequently sheds light on the complex ways in which we think, which often cannot be reduced to straightforward description. The pleasure that we feel in love or friendship is often tinged with pain; hence we know that certain emotions can be both bitter and sweet. The word "village" usually denotes a small settlement; when we place the adjective "global" in front of it, we evoke an entire world that, because of technology, has somehow become smaller, enabling rapid communication and intimate interaction with people far away.

The seventeenth-century poet John Milton is best known for *Paradise Lost* (1667, 1674), in which he reconstructs humanity's fall and expulsion from the Garden of Eden. One of the protagonists in the epic is Satan, who, as the poem begins, has been ejected from heaven because he led an uprising against God. His new abode, hell, is described as

> A dungeon horrible, on all sides round
> As one great furnace flamed, yet from those flames
> No light, but rather darkness visible
> Served only to discover sights of woe,
> Regions of sorrow, doleful shades, where peace
> And rest can never dwell . . .

> *(1.61–66)*

Here, the oxymoronic phrase "darkness visible" distinguishes the light that exists in hell from the radiant light of heaven. Perhaps Milton uses it to replace the positive associations of light—goodness, knowledge, hope—with the more sinister connotations appropriate to hell. The "light" in hell needs to be related to pain, sorrow, and hopelessness. It is light that, ironically, makes the darkness visible.

PERSONIFICATION

Personification occurs when we endow inanimate objects or ideas with human qualities, thoughts, or feelings. People often think of a car in human (and gendered) terms: "Look at my new car . . . isn't she beautiful?" Ships, too, are traditionally referred to as "she": "The *Titanic* began her maiden voyage shortly after noon on April 10, 1912, and within four days she sank." Shakespeare's *The Rape of Lucrece* (1594) provides a more literary example:

> Till sable night, mother of dread and fear,
> Upon the world dim darkness doth display
> And in her vaulty prison stows the day.

(lines 117–19)

Instead of being treated as part of a natural cycle that includes the day, night is here invested with frightening powers, bringing fear and darkness to the world and imprisoning the day.

Personification has a number of uses. Often, as in this example from Shakespeare, elements of nature are treated as having a will and agency of their own, which can make them malicious or benign. Shakespeare presents the night negatively; but the Romantic poet Lord Byron begins "She Walks in Beauty" (1815) by painting it much more brightly:

> She walks in beauty, like the night
> Of cloudless climes and starry skies;
> And all that's best of dark and bright
> Meet in her aspect and her eyes:
> Thus mellow'd to that tender light
> Which heaven to gaudy day denies.

(lines 1–6)

Here the night is associated with beauty and tenderness, with a mild light—qualities that are denied to the day, which is "gaudy" and insufficiently mellow. By personifying night, Byron accentuates these same attributes in the woman about whom the poem is written.

We like to *humanize* the world around us, whether the world of nature or the artificial world of our own construction (cars, ships, planes, buildings). We often talk of "mother Earth," implying that the planet is a living being with her own subjectivity and her own agenda—but an agenda that is part of our larger, human scheme. Many religions, including those of Hindus and the ancient Greeks and Egyptians, personify the gods—Vishnu, Zeus, Isis—in order to make them comprehensible within a human universe. Even in the Judeo-Christian and Islamic traditions, people talk about God in personifying terms that make the deity more accessible. As the Roman Catholic theologian Thomas Aquinas noted centuries ago, this kind of analogy with the human is a way to talk about God, who is otherwise unknowable.

ONOMATOPOEIA

In **onomatopoeia** (literally, "making a name"), words imitate the sounds or actions they describe, as in "splashing" or "crashing" or "smashing." This figure can also be seen in groups of words, as in "The room was full of hushed whispering."

When the sound of a word imitates its sense or meaning, we respond to it not only at an intellectual or conceptual level but also at a bodily level, with our senses. Meaning is effectively transmuted into sensation, producing greater immediacy and vividness and provoking a more intense emotional response. I once heard a bully say to a fellow student in the playground, "I'll smash you up." The threatening quality of this phrase is heightened by its onomatopoeia: we can be sure that the student responded with his entire being!

T. S. Eliot's *The Waste Land* offers an excellent example of onomatopoeia. The poet is describing a symbolic desert scene, suggesting a civilization that is spiritually desiccated:

> If there were the sound of water only
> Not the cicada

And dry grass singing
But sound of water over a rock
Where the hermit-thrush sings in the pine trees
Drip drop drip drop drop drop drop
But there is no water

(lines 353–59)

The line beginning "Drip drop" is onomatopoeic, imitating the sound of water. Brilliantly, in the first line of the quoted passage the poet has invoked the concept of the sound of water—a sound that is absent and longed-for in these arid surroundings.

Another powerful example of onomatopoeia occurs in "Daddy" (1965) by the American poet Sylvia Plath, whose German-born father died when she was eight. In this poem she tries to come to terms with her memory of him, and in this particular section she envisions him as a domineering Nazi figure:

I never could talk to you.
The tongue stuck in my jaw.

It stuck in a barb wire snare.
Ich, ich, ich, ich,
I could hardly speak.
I thought every German was you.
And the language obscene

An engine, an engine
Chuffing me off like a Jew.
A Jew to Dachau, Auschwitz, Belsen.
I began to talk like a Jew.
I think I may well be a Jew.

(lines 24–35)

The first image depicts a child's inability to speak with her father. It is almost as if her own jaw, her own language, becomes a snare and prevents her from communicating. The sound of the German word *ich* (I), when repeated, imitates the speaker's meaning: her inability to advance beyond this pronoun. But then the poet does something more startling with onomatopoeia: she describes the German language itself as a train taking her away to a Nazi extermination camp. The onomatopoeic effect is achieved not only by the repetition of "engine," which mimics the sound of the train moving, but also by the use of "chuffing," which mimics the sound made by the pistons of a steam locomotive. By this seemingly simple literary device, Plath creates a powerful image of language as not only a cultural and familial barrier but also an instrument of oppression and tyranny.

ALLITERATION

Alliteration occurs when a consonant sound is repeated in a phrase or line. For example, the *gr* sound is repeated in "The grass grows greener," and the *k* sound is repeated in "Coca-Cola." A famous example of this device is the first line of Percy Bysshe Shelley's "Ode to the West Wind" (1820), "O wild West Wind, thou breath of Autumn's being," which repeats both the *w* and *b* sounds.

Alliteration may have a musical effect and tends to make phrases more vivid and memorable. For that reason, it often appears in advertising and in brand names, such as "Best Buy." In literature, the effects of alliteration can be both powerful and subtle. On this subject, as many others, the English neoclassical poet Alexander Pope offers excellent advice in *An Essay on Criticism* (1711):

> The sound must seem an echo to the sense.
> Soft is the strain when Zephyr gently blows,
> And the smooth stream in smoother numbers flows.
>
> *(lines 365–67)*

As often in this poem, Pope demonstrates the point he is making. The alliteration of "sound" and "sense" in the first line gives more force to the poetic principle that sound effects should reinforce meaning. That principle is then illustrated by the next two lines, where the repeated *s* sounds emphasize the mildness of the zephyr (by definition, a gentle breeze) and the smoothness of the stream.

ASSONANCE

With **assonance**, vowel sounds—as in, for example, "shine" and "flight," or "home" and "phone"—are repeated. A famous example occurs in William Wordsworth's "I wandered lonely as a cloud" (1807): "A host, of golden daffodils," which repeats the long *o* sound. Similarly, in "Frost at Midnight" (1798) Coleridge repeats the long *e* sound: "Therefore all seasons shall be sweet to thee." Like alliteration, assonance emphasizes the musical quality of words; it creates a kind of understated internal rhyme, whose effects can be more subtle than those of rhyming final syllables.

ANAPHORA

Anaphora is the repetition of the initial word or phrase at the beginning of successive clauses or sentences. One of the most famous examples occurs in the New Testament, in the words spoken by Jesus in the Sermon on the Mount:

> Blessed are the merciful: for they shall obtain mercy.
> Blessed are the pure in heart: for they shall see God.
> Blessed are the peacemakers: for they shall be called the children of God.

> (*Matthew 5:7–9; King James Version*)

The repetition of "Blessed are" not only emphasizes the favored condition of those who follow the path of mercy, purity, and peace but also introduces rhythm into the lines. The virtues of the new, Christian way of life are implicitly opposed to the values of the harsh Roman world in which Jesus is delivering his message. He is stressing that mercy and peacefulness are signs not of weakness but of spiritual strength and virtue; as such, they will be rewarded. Anaphora here adds persuasive power: the repetition is designed to sway people by appealing to their emotions as well as to their logical faculties.

EPIPHORA

The counterpart of anaphora is **epiphora**, the repetition of words or phrases at the end of clauses. We see (and hear) a powerful example of this device in Aemilia Lanyer's "To the Virtuous Reader" (1611).

> As also in respect it pleased our lord and savior Jesus Christ, without the assistance of man, being free from original and all other sins, from the time of his conception, till the hour of his death, to be begotten of a woman, born of a woman, nourished of a woman, obedient to a woman; and that he healed women, pardoned women, comforted women: yea, even when he was in his greatest agony and bloody sweat, going to be crucified, and also in the last hour of his death, took care to dispose of [care for] a woman: after his resurrection, appeared first to a woman, sent a woman to declare his most glorious resurrection to the rest of his disciples. Many other examples I could allege of divers faithful and virtuous women, who have in all ages not only been confessors but also endured most cruel martyrdom for their faith in Jesus Christ.

This prose epistle, published with her poem "Eve's Apology in Defense of Women," is part of Lanyer's attempt to defend Eve and all women from centuries of moral censure by men. In this passage, the repetition of "woman" or "women" highlights and reinforces Lanyer's argument. For example, "born of a woman, nourished of a woman, obedient to a woman" emphasizes the active and crucial roles played by women. The next sentence employs the same technique with the plural "women," as if to universalize the close connection of women with Christ. Again, it's worth observing that this literary device doesn't occur in isolation. It is used in the service of a larger strategy, which is to show the formative role that women have played in the birth and growth of Christianity.

CHAPTER 8

LITERARY LANGUAGE AND FORM: PROSODY

Literature engages in a specialized use of language, whose purpose is not just to communicate a simple message. For example, if we wanted to tell someone about the weather, we might say, "This autumn day is very windy." When we hear this statement, we register its information at a purely conceptual level. We know that it's autumn and we know that it's windy, and that is all we need to know. We don't stop to look at the words that are used or the way in which the information was communicated. But when the we hear "O wild West Wind, thou breath of Autumn's being," we respond to the words not just with our conceptual or intellectual faculties but with our emotions and even our senses: we *feel* the words, their meaning, their sound, their rhythm, their power to point to something far beyond themselves, something deep within us.

Why do these words, the first line of Shelley's "Ode to the West Wind," have this effect? Well, to begin with, they have a *rhythm* that is unlike the rhythms of ordinary language. The sentence

x / x / x / x / x
This Au | tumn day | is ver | y win | dy

follows the usual rhythm of the English language, which is *iambic*: that is, an unstressed syllable (x) is followed by a stressed syllable (/). But the poet's line

$$/ \quad / \quad x \quad / \quad x \quad / \quad x \ / \quad x \quad / \quad x$$

O wild | West Wind, | thou breath | of Au | tumn's be | ing

begins much more emphatically, with a stress on at least the first two syllables (though the stress on the second is greater). Taken together, those stresses make us slow down and pronounce the words more deliberately and more forcefully. This slow movement is accentuated by alliteration—the repetition of the *w* sound, and the repeated *b* in "breath" and "being." But the poetic effects go deeper: to begin with, these words are *addressing* the wind itself (a figure of speech called "apostrophe"). We thus see that the wind here is not treated merely as a force of nature, but has a symbolic significance. Further, the poet uses a metaphor in this line, indicating that the wind is the "breath"—perhaps the life or essence—of the very being or existence of Autumn. We might therefore infer that Autumn itself is a metaphor, perhaps representing age or decay or death.

In analyzing this line's features, we've identified two dimensions of literary language. The first is **prosody**, which deals with the rhythm and meter of language. And the second is the use of literary **tropes**, usually called **figures of speech**. It will be difficult to analyze any piece of literature without knowing something about these two aspects of literary form. Chapter 7 examined some major literary devices; this chapter sets forth some basic elements of prosody.

PROSODY

The word **prosody** comes from the Greek word *prosōdia*, which originally meant "song sung to instrumental music." Prosody refers to the analysis of various elements of verse form: rhythm, meter, rhyme, and structural features (such as the stanza).

Rhythm, from the Greek *rhythmos*, "measured motion" (the root is *rhein*, "to flow"), refers to the cadence or movement of sounds—their rise and fall.

Meter, from the Greek *metron*, "measure," refers to the rhythmic pattern or arrangement of stressed and unstressed syllables in verse.

A **foot** is the basic unit of meter. Examples include the following:

Iamb, or iambic foot: unstressed syllable followed by stressed syllable, x /

$$\begin{array}{c} \text{x} \quad / \quad \text{x} \quad / \quad \text{x} \quad / \quad \text{x} \quad / \quad \text{x} \quad / \\ \text{defeat,} \mid \text{behold,} \mid \text{amuse,} \mid \text{to be,} \mid \text{delete} \end{array}$$

Because the natural movement of the English language is iambic, most departures from this rhythm create emphasis or otherwise draw attention to themselves.

Trochee, or trochaic foot: stressed syllable followed by unstressed, / x

$$\begin{array}{c} / \quad \text{x} \quad / \quad \text{x} \quad / \quad \text{x} \quad / \quad \text{x} \\ \text{happy,} \mid \text{hammer,} \mid \text{making,} \mid \text{little} \end{array}$$

Spondee, or spondaic foot: two stressed syllables, / /

$$\begin{array}{c} / \; / \quad / \; / \quad / \; / \quad / \; / \quad / \; / \\ \text{football,} \mid \text{sunshine,} \mid \text{fresh food,} \mid \text{heartbreak,} \mid \text{dead man} \end{array}$$

Dactyl, or dactylic foot: stressed syllable followed by two unstressed, / x x

$$\begin{array}{c} / \quad \text{x x} \quad / \quad \text{x x} \quad / \quad \text{x x} \quad / \quad \text{x x} \quad / \quad \text{x x} \\ \text{strawberry,} \mid \text{murmuring,} \mid \text{endlessly,} \mid \text{merrily,} \mid \text{tenderly} \end{array}$$

Anapest, or anapestic foot: two unstressed syllables followed by stressed, x x /

$$\begin{array}{c} \text{x x} \quad / \quad \text{x x} \quad / \quad \text{x x} \quad / \\ \text{understand,} \mid \text{it was late,} \mid \text{like the leaves} \end{array}$$

Pyrrhic: two unstressed syllables (sometimes attached to a stressed syllable), x x

x x   x x

to a [man], | with a [pen]

Overall, metrical pattern depends on two elements: the kind of foot that predominates (for example, iambic) and the number of feet per line. So, for example, **iambic pentameter** has five iambic feet:

x /   x /   x /   x /   x /

Four days | will quick | ly steep | themselves | in night

And **trochaic trimeter** will have three trochaic feet:

/ x   / x   / x

Little | Lamb, who | made thee?

Other common line lengths are **dimeter** (two feet per line), **tetrameter** (four feet per line), and **hexameter** (six feet per line).

A **caesura** is a pause or a natural break in the rhythm of a line, indicated by a double line ||. It usually occurs in the middle of a line, though it can fall near the beginning or the end. There are two kinds of caesura, as illustrated by the following couplet from Alexander Pope's *An Essay on Criticism*, Part II (1711):

True ease in writing comes from art, || not chance,
As those move easiest || who have learned to dance.

(lines 363–64)

In the first line a sharp break or pause comes after a stressed syllable; in the second line, the pause is gentler and comes after an unstressed syllable. These are called a **masculine** and a **feminine caesura**, respectively.

Stanzas and verse forms

A **stanza** is a group of lines in verse, often with a consistent metrical pattern and a rhyme scheme.

A **quatrain** is a stanza with four lines, as in the following from Edward FitzGerald's 1859 translation of the *Rubáiyát* (*Quatrains*) of the Persian poet Omar Khayyam.

> Come, fill the Cup, and in the fire of Spring
> Our Winter-garment of Repentance fling:
> The Bird of Time has but a little way
> To flutter—and the Bird is on the Wing.

(lines 25–28)

A pair of two, usually rhyming, lines is called a **couplet**, as in these lines from "Against Love" (1678) by the English poet Katherine Philips:

> Lovers like men in fevers burn and rave,
> And only what will injure them do crave.

(lines 4–5)

Blank verse is another name for unrhymed iambic pentameter, which has been the standard meter for much poetic drama (including Shakespeare). It is close to the natural rhythms of the English language. Perhaps the most famous example is John Milton's epic *Paradise Lost* (1667, 1674), which begins:

> Of man's first disobedience, and the fruit
> Of that forbidden tree, whose mortal taste
> Brought Death into the World, and all our woe,
> With loss of Eden, till one greater Man
> Restore us, and regain the blissful seat,
> Sing Heav'nly Muse.

(1.1–6)

There are basically three types of **sonnet:** the Petrarchan (or Italian), the Shakespearean (or English), and the Spenserian. Each has fourteen lines of iambic pentameter, but they differ in their rhyme schemes.

> **Petrarchan:** *abba abba cde cde*, an **octave** (eight lines) + a **sestet** (six lines)

> **Shakespearean:** *abab cdcd efef gg* (three quatrains + a couplet)

> **Spenserian:** *abab bcbc cdcd ee* (three quatrains + a couplet)

Sonnets often contain a *volta*, or "turn," in the argument or thought or mood. In Petrarchan sonnets, this occurs between the octave and the sestet, and in the Shakespearian sonnet between either lines 8 and 9 or 12 and 13. Clearly, these structures offer the poet many possibilities. For example, a statement in the octave could be met by a counterstatement in the sestet. Or an argument could be developed through three quatrains with the couplet expressing a conclusion. Alternatively, each quatrain could express a different point of view on a given topic and the couplet might offer a summary or a question.

Terza rima is a verse form comprising three-line stanzas (**tercets**) with the rhyme scheme *aba bcb cdc . . . yzy z*. It was made famous by the Italian poet Dante Alighieri, who used it in his *Divine Comedy* (1307–21). A poem in English in this form is Richard Wilbur's "First Snow in Alsace" (1947), which begins:

> The snow came down last night like moths   *a*
> Burned on the moon; it fell till dawn,   *b*
> Covered the town with simple cloths.   *a*
>
> Absolute snow lies rumpled on   *b*
> What shellbursts scattered and deranged,   *c*
> Entangled railings, crevassed lawn.   *b*
>
> As if it did not know they'd changed,   *c*
> Snow smoothly clasps the roofs of homes   *d*
> Fear-gutted, trustless and estranged.   *c*

> *(lines 1–9)*

Ottava rima is an eight-line stanza that rhymes *abababcc*. A well-known example is W. B. Yeats's "Sailing to Byzantium" (1927), which begins:

> That is no country for old men. The young   *a*
> In one another's arms, birds in the trees,   *b*
> —Those dying generations—at their song,   *a*
> The salmon-falls, the mackerel-crowded seas,   *b*
> Fish, flesh, or fowl, commend all summer long   *a*
> Whatever is begotten, born, and dies.   *b*
> Caught in that sensual music all neglect   *c*
> Monuments of unageing intellect.   *c*
>
>   *(lines 1–8)*

The **villanelle** consists of five tercets and one quatrain. The first and third lines of the first stanza are repeated alternately in the following stanzas, with the rhyme scheme *aba aba aba aba aba abaa*. A good example is Elizabeth Bishop's "One Art" (1976).

> The art of losing isn't hard to master;   *a*
> so many things seem filled with the intent   *b*
> to be lost that their loss is no disaster.   *a*
>
>   Lose something every day. Accept the fluster   *a*
> 5   of lost door keys, the hour badly spent.   *b*
>   The art of losing isn't hard to master.   *a*
>
> Then practice losing farther, losing faster: *a*
> places, and names, and where it was you meant   *b*
> to travel. None of these will bring disaster.   *a*
>
> 10   I lost my mother's watch. And look! my last, or   *a*
> next-to-last, of three loved houses went.   *b*
> The art of losing isn't hard to master.   *a*
>
> I lost two cities, lovely ones. And, vaster,   *a*
> some realms I owned, two rivers, a continent.   *b*
> 15   I miss them, but it wasn't a disaster.   *a*

—Even losing you (the joking voice, a gesture	*a*
I love) I shan't have lied. It's evident	*b*
the art of losing's not too hard to master	*a*
though it may look like (*Write* it!) like disaster.	*a*

All of the above are traditional forms, with which poets continue to experiment. By far the most widely used form now is **free verse** (in French, *vers libre*), which has no regular meter or rhyme scheme or line length, and which usually expresses the rhythms of everyday speech. While free verse was developed in modern times by, among others, Walt Whitman, and the modernist poets T. S. Eliot, Ezra Pound, Gertrude Stein, and William Carlos Williams, there are foreshadowings of it in the King James Version of the Bible, as well as in the Romantic poets and in the French poet Charles Baudelaire. Here's a well-known example of free verse from Marianne Moore's poem "Poetry" (1919):

> I too, dislike it: there are things that are important
>   beyond all this fiddle.
>   Reading it, however, with a perfect contempt for it,
>   one discovers in
>   it after all, a place for the genuine.

(lines 1–3)

Clearly, the rhythms here are those of everyday speech, largely iambic and conversational, and there is no use of symbolism or imagery that draws attention to itself. Free verse is said to create its own rhythms and its own patterns. Thus Moore's lines have a slow, meditative cadence, with substantial pauses after "dislike it," "however," and "after all."

SCANSION

When we **scan** a poem, we look at it in terms of its metrical pattern, its arrangement of stressed and unstressed syllables, just as we did the line from Shelley's poem at the start of this chapter, in order to understand how it achieves certain effects. In doing so, we must keep in mind that scansion—the analysis of rhythmic structure—is not a mechanical exercise. The stress we put on a word will be affected both by its meaning and by the other words around it. For example, in the phrase "O wild West Wind," we might stress all four syllables, but perhaps not equally. How we scan a line of verse or a poem will depend on our interpretation of the poem. So, as always, what we say about the style or *form* of a poem is intrinsically connected to how we interpret its *content*.

Scanning "The Tyger"

Let's look at the first stanza of a poem that we've already read. William Blake's "The Tyger" is a particularly interesting example, because it shows how regular meter can be varied to achieve certain effects.

```
   /  x   /  x    /  x    /
Tyger! | Tyger! | burning | bright          a
  /  x   /  x    /  x    /
In the | forests | of the | night,          a
    /  x   /  x   /  x   /
What im | mortal | hand or | eye            b
   x   /   x   /   x  /   x  /
Could frame | thy fear | ful sym | metry?    b
```

(lines 1–4)

We see right away that this stanza is a quatrain, with the rhyme scheme *aabb*. In the first line, the stress naturally falls on the first syllable of the word "Tyger." So this word is a trochee, and it is repeated. The third word, "burning," is also a trochee. This pattern of trochaic feet suggests that the regular meter here would be trochaic tetrameter—that is, an eight-syllable line of four trochaic feet. But we can see that these lines are only seven syllables long—the last syllable of the tetrameter is missing. Such elision or omission of the last syllable is called **catalexis**.

What is the effect of Blake's variation on trochaic tetrameter? With the unstressed syllable omitted, each line now ends with a stressed syllable: the words "bright," "night," and "eye" are thereby given special weight. And because of the trochaic rhythm, the words "Tyger" (line 1) and "What" (line 3) receive emphasis. However, the fourth line begins not with a trochee but with a regular iamb, which emphasizes the word "frame" and thus God's act of (symmetrical) creating. Also, the imperfect rhyme of "eye" with the last syllable of "symmetry" might draw attention to the contrast between divinely created symmetry—which is perfect—and human attempts at symmetry, which are inevitably flawed. More broadly, the trochaic rhythm, which stresses the first syllable of each word, and the shortness of the tetrameter lines make the stanza read almost like a nursery rhyme, in which childlike (but difficult) questions are posed about the nature of God—the God who could create something as fierce as a tiger.

Scanning "The Charge of the Light Brigade"

Tennyson wrote this poem in 1854 to celebrate the courage of a British cavalry force that was mistakenly commanded to charge against Russian artillery in the Crimean War (1853–56). The charge proved to be disastrous.

<pre>
     / x   x   / x   x
  Half a league, | half a league,
       / x   x   / x
     Half a league | onward,
   / x   x   / x   x   /
  All in the | valley of | Death
       /   x   x   /   x
     Rode the six | hundred.
     /   x   x   / x   x
  "Forward, the | Light Brigade!
        /   x   x   /   x   x
  "Charge for the | guns!" he said:
  / x   x   / x   x   /
  Into the | valley of | Death
        /   x   x   /   x
     Rode the six | hundred.
</pre>

(lines 1–8)

We noted above that the natural rhythm of English is iambic, with syllables paired in the order unstressed (x), stressed (/), and that disrupting this rhythm tends to create some kind of emphasis. Hence, in the first line, the first word, "Half," receives this emphasis, which is repeated in the second line. Perhaps the point is that life and death are not very distant (half a league, a metaphor for impending death, is only about one and a half miles). And in the third line, the emphasis falls on the word "All," suggesting that the valley of death will hold everyone making this charge. Indeed, in the second half of this line, the trochaic rhythm is itself broken to emphasize the word "Death."

In the fourth line, emphasis falls first on the act of riding; and we could read its second part as scanned above or we could stress "six" as well as the first syllable of "hundred." Either way, we are emphasizing the sheer number of men about to meet their doom. Toward the end, the trochaic meter seems appropriate for the commands "Forward" and "Charge for." In the stanza's penultimate line, if we stress the first syllable of "Into," we draw attention again to the line between life and death and to the act of crossing it. Finally, if we let ourselves feel the overall trochaic rhythm of the stanza, we can almost hear the beat of hooves as the horses charge with their riders toward their bloody end.

A coherent statement of these observations might look something like this:

> The trochaic rhythm of this stanza serves a number of functions. It mimics the rhythm of the cavalrymen's ride toward their death. It also emphasizes the disastrous orders given to the men by their commander ("Forward" and "Charge for"). Finally, it places appropriate stress on certain words: "Half," which indicates the nearness of death; "All," suggesting that no one will survive; and "Rode," which draws attention to the act of riding forward. But occasionally, the trochaic rhythm is itself broken—for example, to give more prominence to the word "Death."

Scanning "We Real Cool"

Gwendolyn Brooks's poem (1959) about a group of teenagers playing pool is intriguing because it's composed entirely of one-syllable words and its stress pattern can be interpreted in various ways. "We Real Cool" is a good example of how the way we scan a poem depends on our interpretation of it.

THE POOL PLAYERS.

SEVEN AT THE GOLDEN SHOVEL.

x / / x
We real cool. We

/ / x
Left school. We

/ / x
Lurk late. We

/ / x
Strike straight. We

/ / x
Sing sin. We

/ / x
Thin gin. We

/ / x
Jazz June. We

/ /
Die soon.

The poem is set in a pool hall, which we could argue is an integral part of the identity of these teenagers: it is where they hang out, where—at least to themselves—their "coolness" is realized. The poem seems to be about identity: these seven are the collective persona of the poem. But how do we read this assertion of their identity? Is it confident and defiant? Is it really proceeding from them?

Listen to Brooks reading this poem on YouTube, and you can hear that she places the most stress on the first word of the line, giving a secondary stress to the second word and no stress to the word "we" at the end of each line, treating it almost as if it were a suffix of the preceding word (like the "-ly" in "really"). Other readers, however, *do* stress the "we"—creating a poem in which every word is stressed. In normal conversation, in a phrase like "We left school," the "we" would not be stressed. But Brooks uses enjambment—the running over from one line to the next—tying the subject (*We*) on one line closely to its verb (*Left*) on the next line. In the interpretation suggested by stressing "We," the voice of the gang is defiant and assertive and proud of having left school, of hanging out late at night, of its pool-playing ability ("Strike straight"), of celebrating transgressions ("Sing sin"), and of drinking cheap alcohol ("Thin gin"). Some see the pool players as proud of sexual exploits ("Jazz" is street slang for sexual intercourse and "June" is a girl's name), though Brooks herself claimed to have been thinking of music; the poem might be seen as imitating the rhythms of jazz, foregrounding its African American heritage. However "we" is treated, the first word, the verb of doing or acting, is stressed, creating a tone of rebelliousness: "This is who we are, whether you like it or not."

But this is not the only way to read the poem. Clearly, the poem's speaker cannot literally be the seven pool players. The words attributed to them are a projection of how the poet characterizes or even stereotypes them. In this reading, the tone of defiance and assertiveness remains, but it is being self-consciously mimicked by the poet speaking on their behalf, who is controlling what they say and forcing it to be overheard. In this scenario, the life of these teenagers is presented as pathos, as a protest against a world that they reject because it has rejected them. In removing emphasis from the final "we" of each line, Brooks mimics the larger erasure of their identity by a system of discrimination and oppression. They strain to assert their identity, but the world hears their efforts as desperation—and indeed they are portrayed as accepting their own desperate condition ("We / Die soon").

There are numerous other elements we could analyze here, such as alliteration ("Lurk late," "Strike straight") and the poem's use of internal rhyme. In any case, how we formulate our thesis—one possibility might be "This poem gives voice to the identity of disenfranchised black youth through both its images and its use of meter and rhyme, but this identity itself is presented as fragile"—will depend on how we scan the poem.

QUESTIONS ABOUT METER

- What is the predominant meter of the poem?
- How (if at all) does the poet vary this meter?

- What is the rhyme scheme?
- What are the most obvious effects created by the meter and rhyme?
- How do these effects help to convey the meaning (of individual words, phrases, lines, and the poem as a whole)?

In general, it's worth remembering that prosody is something that does not exist, and should not be considered, in isolation. A poem's meter and rhythm contribute significantly to its overall effect and meaning.

PART FOUR

HISTORICAL PERIODS

The uniqueness of every work of literature arises from its author's talent and vision. But literary works also exhibit aspects of style and content that are characteristic of the age in which they were written. Knowing something about the time in which a literary work was produced can deepen our experience and understanding of it.

The chapters in Part Four offer brief introductions to the historical periods, beginning with the ancient and classical eras and moving through the Middle Ages, the Renaissance, the seventeenth century, the Enlightenment, neoclassicism to Romanticism, the later nineteenth century, and the modern, postmodern, and contemporary periods. Each looks at examples of often-studied literary texts, showing how they relate to and reflect—and sometimes challenge—their time.

CHAPTER 9

THE ANCIENT WORLD THROUGH THE CLASSICAL ERA

For our purposes, we can divide ancient Greek and Roman literature into the **preclassical period** (ca. 800–ca. 500 B.C.E.) and the **classical period** (500 B.C.E.–17 C.E.). In Greek literature, the classical period proper is limited to the fifth and fourth centuries, and is followed by the Hellenistic period (323–30 B.C.E.), when the conquests of Alexander the Great and the fragmentation of his empire spread Greek (Hellenistic) culture throughout the Mediterranean and Middle East. Latin literature begins in the third century B.C.E.; it can be divided into a golden age (70 B.C.E.–17 C.E.), a silver age (17–130 C.E.), and late Latin, giving way at the end of the Roman Empire (476 C.E.) to the Middle Ages.

THE PRECLASSICAL PERIOD
(ca. 800–ca. 500 B.C.E.)

This period gave rise to several of the literary forms at the foundation of the Western literary tradition: the epic, lyric poetry, and drama (tragedy and comedy), as well as various genres of prose and fable. To this era belonged the epic poets Homer and Hesiod and the lyric poets Archilochus, Sappho, and Pindar. During this time, most poetry was composed for oral performance, and in some cases (notably, Homeric epic) was not written down until centuries later. Its subject was myth, legend, and folk-tale; and it sometimes included accounts of historical events, as well as stories about gods and goddesses.

ANALYZING A PRECLASSICAL TEXT

Homer, *Iliad* (ca. 8th c. B.C.E.)

All the characteristics of an epic poem summarized in chapter 5 are found in the works traditionally ascribed to Homer, the *Iliad* and the *Odyssey*, which established the conventions of the epic in European literature. Many of these "epic" qualities arise from the fact that, like the Akkadian-language *Epic of Gilgamesh* (late 2nd century B.C.E.), the *Iliad* and the *Odyssey* were not written but oral compositions. To us it may seem astonishing, but poems in an oral tradition were actually composed by a poet or storyteller *during* a performance. He would draw on well-known stories whose basic themes and plots had been passed down through generations. But the poet would add his own touches, modifying certain elements as he went along.

Here's the beginning of book 1 of the *Iliad*; it illustrates a number of epic qualities and conventions that are deeply tied to the framework of ancient Greek religion and culture.

> Rage:
>   Sing, Goddess, Achilles' rage,
> Black and murderous, that cost the Greeks
> Incalculable pain, pitched countless souls
> Of heroes into Hades' dark,
> And left their bodies to rot as feasts
> For dogs and birds, as Zeus' will was done.
>   Begin with the clash between Agamemnon—
> The Greek warlord—and godlike Achilles.
>
>   Which of the immortals set these two
> At each other's throats?
>   Apollo,

Zeus' son and Leto's, offended
By the warlord. Agamemnon had dishonored
Chryses, Apollo's priest, so the god
Struck the Greek camp with plague,
And the soldiers were dying of it.

(1.1–16; trans. Stanley Lombardo)

Epic features

- **Invocation to the muse.** Where today we might talk of "inspiration," the poet here literally asks the muse or goddess to sing through him. We see immediately how dependent the ancient Greeks were on the gods for any kind of enterprise, even the creation of a poem. Indeed, as these first lines reveal the foundation of the poem's basic plot—the destruction caused by Achilles' anger and his quarrel with Agamemnon—they emphasize that all this was the "will" of Zeus, the most powerful of the Greek gods. In the world of ancient Greece humans cannot operate independently of the gods.

- **Epithets.** The original Greek describes Agamemnon as "master of men" or "lord of men." Achilles is described as "godlike." These epithets, or descriptive adjectives, serve as a kind of shorthand, revealing some of a character's essential traits. Such descriptions are tied to the Greek worldview. We wouldn't dream of calling anyone godlike today (except if we're speaking hyperbolically!); but the ancient Greeks saw continuity between the world of gods and the world of humans. Achilles, for example, is godlike not only in his appearance but in his lineage, for his mother was the goddess Thetis.

- **Rhetorical questions.** In the passage, the speaker asks how the clash between Agamemnon and Achilles came about. This is a rhetorical question (that is, a question to which the speaker knows the answer), because the speaker himself tells us the cause: the god Apollo. Here we find another common epic theme, the offending of the gods by humans. In this case, Agamemnon has dishonored Apollo's priest Chryses by refusing to accept ransom for the priest's daughter and by speaking insultingly to him.

- **Epic formulae.** A few passages later, we encounter Chryses offering up a prayer to Apollo, asking the god to wreak vengeance (1.37–42). The formula of his prayer ("If I ever sacrificed to you . . . hear my prayer") is intrinsically tied to the nature of ancient Greek religion. The connection between humans and gods was essentially one of bartering, the exchange of favors or services.

- **Similes.** The poem tells us that in response to Chryses' prayer, "the angry god [Apollo] moved *like* night down the mountain" (1.44, 47). Later, Achilles' mother Thetis is described as rising "from the white-capped sea *like* a mist" (1.359). Such similes are not merely literary devices; they are also a key to the author's conception of the world. Although the Greek gods were anthropomorphic (that is, took human shape), they were also supernatural forces.

In many other places in the *Iliad*, epic conventions are tied to the Greek worldview. For example, there are scenes of ritual sacrifice and feasting (1.458–76), the recounting of history and myth (1.263–72), and accounts of conflicts between the gods (1.540–67). Other passages tell us about Zeus's lineage and show that the Greek gods and goddesses were by no means omnipotent (unlike the God worshipped by Jews, Christians, and Muslims). Rather, the Greek gods had varying degrees of power and frequently argued and struggled among themselves.

THE CLASSICAL PERIOD (ca. 500 B.C.E.–17 C.E.)

The great writers of the classical period include the tragedians Euripides, Aeschylus, and Sophocles, as well as the comic playwright Aristophanes. The philosophers Socrates, Plato, and Aristotle also lived and taught during this era of Athenian democracy and power. Poetry had a much greater public function in ancient Greece than it does now: it was a repository of traditional wisdom and myth, and it expressed a collective vision of the deities who ruled the Greek universe, of morality, and of the ideals of courage and strength. In fact, for centuries the Homeric epics were the basis of the Greek educational system.

Also important in classical Athens was **rhetoric**, or the art of public speaking. It was taught by professional teachers who became known as

Sophists (from the Greek word *sophia*, "wisdom"). As we see today, rhetoric is important in any society that allows the expression of divergent viewpoints. Those able to speak effectively, to persuade, can influence public policy, the internal and foreign affairs of a state, as well as their everyday encounters.

In ancient Athens, the teachers of rhetoric groomed young males from the upper class to participate in public or civic life. They taught their students how to look at an issue from various perspectives, to argue both sides of a case, and, interestingly, to care less about truth than about presenting the strongest argument possible. They also instructed them in how to speak persuasively in front of any kind of audience. Hence, they offered a vision that was essentially humanistic and secular (nonreligious), a vision still alive in democratic societies today. Two classical philosophers who largely rejected the Sophists' approach are Plato and Aristotle, whose writings are foundational to Western thought.

Plato (ca. 427–ca. 347 B.C.E.)

Plato's work explores many of the questions that have preoccupied philosophers for centuries: What is the nature of truth? How can we define basic concepts such as goodness, virtue, love, piety, and justice? What is the connection between soul and body? What is the best kind of political state? What function is served by literature and the arts? Many of Plato's ideas came from his great teacher Socrates, who himself wrote nothing but is the major character in most of Plato's dialogues, in which he represents Plato's own positions.

The **theory of Forms** underlies Plato's worldview: it holds that the physical world, the world of the senses that surrounds us, is not real. This world of "appearances," as Plato calls it, is merely an imperfect copy of a higher world of Forms or pure ideas (though these are not ideas in anyone's mind). Any object in the material world—he uses the example of a bed—is a copy of the Form or idea or essence of the bed that exists in the higher world. A woman is tall or good because she participates in the Form of "tallness" or "goodness." Plato also used examples from geometry: a triangle drawn with instruments in the physical world can never be perfect; it is an imperfect copy of the perfect triangle, which is in fact not an object but a concept. According to Plato, the world of Forms is the true reality: eternal and changeless, it is apprehended by reason, not by the senses. The physical world is the world of change and decay, the world we know through our bodies. Poetry, according to Plato, is flawed because it represents or imitates the physical world—which is already an imitation of the world of Forms. So poetry, he famously remarks at the beginning of *Republic* 10, is at a third remove from truth.

One of Plato's best-known explanations of this theory is his allegory of the cave, which opens book 7 of the *Republic*. Imagine, he says, people shackled so that they can see only the wall of a cave. There is a fire far above and behind them, and they watch the shadows cast on the wall by statues of people and objects passing behind them. Because they have lived like this all their lives, they think these shadows—appearances—are reality. Only if someone is dragged out of the cave and into the light of the sun will he be able to see things as they are, in the real world. The cave represents the physical world, and reality—the world of Forms—is outside it.

At first glance, Plato's theory might seem strange. Surely the real world is what we see and feel and hear. But think about a familiar scenario: a seminar in a college classroom. We would probably agree that what is most "real" in that situation is not the physical objects—chairs, desks, whiteboard—but the exchange of ideas, thoughts, and emotions, which we cannot see or feel. And what we physically "hear" is merely the outward sign of some deeper internal transformation that is not physical at all. So in an important sense, Plato may have been right.

Aristotle (384–322 B.C.E.)

Aristotle's influence on Western thought was at least as extensive as that of his teacher, Plato. Aristotle's contributions range over logic, metaphysics, ethics, politics, psychology, poetry, and rhetoric. Whereas Plato's emphasis on timeless Forms led him to value mathematics and geometry as means to understand the immaterial realm, Aristotle was interested in the phenomena of the natural world, including biology and zoology. A number of Aristotle's basic notions have profoundly affected subsequent thought in many fields and much modern philosophy.

Aristotle suggested that our view of the world is filtered through ten categories, which include space, time, quantity, quality, and relation. Underlying all these categories is **substance** or **essence**, the primary reality. In many ways, we still think of objects in terms of these categories; and we still think of objects and concepts as having an identifiable essence. We might, for example, define the essence of a table as a flat surface with four legs, or the essence of love as self-sacrifice. Also influential were Aristotle's formulations of **logic**, especially the three so-called laws of logic: the laws of identity, noncontradiction, and the excluded middle.

Aristotle also wrote the single most influential text in the history of literary criticism, the *Poetics* (ca. 330 B.C.E.). His understanding of tragedy, his perception of a hierarchy of literary genres, his views of imitation, his insistence on the unity of action and of time in drama, his view of poetry as expressing universal truths, his view that a literary work should have organic unity, his understanding of the moral and educational function of literature, and his assessment of the role of the audience have shaped the thinking of Western writers and critics for two millennia.

ELEMENTS OF CLASSICISM

Aristotle's *Poetics* is the source of the most important elements of classicism.

- **Poetry as imitation.** What does poetry imitate? Aristotle's answer is subtle. Poetry does not represent the outside world or even the human mind. Rather, it imitates human action: specifically, action that has a *moral* import. For Aristotle, poetry has a moral and educational function.

- **Realism.** The action that poetry represents must have some "probability" or "necessity." Literature should not talk about fantastic or imaginary beings or events. Rather, it should imitate or express what is central to actual human experience.

- **Universal truths.** Unlike history, which narrates particular actions and events, poetry must express general truths, portraying actions whose significance can be applied more widely to other situations.

- **Objectivity.** Poetry should express not something subjective or personal but rather some feature of the objective human situation.

- **Definition of tragedy.** Aristotle defines tragedy as the imitation of an action that is serious, complete, and of a certain magnitude. By "serious" he means *morally* serious: the action imitated must be important, with significant consequences. (His discussion of comedy has been lost.)

- **Dramatic unities.** Though neoclassical critics would later propose three dramatic unities—of time, of place, and of action—Aristotle writes of only two in the *Poetics*. The action represented on the stage should be restricted in time to "one revolution of the sun or a little bit more," a span interpreted by some critics as twelve hours and by others as twenty-four hours. Moreover, there must be unity of plot—the presentation of one action in its entirety, with all of its parts necessarily connected. The plot includes "recognition" (a character suddenly realizing something) and *peripeteia* or "reversal" of a situation. Tragedy will produce a release of the emotions of pity and fear in an audience (*catharsis*).

- **Clarity.** In his treatise *On Rhetoric* (ca. 340 B.C.E.), Aristotle calls clarity the chief virtue of style: it is crucial that an audience understand what a speaker or poet is saying.

- **Propriety or decorum.** The style must be appropriate to the subject matter. A youth, for example, must not speak like an old man.

What we call classicism in literature also drew largely on the *Ars Poetica* (ca. 10 B.C.E., *Art of Poetry*) by the Roman poet and critic Horace; indeed, over the past two thousand years the *Ars Poetica* has enjoyed an influence sometimes greater than that of Aristotle's *Poetics*. Horace was a poet, and his *Ars*—itself a poem—insists strongly on the labor or **craft** required to compose poetry. He urges the poet to revise his or her work, to show it to qualified people, and to publish it only after strenuous improvement. Horace offers a famous warning against the hazards of publication: "the voice once sent forth can never be called back." His prescriptions for poetry are summed up in his idea that poetry should give **pleasure** and offer **moral instruction**, a combination often channeled into the influential formula that poetry should "teach and delight."

ANALYZING A CLASSICAL TEXT

Virgil, *Aeneid* (29–19 B.C.E.)

Virgil's *Aeneid*, a later poem written in Latin, is modeled in many ways on the Homeric poems, but it is a different kind of epic. Whereas Homer's heroes Achilles and Odysseus act largely on behalf of themselves and their immediate families or companions, the *Aeneid* situates its hero, Aeneas, within a larger historical context and insists on his responsibility to causes other than self-interest. The word used to describe Aeneas's obligation is *pietas*, which denotes devotion to family, community, country, and the gods, and his epithet is *pius*.

These classical attributes are illustrated in one of the many powerful episodes in the *Aeneid*, the love affair between Aeneas and Dido, the queen of Carthage. After listening, spellbound, to Aeneas's story of his escape from Troy, Dido falls in love with him, and Aeneas appears to return her feelings. He even helps build the walls of Carthage. It's at this point that Jupiter sends his messenger Mercury to remind Aeneas of his mission, which is to prepare the foundations of Rome "and bring the entire world beneath the rule of law" (4.231). Aeneas resolves to leave Carthage. When Dido confronts him, he says:

> My father, Anchises, whenever the darkness shrouds
> the earth in its dank shadows, whenever the stars
> go flaming up the sky, my father's anxious ghost
> warns me in dreams and fills my heart with fear.
> My son Ascanius . . . I feel the wrong I do
> to one so dear, robbing him of his kingdom,
> lands in the West, his fields decreed by Fate.
> And now the messenger of the gods—I swear it,
> by your life and mine—dispatched by Jove himself

has brought me firm commands through the racing winds.
With my own eyes I saw him, clear, in broad daylight,
moving through your gates. With my own ears I drank
his message in. Come, stop inflaming us both
with your appeals. I set sail for Italy—
all against my will.

(4.438–52; trans. Robert Fagles)

This passage exhibits several features of a classical worldview.

- **Emphasis on human limitation.** Aeneas acknowledges his inability to resist larger forces and pleads that he is not following his own will.

- **Historical contextualization.** Aeneas is beginning to situate his life within the movement of history. The past is embodied in his dead father, Anchises, while the future is represented by his son, Ascanius. We witness here the workings of a conscience ("I feel the wrong I do"), whereby an individual rises above his own desire or self-interest to reflect on his potential impact on others and on the future.

- **Duty.** Aeneas is driven by *pietas*, a sense of duty to his family, his people, and the gods. This devotion requires considerable sacrifice on his part: he cannot help hurting Dido, and his own heart is equally pained.

- **Contrast with Dido.** While Aeneas represents the classical virtues of civilization—law, rationality, the perception of oneself as a social being with responsibilities to family and community, the recognition of one's relation to fate and the gods, the ability to master one's emotions—Dido presents a counterpoint to these values. From the beginning of book 4, Dido is described as "consumed by . . . fire" (4.3), "mad with love" (4.83), in a state of "frenzy" (4.87), and as "the restless queen" (4.10).

Overall, the *Aeneid* exhibits a classical preoccupation with universal themes such as the search for a home, as well as a classical emphasis on human limitation, a collective vision, and a concern with history and tradition. It also pays attention to the ideals—and costs—of civilization. Such ideals include law, rationality, moral virtue, fortitude, and moderation, all exercised in the commitment to causes higher than mere survival or personal glory.

CHAPTER 10

THE MIDDLE AGES

THE EARLY MIDDLE AGES (ca. 476–1050 C.E.)

The Middle Ages stretch from the fall of Rome in 476 until the beginnings of the Renaissance ("rebirth") in the fifteenth century. Why do we call this period the "middle" ages? It was in fact Italian Renaissance thinkers who coined the term *medium aevum* (Middle Age). Seeing their own era as one of rebirth and rediscovery of classical values, they wanted to distinguish themselves from the intervening thousand years, which they disparaged as an age of darkness and superstition. Indeed, until quite recently the early Middle Ages were often spoken of as the "Dark Ages." Following are some important aspects of the early Middle Ages:

- **Christianity.** Thanks to the conversion of the emperor Constantine around 312, Christianity was increasingly tolerated in the Roman Empire. By 381 it was recognized as the empire's official religion. After the empire's disintegration into warring tribes and kingdoms, Christianity was the only unifying force. Early in the life of the church, its central doctrines were often the subject of bitter dispute, and there were numerous Christian sects. It was only at the Council of Nicaea in 325 that the notion of the Trinity— the unity of Father, Son, and Holy Spirit as three persons in one

Godhead—was adopted as orthodox doctrine. The doctrine of Incarnation—that God took bodily form in the person of Jesus Christ—was adopted at the Council of Chalcedon in 451. The organization of the church became increasingly centralized under the authority of the pope in Rome.

- **Germanic culture.** Medieval civilization in western Europe was also shaped by the Germanic tribes who had overrun the empire. These tribes included Scandinavians, Goths, Vandals, Franks, Angles, and Saxons, who had settled throughout the Western Roman Empire long before the sack of Rome in 410 by the Visigoths. The typical tribe consisted of a king or chieftain surrounded by his "royal clan" of councilmen or retainers. This structure eventually developed into the system of feudalism, which involved sworn obligations between rulers and subjects, lords and vassals. Feudal societies stressed values such as courage, honor, loyalty, protection, and obedience. We see these values expressed in poems such as *Beowulf* (ca. 9th century), often in uneasy coexistence with Christian values such as humility and trust in divine providence. After the German chieftain Odoacer deposed the last Roman emperor in 476, the Germanic peoples gradually converted to Christianity.

- **Classical heritage.** The intellectual life of the early Middle Ages was largely shaped by the interaction between the classical legacy and evolving Christian theology. Some Christian thinkers tried to free their religion of pagan notions and influences, but other theologians such as Augustine attempted to integrate useful features of classical philosophy and rhetoric into a Christian framework.

When analyzing texts from the early Middle Ages, it's useful to remember the major components of medieval civilization mentioned above: Christianity, Germanic culture, and the legacy of the classical world. Most early medieval texts will contain some interplay between these elements.

ANALYZING AN EARLY MEDIEVAL TEXT

Augustine, *Confessions* (ca. 400 C.E.)

Augustine is usually seen as belonging to two worlds, with one foot in the ancient world and the other stepping into the medieval world. During his lifetime, the Roman Empire was collapsing, and at the end of his life Vandals laid siege to Hippo (in modern-day Algeria), where he was bishop. Augustine's *Confessions* is a personal work, directly addressed to God. But it's also aimed at all people who would take the path of salvation. Describing his long and tortuous journey toward Christianity, Augustine shows us that religious conversion is a difficult process, involving regression, doubt, lapses of faith, and outright sinning. His story, as in so many ancient texts, is of a journey. Augustine moves from the classical and worldly pursuits of rhetoric, grammar, and law, from indulgence of bodily appetites and lust, from pleasure in committing sins such as stealing, to a reunion with his higher spiritual self, as commanded by God. During this process, Augustine sheds light on the nature of sin, showing how, from an earthly standpoint, it can appear beautiful. The following passage from book 7 is central to Augustine's journey:

> Thus I was sick at heart and in torment, accusing myself with a new intensity of bitterness, twisting and turning in my chain in the hope that it might be utterly broken, for what held me was so small a thing! But it still held me. And You stood in the secret places of my soul, O Lord, in the harshness of Your Mercy redoubling the scourges of fear and shame lest I should give way again and that small slight tie which remained should not be broken but should grow again to full strength and bind me even closer than before. For I kept saying within myself: "Let it be now, let it be now," and by the mere words I had begun to move toward the resolution. I almost made it, yet I did not quite make it. But I did not fall back into my original state, but as it were stood near to get my breath. And I tried again and I was almost there, and now I could all but touch it and hold it: yet I was not quite there,

I did not touch it or hold it. I still shrank from dying unto death and living unto life. The lower condition which had grown habitual was more powerful than the better condition which I had not tried. The nearer the point of time came in which I was to become different, the more it struck me with horror; but it did not force me utterly back nor turn me utterly away, but held me there between the two.

(trans. F. J. Sheed)

As always, let's start by asking questions.

What is the **historical context**?

- The medieval worldview was otherworldly in orientation, viewing earthly life as a preparation for the next life, the life of the spirit.
- Augustine lived at an important historical turning point—the Roman Empire poised between paganism and Christianity. He presents this shift as a movement within his own life and psychology.

What is the **theme**?

- The main theme that structures this passage seems to be Augustine's sense of internal dividedness, of being torn between his old ways and new possibilities. Or perhaps the primary theme is the nature of sin.

What are the **stylistic features**?

- Consider Augustine's language. He describes himself as "twisting and turning," as "almost there" but "not quite there."
- Augustine makes his description immediate and graphic by using direct speech, letting us know what he is saying to himself internally ("Let it be now, let it be now"), giving us a sense of his impatience but also of his hesitancy.

How can we **relate this passage to other parts** of the text?

- What does Augustine mean by "chain"? In an earlier passage, he says, "I had grown deaf from the clanking of the chain of my mortality, the punishment for the pride of my soul: and I departed further from You" (book 2.2). Perhaps the "chain" is mortality—the fact that he will die, the consequence of original sin as inherited from Adam and Eve. Mortality binds him to earthly life so that he cannot direct his thoughts to the hereafter. This is what Augustine seems to mean when he talks of "dying unto death and living unto life." Death is the life on earth; he must kill that lower life within himself and be reborn in his higher or spiritual life.

Moving from notes to thesis

Basically, we've made notes on historical context, theme, and style. Let's say you were asked to write about how Augustine reconciles classical and Christian values. The opening paragraph of your essay might run something like this:

> In expressing his inner turmoil, Augustine is expressing a medieval attitude which subordinates this world to the next, and body to spirit or soul. He is caught between two worlds, struggling to become a Christian but still attracted to his old ways. This anguish is captured in his language, which describes him as pulled in two directions. However, Augustine's classical background, his training in rhetoric, helps him in this journey; as he tells us in book 3, a book by the Roman orator Cicero inspired him to turn away from worldly pleasures. So, in Augustine, there is some attempt to reconcile classical and Christian values.

This paragraph, which ends with the thesis statement, will furnish a sound basis for the rest of the paper, Of course, many other readings are possible. You might want to focus on the psychology of Augustine's conversion. Or you might want to talk about how Augustine explores the meaning of "sin."

ANALYZING AN EARLY MEDIEVAL TEXT

Beowulf (ca. 9th c.)

The epic poem *Beowulf* is now thought to have been composed by a Christian poet as early as the year 700, but the only surviving manuscript was written around the year 1000. Though *Beowulf* is written in Old English, it describes events that took place in the sixth century concerning heroes from Germanic culture, specifically the south Scandinavian tribes of the Danes and the Geats. The initial invasion of England by the Germanic tribes occurred in the mid-fifth century, and their conversion to Christianity was completed during the seventh century. So, naturally, in this poem we find a mixture of Christian and pagan Germanic values. Sometimes these values coincide; at other times they conflict sharply.

Let's analyze a passage toward the end of the poem. Much earlier, Beowulf defeated the monster Grendel and its mother; he has ruled as king over the Geats for fifty years. Now he faces the prospect of dueling yet another monster, the dragon. This creature, which stands guard over a hoard of treasure, has destroyed Beowulf's village in revenge for the theft of a cup. The poet describes Beowulf's state of mind:

> Then Beowulf was given bad news,
> the hard truth: his own home,
> the best of buildings, had been burned to a cinder,
> the throne-room of the Geats. It threw the hero
> into deep anguish and darkened his mood:
> the wise man thought he must have thwarted
> ancient ordinance of the eternal Lord,
> broken His commandment. His mind was in turmoil,
> unaccustomed anxiety and gloom
> confused his brain; the fire-dragon
> had razed the coastal region and reduced
> forts and earthworks to dust and ashes,
> so the war-king planned and plotted his revenge.

(lines 2324–36; trans. Seamus Heaney)

And now for some questions.

What is the **historical context**?

- Although the poem was written by a Christian, it refers to actions of Germanic heroes centuries earlier. So it may contain an unreconciled mixture of pagan Germanic and Christian values.

What is the **theme** of the passage?

- Is the theme the conflict between good and evil? It's clear that Beowulf represents the good. He has been appointed by God to fight Grendel and he has put his trust in God (lines 665–70). The dragon is called "the scourge of the people" (line 2278).

- The monsters that Beowulf has already fought—Grendel and his mother—represent evil. They are described as descended from the first murderer, Cain, who killed his brother Abel (lines 104–14). Grendel is described as "God-cursed" (line 121).

What are the **Christian elements** of the poem?

- Beowulf is viewed as a type of Christian savior. He is described as devoted to truth, justice, peace, friendship, and humility (lines 1700–701, 1760, 1838, 1857). All these are qualities compatible with Christianity.

- Beowulf is described by his comrade Wiglaf in explicitly Christian terms as "the shepherd of our land" (line 2644).

- Feeling "deep anguish," "turmoil," and "anxiety," Beowulf wonders if he has disobeyed the commandments of "the eternal Lord."

What are the **Germanic elements** of the poem?

- Beowulf is described as achieving immortality through "glorious action" (lines 953–54), as devoted to tradition (line 1701), and even at the end of the poem as "keenest to win fame" (line 3182).

- Beowulf reverts to his Germanic role as a "war-king" and "warriors' protector" (lines 2336, 2337) and plots revenge against the monster. Vengefulness, of course, is not a Christian quality.

- Beowulf seeks glory. He is "too proud" to summon the aid of others and is eager to fight the monster single-handedly.

Moving from notes to thesis

What are we to make of this conflict between Christian and Germanic values? Such differences between the religious and the secular have characterized many societies, including our own. How should these tensions be resolved? Or can they? We could formulate a thesis that reflects this contradiction:

> *Beowulf* embodies an unreconciled conflict between pagan and Christian values. On the one hand, Beowulf is presented as possessing Christian virtues such as love, devotion to peace, and a moral conscience. On the other hand, he is motivated by a desire for vengeance and glory and by the wish to protect his people.

Or we could argue that one set of values wins out over the other. In that case, the thesis might look like this:

> Despite the apparent conflict in *Beowulf* between pagan and Christian values, the Christian vision ultimately supersedes the Germanic elements: the dragon is perhaps a symbol of death, and while Beowulf does kill it, he does so only by yielding his own life, his own attachment to worldly things.

Whatever thesis you develop, the overall structure of your paper might look something like this:

- A statement of the **relevant** historical context (the slow spreading of Christianity through a pagan culture, resulting in the coexistence of contradictory values)
- A statement of the **main theme**, as expressed in your thesis
- One or two paragraphs on the **Germanic** elements of the passage
- One or two paragraphs on the **Christian** elements of the passage
- One or two paragraphs justifying your own argument as to which set of values is dominant

THE LATER MIDDLE AGES (ca. 1050–1500)

Many elements from the early medieval period continued to shape life and thought in the later Middle Ages. The influence of Christianity and classicism became even more profound, but the structure of Germanic tribal culture evolved into the feudal system. A number of new intellectual movements and social features, enabled by the growth of universities and religious schools, characterized the later Middle Ages.

- **Allegorical criticism**, which arose in the early Middle Ages, is a way of reading a text on several different levels. These levels are usually described in Christian thought as literal, moral, and spiritual. Allegory was used to reconcile the Old with the New Testament, as well as Christian doctrine with classical thought. Medieval allegory embodies the belief that things in this world have a significance beyond themselves in that they refer to elements in the larger spiritual order of the universe. For example, in *The Divine Comedy*, Dante uses a she-wolf, a lion, and a leopard to represent lust, violence, and fraud, respectively.

- **Scholasticism** was a school of thought that tried to understand Christian scripture by reconciling the doctrines of Christian faith with the rational methods of classical philosophy, especially the philosophy of Aristotle. The central figure of this school was St. Thomas Aquinas (1225–1274), the most important thinker of the Roman Catholic Church.

- **Humanism** rests on the notions that the world is centered not on a divine plan but on human values and schemes of thought, and that human beings possess free will and moral responsibility. Thus a humanist views events in the world not as ordained by God but as caused by human actions and natural phenomena. Humanism flowers fully in the Renaissance, but it's important to recognize its medieval roots. For example, we see humanism in the works of Chaucer and the medieval feminist thinker Christine de Pizan.

- Our idea of the university, with its various departments and curricula, was formed in the Middle Ages, and the **liberal arts** have their roots in the classical world. The Roman philosopher and tragedian

Seneca saw these disciplines as "liberal" because they are worthy of freeborn (*liber*) men, who need not make money.

- **Feudalism** is a term that came into use long after this period and derived from the medieval Latin *feudum*, which means "fief"—that is, a piece of land or sometimes an office that was not owned outright but held on condition of service to a superior lord ("in fee"). The lord who owned the land provided protection and patronage. Hence feudalism was a huge system of interrelated contracts between lords and vassals, taking the place of a centralized authority. It later would be seen as a strict and largely static hierarchy, ranging from the king through the nobility, through a small middle class of merchants and craftsmen, to the peasantry, which composed the vast majority of the population.

Familiarity with these terms will help you not only understand medieval literary texts but also grasp how the modern world came into being. Theories such as Marxism are based on an interpretation of how the capitalist democracies of today emerged as reactions against the economic and social constraints of the feudal system.

ANALYZING A LATER MEDIEVAL TEXT

Dante, *Inferno* (ca. 1307–21)

Dante's epic poem *The Divine Comedy* provides a good illustration of how allegory works. Allegory operates in it on many levels and informs its overall structure, whose three-part division echoes the Christian Trinity. And Dante is guided in his journey first by his poetic mentor Virgil, who represents human reason, and later by Beatrice, who embodies Divine Love, through hell and purgatory to the ultimate vision of God in paradise.

In his prose writings, Dante explains that *The Divine Comedy* is "polysemous," or characterized by several layers of meaning: the literal sense points to three other levels of meaning. Dante classifies all three levels as allegorical, though he also divides them into the allegorical sense (the truth beneath a beautiful fiction), the moral sense (the example or lesson that can be learned), and the anagogical sense (the spiritual meaning, expressing the otherwise inexpressible mysteries of God). We can see, then, that allegory conveys a vision of the world in which the true significance of things is referred to a spiritual realm.

Let's look at one of the most famous passages in the *Inferno*: the punishment of the adulterous lovers Paolo and Francesca in canto 5. When Dante enters the second circle of hell, he describes it as follows:

> I came to a place where no light shone at all,
>> bellowing like the sea racked by a tempest,
>> when warring winds attack it from both sides.
>
> The infernal storm, eternal in its rage,
>> sweeps and drives the spirits with its blast:
>> it whirls them, lashing them with punishment.
> . . . .
> I learned that to this place of punishment
>> all those who sin in lust have been condemned,
>> those who make reason slave to appetite.
>
> *(lines 28–39; trans. Mark Musa)*

For the most part, we don't need specialized knowledge to see how the allegory works here, where the lustful are punished. Still, as always, the best strategy is to come up with the right questions.

What is the **historical and structural context** of Dante's allegory?

- Dante's poem is informed by a medieval worldview that considers life in this temporal world as preparation for life in the hereafter. Actions that appear attractive on earth—such as adultery—may take on very different appearances when considered in an eternal context.

- Paolo and Francesca decided to be lovers. Francesca relates that their affair started while they were reading: "our eyes were brought together" (line 130). But this connection and their affair reverberate in eternity. The lovers chose each other instead of God, and their punishment is precisely that they have each other forever—but not God.

- Dante's worldview is informed by Scholasticism, by the insistence that reason is an important component of our spiritual condition. Paolo and Francesca allowed reason to be subordinate to their appetites and desires.

What are the **elements of allegory** in this passage?

- There is "no light." What does darkness represent? Ignorance? Being morally lost?

- What does the tempest or storm represent? Perhaps the upheaval of desire or lust? And why "warring winds"? Violent and confusing emotions, even those of love, can make us feel torn in opposite directions.

- The fact that the lovers are "whirling" in a circle may represent their spiritual aimlessness.

Moving from notes to thesis

Now that you have these notes, you can organize them according to whatever perspective you adopt.

Dante's allegory operates on both structural and textual levels. It is broadly informed by a medieval vision that values knowledge and reason and places earthly action in the context of eternity. This passage represents the spiritual condition of those who have given in to lustful appetites and uses physical phenomena such as the wind and storms as symbols of this condition.

Then you might organize your paper as follows:

- Give a statement of the **relevant** historical context (how the medieval worldview places earthly life in relationship to eternal life and divine judgment).

- Explain how **allegory** embodies this worldview.

- Provide a **thesis** about Dante's allegory.

- Demonstrate the **structural** operation of Dante's allegory.
- Show how Dante's allegory works in the text.

ANALYZING A LATER MEDIEVAL TEXT

Christine de Pizan, *The Book of the City of Ladies* (1405)

Christine de Pizan was one of the most powerful voices of the Middle Ages. Indeed, it can be argued that her feminism and humanism mutually shaped and refined each other in a unique and pioneering manner. Her most famous work, *The Book of the City of Ladies*, challenges history as it has been written by men and rewrites the history of women, refuting the stereotypes of women as deficient in both intellect and morals and as unsuited to public and political life.

The *Book* is written as a conversation between Christine and three allegorical personae. Christine begins by reflecting on the numerous treatises written by men that characterize women's behavior as wicked. She reflects that such negative views are contradicted by her own experience of women. But she finds herself distrusting her own intellect and relying more on the judgments of others—the male "authorities" she has read. Doubting herself, she begins to despair and wonders why God created woman if she is so bad.

At this point, three "crowned ladies" appear to Christine: Reason, who guides people to the right path by showing them a mirror of themselves and the world; Rectitude, who promotes righteousness against the work of evildoers; and Justice, who judges people according to their actions. Collectively, their mission is to urge Christine to build a "City of Ladies" that will be a place of refuge for women. Christine's city is explicitly metaphorical: she must "build" it with her pen.

The first to address Christine is Reason, who encourages her to trust her own experience and says the following about the tradition of male thinking:

> Now, if you turn your mind to the very highest realm of all, the realm of abstract ideas, think for a moment whether or not those philosophers

whose views against women you've been citing have ever been proven wrong. In fact, they are all constantly correcting each other's opinions, as you yourself should know from reading Aristotle's *Metaphysics*, where he discusses and refutes both their views and those of Plato and other philosophers. Don't forget the Doctors of the Church either, and Saint Augustine in particular, who all took issue with Aristotle himself on certain matters, even though he is considered to be the greatest of all authorities on both moral and natural philosophy. You seem to have accepted the philosophers' views as articles of faith and thus as irrefutable on every point.

(trans. Rosalind Brown-Grant)

Regarding the qualities that men have attributed to women in their writings, Reason points out that Christine's own experience will tell her that "it's all a pack of outrageous lies." Now let's pose some questions.

What is the relevant **historical and biographical context**?

- In the Middle Ages, many women received no education; those who received formal schooling did so largely in convents. Some in the upper class attended court schools, while others were tutored at home.

- Christine was born into a high-ranking family. Her father was astrologer to Charles V, and she studied at the French court. Thus she was able to explore not only the traditions of male thinking but also the neglected contributions of women to both history and literature.

- In fact, nearly all of Christine's work challenged the predominant attitudes toward women and urged that women be educated.

What are the **features** of Christine's humanism?

- One humanistic feature of the passage is its championing of reason and overt challenge of faith and authority. But unlike much Renaissance humanism, which returned to the values of classical culture, Christine questions the authority of the classical writers themselves—most notably Aristotle.

- Another humanistic feature is the appeal to the evidence of one's own experience, even if it contradicts what thinkers have said in their books.

- In fact, Reason challenges the entire male philosophical tradition, showing that it is internally self-contradictory (philosophers disagree with one another) and that its views are not infallible and are sometimes easily refuted.

- All these factors are concerned not just with Christine's humanism but also with her feminism. How does the feminist element of her humanism make it different from other kinds of Christian humanism? Does Christine's appeal to Christianity undermine her feminism?

What **rhetorical strategies** does Christine use?

- The most obvious strategy is allegory, which structures *The Book of the City of Ladies* and which, characteristically, uses personification. "City" refers to an intellectual enterprise, while human reason, rectitude, and justice are personified. In using allegory, Christine deploys a traditional medieval strategy for her own purposes. For example, in personifying reason as female, she appropriates for women a faculty that men have traditionally claimed for themselves.

- Christine's strategy is ingenious: she places herself in the position of a woman who lacks confidence. The voice that challenges the male tradition is outside of her: it speaks to her and comes to her from God. In essence, she is projecting her own voice into these divinely sent figures.

Moving from notes to thesis

How you proceed depends on *your* point of entry into Christine's text. What is it that interests you most? What do you find striking or original or controversial? Perhaps you find her embodiment of "reason" in a female, and her deconstruction and reconstruction of authority, appealing. If that interests you, you might come up with something like this:

> For thousands of years, one of the dominant male stereotypes about women has been that they lack "reason," which has been deemed to be an essentially male faculty. What gives power to Christine's undermining of this stereotype are not just her counterarguments but also the form those counterarguments take. Reason is personified as a woman who is sent as a messenger from God. This strategy (a) immediately removes "reason" from the male tradition, (b) enables "reason" to speak with a more authoritative voice, and (c) allows "reason" to connect intimately with the narrator.

This paragraph offers an initial direction for a paper. But we could follow many other paths. We could ask questions about the connections between Christine's feminism and her Christian beliefs. How does her feminism change her beliefs? Exploring this might raise the broader question of whether Christianity and feminism are compatible.

ANALYZING A LATER MEDIEVAL TEXT

Geoffrey Chaucer, *The Canterbury Tales* (ca. 1386–1400)

Chaucer's writing is known for its complex narrative techniques, detailed character portrayal, and a moral and spiritual outlook that is both humanistic and modern. An interesting difference between Dante's religious and Chaucer's humanistic outlooks is found in their approaches to description. Dante *never* describes what people look like, even Virgil or Beatrice. He is interested only in describing a person's *moral* and *spiritual* condition. In contrast, Chaucer's definition of the "human" is broader, including not only the moral complexity of people (they are not just good or bad) but the sheer range of their character and personality. He tells us about their origins, appearance, speech, dress, habits, self-image, and behavior.

Chaucer's narrative technique often points toward the *ideal* through a description of the *real*. Chaucer anticipates a realism that moves beyond and even shuns allegory in favor of uniqueness and detailed description, a realism that avoids moral stereotyping. Where Dante presents a moral hierarchy, Chaucer offers a social one. He gives us a cross-section of feudal English society. Moreover, unlike Dante, he refrains from judging most of his characters, often allowing the reader to make the final assessment. For all these reasons, we may relate to Chaucer more easily than we do to Dante: for the most part, we don't care just about a person's morality but also about their appearance, manners, dress, and speech, as well as their profession. Chaucer's portrayal of characters in the General Prologue to *The Canterbury Tales* perfectly illustrates his humanistic narrative technique. Here is a wonderful description, that of the Prioress:

> There was also a Nun, a Prioress,
> Who in her smiling was simple and gracious;
> . . . .
> Quite well she sang the liturgy divine,
> Intoning it in her nose quite properly;
> And French she spoke quite well and elegantly,
> After the school of Stratford-at-the-Bow,
> Because Parisian French she did not know.
> In dining, she was well taught overall;
> She let no morsel down from her lips fall,
> . . . .
> And truthfully, she was so very pleasant,
> And amiable, her manners excellent;
> She pained herself to imitate the ways
> Of court, and to be stately all her days,
> And to be held worthy of reverence.
> . . . .
> Her eyes blue gray as glass, her nose well-shaped,
> Her mouth quite small, and also soft and red.
> But, certainly, she had a fair forehead;
> It was almost a span in breadth, I own;
> For, truth to tell, she was not undergrown.
>
> (lines 118–56; trans. Sheila Fisher)

Asking the following questions will help us explore Chaucer's narrative technique.

What is the **historical context**?

- Chaucer was writing in the late Middle Ages, when an "other-worldly" attitude toward life, which tended to devalue earthly life, still prevailed.

- However, more humanistic and secular (nonreligious) attitudes were emerging. Commerce and communication across countries were expanding, cities were growing, and the Roman Catholic Church, as Chaucer shows through his portraits of the clergy, was becoming somewhat corrupt.

- Medieval nuns were bound by vows of poverty, chastity, and obedience. Aside from wanting to devote their lives to the church, women had various motivations for becoming nuns: the wishes of their families, the desire to be respected at a time when women had few options, and perhaps a need for independence from men. Nuns from wealthy families would sometimes break their vows by enjoying fine food, wearing rich clothing, and keeping dogs.

What are the **humanistic features** in Chaucer's portrait of the Prioress?

- The Prioress's skills and manners as a lady: her smiling, singing, and (dubious) ability to speak French. Chaucer spends at least ten lines describing her eating habits. Why?

- The Prioress's appearance: we get a detailed description of her face. Her nose is mentioned twice, her mouth is portrayed somewhat sensuously, and overall she is not small.

- Her character is summed up in the great lengths to which the Prioress goes to "imitate" the ways of court—not the ways of the church. Indeed, Chaucer talks very little about her religious or spiritual qualities.

- Chaucer's portrait does not pass moral judgment on the Prioress. He leaves that to us, the readers. How do we react? Many people find her to be an attractive character, in spite of her laxity as a nun. Perhaps we like her for her very weaknesses.

What can we say about the **style** of Chaucer's poetry?

- The most obvious feature is realism. Chaucer's descriptions are detailed and show people in their actual moral complexity. Most people are not good or bad but are somewhere in between. Chaucer shows us people who are like us.

- Chaucer's language seems to be mostly literal. There is no symbolic reference to another world. So Chaucer has moved away from allegory as a literary device and as a way of thinking about the world. This suggests a large change in worldview, with earthly life being regarded as important in its own right.

Moving from notes to thesis

From these notes, we could develop many different theses. One might read:

> Chaucer's portrait of the Prioress embodies a worldview that is humanistic and secular, as expressed both in its content and in its narrative technique.

The paper could be organized something like this:

- A statement of the **relevant historical context** (how a humanist and secular view of the world was beginning to supplant medieval "otherworldliness")

- A **thesis** about Chaucer's humanism

- A discussion of how this humanism is expressed in the **content** of Chaucer's portrait

- A demonstration of humanist features in the **form** of Chaucer's narrative technique

There are, of course, many ways in which we could analyze Chaucer's tale. We could examine how he presents a cross-section of the social ranks of feudal society. We could look at the use of allegory in other medieval texts, from both Western and Eastern cultures, such as *Sir Gawain and the Green Knight* and the *Thousand and One Nights*.

CHAPTER II

FROM THE EARLY MODERN PERIOD TO THE LATE NINETEENTH CENTURY

THE EARLY MODERN PERIOD

The early modern period, conventionally called the Renaissance, began in the fourteenth century and lasted until the middle of the seventeenth century. The term "Renaissance," or "rebirth," indicates a return to the classical values and styles and, in general, the humanism of ancient Greece and Rome. Reacting against medieval "otherworldliness," Renaissance thinkers placed emphasis on *this* world and on science, investigating all aspects of life in human terms rather than referring everything to God. They also tended to attach greater importance to the individual. All of these characteristics are associated with humanism, a broad outlook that places the human being rather than God at the center of explanations, focusing on human achievements rather than theological issues and dilemmas. Many of these characteristics can be seen in the works of the great writers of the period, such as Christopher Marlowe and William Shakespeare in the sixteenth century. Here are some of the important dimensions of early modern humanism.

- **A new cosmology.** Medieval cosmology, following the first-century C.E. thinker Ptolemy, placed the Earth at the center of the universe, surrounded by the other planets, beyond which lay the empyrean— the heavenly sphere—and the throne of God. In the early fifteenth century, the Polish astronomer Copernicus formulated a heliocentric theory (published in 1543), which argued that the Sun was at the center of the planets' rotation. This theory was verified in the next century by Galileo.

- **Scientific and empirical methods.** Whereas most medieval thinkers had spiritual and idealistic views of the world and of the "human," based on the idea of God's providence, Renaissance thinkers tended to base their inquiries on reason and the observation of natural phenomena. The greatest philosopher of this period, Francis Bacon, advocated the empirical method of induction as against the scholastic reliance on deduction, authority, and faith (for definitions of "inductive" and "deductive" reasoning, see chapter 19).

- **The Protestant Reformation.** This huge transformation, which was followed by the Catholic Counter-Reformation, caused a rift within Christendom, as most of northern Europe broke away from the authority of the pope. The German theologian Martin Luther attacked the Catholic Church for its financial abuses (publishing his Ninety-Five Theses in 1517) and for its view that humans could not attain salvation without divine grace, which was conferred through the sacraments administered by the clergy. Instead, Luther held that humans had a direct relationship with God, emphasizing the importance of individual conscience and of returning to the doctrines—and texts—of the scriptures. Another reform movement was begun by the Frenchman John Calvin in Switzerland, and the Church of England was started by King Henry VIII in 1534. The Protestant Reformation reflected many tendencies of the early modern period: it gave increased sanction to worldly activity, promoting both individualism and nationalism as well as trade.

- **Expansion of commerce.** The expansion of trade and markets, manufacture, and capital investment eroded the medieval social structure, and the growth of a wealthy merchant class overturned many economic restraints.

- **Changing views of literature.** Whereas medieval thinkers tended to place literature in a theological context, Renaissance writers emphasized style and form, stressing the moral and educational value of poetry and rhetoric. Though the humanists returned to the classics, they also promoted their vernacular languages. Great writers such as Christopher Marlowe, Ben Jonson, and Shakespeare analyzed human character with a depth that far exceeded narrow moral categories. Gutenberg's invention of the printing press in the mid-1400s revolutionized the conditions of reading by vastly extending the sphere of the reading public.

ANALYZING EARLY MODERN LITERATURE

Francis Petrarch, Sonnet 333

Strictly speaking, Petrarch (1304–1374) lived in the Middle Ages, but many see him and his work as precursors of Renaissance humanism. His verse displays modern traits, including a concern with the self, which he views as changing rather than fixed; he is torn between the demands of this world and the next, between sensuous longing and spirituality. Petrarch inaugurated a long tradition of introspective love poetry. Here is Sonnet 333 from his *Rime Sparse* (*Scattered Rhymes*):

> Go, grieving rimes of mine, to that hard stone
> Whereunder lies my darling, lies my dear,
> And cry to her to speak from heaven's sphere.
> Her mortal part with grass is overgrown.
>
> 5 Tell her, I'm sick of living; that I'm blown
> By winds of grief from the course I ought to steer,
> That praise of her is all my purpose here
> And all my business; that of her alone
>
> Do I go telling, that how she lived and died
> 10 And lives again in immortality,
> All men may know, and love my Laura's grace.

> Oh, may she deign to stand at my bedside
> When I come to die; and may she call to me
> And draw me to her in the blessèd place!

(trans. Morris Bishop)

Let's ask some questions about the worldview of the poem and how it is conveyed through content and form.

What is the **humanistic content** of the poem?

- What preoccupies the poet is not anything spiritual but the loss of his lover, whose death has made him weary of life.

- His only purpose is to praise her, so that the world will know of her "grace."

- He admits that he is distracted by grief from the more spiritual path he "ought to steer."

- His only access to spirituality seems to be through her: she is to "speak from heaven's sphere," and at his death she will call him to "the blessèd place."

- Is he redefining religion and spirituality in human terms? His paradise is to be with her; and her "immortality" may well be achieved through his verse.

- The poem is just as much about him, about his feelings and his own fragmented sense of self, as it is about the woman—about her we are told nothing except that she has "grace."

What **elements** of the poem's form reinforce its humanistic content?

- **Rhetorical situation.** The poet addresses not the woman but his *own* poetry, telling his "grieving rimes" to visit her grave.

- **Word patterns.** The translator cleverly places "Whereunder" and "darling" beneath the "hard stone." Moreover, "stone" rhymes with the "overgrown" grass covering the beloved. The translator thus replicates Petrarch's Italian, where *loco oscuro et basso* (low, dark place) rhymes with *duro sasso* (hard stone). Also, as in the Italian, the word "live" is repeated in lines 9 and 10, stressing that although the beloved has died, she lives again in his verse.

- **Structure.** A Petrarchan sonnet has the rhyme scheme *abba abba cde cde*, divided into an octave of eight lines and a sestet of six. As noted in chapter 8, there is a "turn" of thought or mood (known as the *volta*) between the octave and the sestet. Here, we see a transition from what the "grieving rimes" tell the dead beloved to the poet's own telling—his continued narration, which continues her life.

Moving from notes to thesis

From these notes, we could come up with several different theses. We could talk about how Petrarch's humanism is expressed through both the content and the form of his verse. His humanistic vision is introspective; it redirects spiritual longing toward an earthly being. Or we might want to approach the sonnet from another perspective, showing that, notwithstanding the speaker's praise of the woman, he actually tells us more about himself. He is obsessed with his feelings and with the power of his verse. Or we might want to explore how Petrarch exploits the formal possibilities of a sonnet.

ANALYZING EARLY MODERN LITERATURE

Louise Labé, Sonnet 18

The French poet Louise Labé (ca. 1520–1566) was one of the most celebrated writers of the Renaissance. Her work provoked scandal and controversy. To this day some scholars question whether she wrote the texts attributed to her. Labé moved in a circle of humanist poets, and her feminist voice, like that of the medieval writer Christine de Pizan, added a new dimension to contemporary writing—in her case, humanism and the tradition of sonnet writing as established by Petrarch. Here is Sonnet 18, one of her best-known poems, followed by the first stanza of the original French:

Kiss me again, rekiss me, and then kiss
me again, with your richest, most succulent
kiss; then adore me with another kiss, meant
to steam out fourfold the very hottest hiss
5   from my love-hot coals. Do I hear you moaning? This
is my plan to soothe you: ten more kisses, sent
just for your pleasure. Then, both sweetly bent
on love, we'll enter joy through doubleness,
and we'll each have two loving lives to tend:
10   one in our single self, one in our friend.
I'll tell you something honest now, my love:
it's very bad for me to live apart.
There's no way I can have a happy heart
without some place outside myself to move.

(trans. Annie Finch)

Baise m'encore, rebaise-moi et baise;
Donne m'en un de tes plus savoureux,
Donne m'en un de tes plus amoureux:
Je t'en rendrai quatre plus chauds que braise.

Again, we can begin by asking questions.

What is the **humanistic content** of the poem?

- Even more than Petrarch's poem, Labé's sonnet focuses on earthly life rather than on spiritual concerns.
- The poem redefines the "human" in entirely human terms: earthly passion wins out over orientation toward God or moral action. Happiness is attained through "doubleness," through a relation to another human being.

What are the **feminist features** of the poem?

- Perhaps the most obvious feminist feature is the honest expression of female desire. This goes against centuries of religious teaching that attempted to repress sexuality, especially that of women. The French word *baise* can mean "kiss" but may also have a more explicitly sexual connotation.

- We might even argue that the sonnet's conception of love is feminist inasmuch as it involves not "conquest" or "subjugation"—goals that underlie much male love poetry—but mutual recognition, a sharing, between the two partners.

What **formal aspects** reinforce or shape the poem's humanist and feminist outlook?

- The voice is distinctly Labé's. Writing a love poem can often be a mode of possession, of controlling someone by reducing them to an object. Here, the poet takes control of the language and the form. Although on the surface she writes in the manner of Petrarch (the translator keeps the rhyme scheme of the French), her tone is direct and refuses poetic adornments. Even the metaphor of the "love-hot coals" is sexualized.

- The insistent repetitions ("Kiss me again, rekiss me") show that the female persona is in control. There is no sense of deference or undue reverence; she is confident and assertive, while retaining empathy for her lover's feelings ("This is my plan to soothe you").

Moving from notes to thesis

Perhaps the most obvious way into this poem is to look at how Labé is not just inserting herself into a largely male poetic tradition but is actively disrupting it by using the Petrarchan sonnet for her own purposes. You might talk about how she redefines not only love but the very notion of the "human" as needing to exist in relation with others. It would be interesting to write a comparison between this sonnet and one of Petrarch's. Alternatively, even without knowing French, you could compare this translation with other translations to see how different treatments of phrases and stanzas yield varying interpretations.

THE SEVENTEENTH CENTURY

In many ways, the seventeenth century is part of the early modern period, since in it we see the fruition and sometimes negative consequences of trends that began in the fifteenth and sixteenth centuries. This century saw the continued growth and impact of science and further expansion of commerce and trade. Printing, which had been invented in the fifteenth century, came to be widely used for religious and political purposes. Perhaps most importantly, in the wake of the Protestant Reformation, numerous religious conflicts erupted, which were tied to political struggles; in particular, the rise of absolute monarchies throughout much of Europe and their eventual defeat by parliamentary and popular forces helped move the political landscape of Europe toward a more modern outlook. Here are some of the broad characteristics of the seventeenth century.

- **The continued advance of science.** The humanism of earlier centuries found expression in the growth of a scientific and rational worldview. This growth was encouraged by the writings of the French philosopher René Descartes, who insisted that all knowledge must arise from reason (not tradition, authority, or faith). The English mathematician Isaac Newton exerted enormous influence through his view that the universe does not operate according to divine providence but is a "machine" subject to regular laws, such as the law of gravitation. The English philosophers Francis Bacon and John Locke argued that all knowledge comes from induction (rather than deduction) and experience (see chapter 19).

- **Economic transformations.** Capitalism continued to emerge through the accumulation of wealth invested for profit, the development of banking, the erosion of feudal manufacturing guilds, and the growth of new industries. These trends were fueled by economic nationalism and imperialism. By the seventeenth century, trade had become worldwide and England, France, Italy, Spain, Portugal, and Holland had become imperial powers. By the end of the century, the middle classes of merchants and traders had become wealthy, and bourgeois ideals—such as religious toleration, separation of church and state, freedom of trade, and popular sovereignty—were beginning to be realized.

- **The English Civil Wars (1642–51) and the Restoration (1660).**
  The power of the English monarchy reached its height under the Tudors Henry VIII and Elizabeth I. The Stuart kings James I and Charles I continued autocratic rule, which (together with rebellions by the Scots and Irish) precipitated the civil wars between the Royalists, loyal to the king, and the Parliamentarians, led by Oliver Cromwell. The Parliamentarians were victorious, and Charles I was beheaded in 1649. England was briefly a republican commonwealth, with Cromwell its "lord protector." However, faced with instability after Cromwell's death, in 1660 Parliament placed Charles II upon the throne in the "Restoration." James II, Charles II's brother and successor, was deposed because of his overt Catholicism in the Glorious (because bloodless) Revolution of 1688, and James II's daughter Mary and her husband, William of Orange (*stadtholder* in the Netherlands), became the rulers of England. These events shifted the balance of power in England from the monarchy to parliamentary government. Similar struggles would take place in much of Europe a century later, and the English Bill of Rights (1689)—the act that formalized the succession of the Crown—anticipated the demands of the American and French revolutionaries.

- **Religious conflicts.** The Reformation precipitated religious and political strife that continued through the seventeenth century. Public debates raged over religion and issues such as censorship, with conflicting views spreading through the developing technology of printing. Much religious and devotional literature circulated, including sermons. King James commissioned a translation of the Bible, which was published in 1611.

- **Literary trends.** Genres such as satire, elegy, epistle, religious lyric, and essay flourished in the seventeenth century. Of great influence were the so-called Metaphysical poets—John Donne, George Herbert, Andrew Marvell, Henry Vaughan—whose poetry was marked by intellectual difficulty, logical argument, conceits (elaborate extended metaphors), hyperbole (exaggeration), paradox, and a concern with love and death.

ANALYZING A METAPHYSICAL POEM

John Donne, "The Flea" (1633)

Donne is the most famous of the Metaphysical poets, and the characteristics of Metaphysical poetry are readily apparent in "The Flea."

> Mark but this flea, and mark in this,
> How little that which thou deniest me is;
> It sucked me first, and now sucks thee,
> And in this flea our two bloods mingled be;
> 5 Thou know'st that this cannot be said
> A sin, nor shame, nor loss of maidenhead,
>   Yet this enjoys before it woo,
>   And pampered swells with one blood made of two,
>   And this, alas, is more than we would do.
>
> 10 Oh stay, three lives in one flea spare,
> Where we almost, nay more than married are.
> This flea is you and I, and this
> Our marriage bed, and marriage temple is;
> Though parents grudge, and you, we are met,
> 15 And cloistered in these living walls of jet.
>   Though use make you apt to kill me,
>   Let not to that, self-murder added be,
>   And sacrilege, three sins in killing three.
>
> Cruel and sudden, hast thou since
> 20 Purpled thy nail in blood of innocence?
> Wherein could this flea guilty be,

Except in that drop which it sucked from thee?
Yet thou triumph'st, and say'st that thou
Find'st not thy self, nor me the weaker now;
25   'Tis true; then learn how false, fears be:
Just so much honor, when thou yield'st to me,
Will waste, as this flea's death took life from thee.

As is typical of Donne's poetry, "The Flea" offers an intellectually rigorous argument. We might begin by asking questions about its context and then looking at the use of the flea as an extended metaphor.

What is the **context** of the poem?

- **Date of composition.** Most scholars agree that this poem was written in the 1590s, when Donne, a Catholic, traveled across Europe and had a reputation as a womanizer. Later, he would convert to Anglicanism. As dean of St. Paul's Cathedral (1621–31), he became known as the finest preacher in England.

- **Donne's secret marriage.** When he was in the service of Sir Thomas Egerton, lord keeper of the great seal of England, Donne fell in love with and in 1601 secretly married Ann More, the niece of Egerton's second wife. Once the marriage was discovered, Donne was briefly imprisoned; the poem's words "Though parents grudge" allude to the disapproval of his wife's family. He failed to gain any substantial position until after he was ordained in 1615.

- **Images.** Fleas were a common part of life in the seventeenth century; as such, they are found in much poetry. Sexual intercourse was thought to involve the mingling of bodily fluids.

How is the flea used as a **conceit,** or extended metaphor?

- **Unites their fluids.** The flea literally contains the blood of both the speaker and his prospective mistress. This combining of fluids, as noted above, was characteristic of sex. So the flea becomes a symbol, and a projection, of sexual union.

- **Embodies their marriage.** Here the flea is not only the couple's "marriage bed" but their very identity as a unified pair ("This flea is you and I").

- **Becomes a symbol of innocence.** Though the flea has bitten the woman and the speaker, it is still regarded as "innocent" and has caused no sin or shame or loss of virginity. In fact, "three lives in one" might allude (perhaps comically or sarcastically) to the Christian Trinity.

Thus the conceit of the flea advances a supposedly logical argument: (1) our bloods have already mingled in the flea; (2) therefore, it is the site of our sexual union and marriage; (3) this has resulted in no sin, and the flea's death has not diminished the lady's integrity. When simplified like this, the argument is hardly valid, though the speaker's tone makes it seem so.

Moving from notes to thesis

We could approach this poem in a number of ways. We could see it as a call to *carpe diem* (seize the day). Such a call is secular because it urges men and women to focus on the moment at hand rather than the hereafter. But Donne's assault on religious orthodoxy goes even further when he argues that virginity or chastity—prized by the church and by seventeenth-century social traditions—is overvalued and is something to be overcome.

Another focus might be the poem's dramatic situation, in which the speaker is talking directly to a woman and modifies his stance according to her actions (such as killing the flea). We could look at the rather bawdy humor (the letter *s* used to be printed ſ in the beginning and middle of words; it doesn't take much imagination to see the potential humor of "It sucked me first, and now sucks thee"). We could also examine the poem's form and how its rhyme scheme (*aa bb cc ddd*) mimics the union of two beings in a third entity (*a*, *b*, and *c* in *ddd*); again, this might be a commentary on the Trinity. What appeared to be a poem about a flea proves to be subversive of deeply engrained traditions.

NEOCLASSICISM

While the Renaissance was marked by a "rebirth" of classical values and literary styles, neoclassicism, which lasted from around the mid-seventeenth until the mid-eighteenth century, was stricter in its return to the classical. Renaissance writing often drew on elements of fantasy and romance, sometimes in an elaborate style. The neoclassicists favored adherence to the classical values of realism, moderation, and rationality and the observation of the Aristotelian dramatic unities of action and time. The important features and emphases of neoclassicism include

- **Stress on human limitations.** Whereas Renaissance thinkers celebrated the belief that humans are the measure of all things, the neoclassicists insisted on a sharp distinction between the human (limited) and the divine (omniscient and omnipotent). The theological concept of "pride"—driving humans to transcend their appropriate station—is central, for example, to both Alexander Pope's worldview and his literary criticism.

- **A distinction from the Enlightenment.** The neoclassic period is often confused with the Enlightenment, since they overlapped historically. Although neoclassicism was influenced by Newton's view of the universe as a vast machine subject to laws, it was conservative, whereas Enlightenment thought was progressive. The neoclassical concept of reason differs from the individualistic reason of the Enlightenment thinkers. Neoclassicists appeal to the reason of classical philosophers like Aristotle, who regarded it as a universal human faculty that offers access to universal truths. They see reason as finite and liable to cause disaster if employed in an individualistic manner. Reason in this sense underlies the classical virtues of moderation, self-knowledge, and restraint.

- **The Quarrel between the Ancients and the Moderns.** Around the beginning of the eighteenth century, writers such as Jonathan Swift, Nicholas Boileau, and Alexander Pope argued for the classical merits of order, balance, and moderation, while the "moderns," who included Charles Perrault and William Wotton, argued that modern knowledge was more enlightened and stressed individual creativity, the mixing of genres, and originality.

- **Characteristic view of nature.** For neoclassical writers, the term "nature" had many levels of significance. It included what was normal, universal, and morally sound in human experience; thus actions such as murder and extreme lust were viewed as "unnatural." But more comprehensively, "nature" encompassed the structure and order of the cosmos, from God at the summit through the angels, humans, animals, and plants to inanimate objects. This cosmic order set the terms for a heavily stratified social and political order. So, nature also referred to one's position and actions within this larger order: Pope warned against the pride that tempted humans to reach beyond their natural state.

- **Stress on imitation.** Neoclassicism emphasized both the imitation of "nature"—of human action and the external world—and the imitation of classical models such as Homer and Virgil. Some neoclassical poets, including Pope, actually equated copying nature with copying the ancients.

- **Verse forms and literary techniques.** The neoclassicists used strict verse forms, most famously the heroic couplet (a couplet of rhyming iambic pentameters). Among their preferred literary techniques were wit, satire, antithesis, parallelism, and irony.

- **Emphasis on clarity.** During the seventeenth and eighteenth centuries, many tried to standardize language and the meanings of words. The Académie Française, established in 1635, sponsored work on a dictionary and grammar. Samuel Johnson's *Dictionary* was published in 1755. The philosopher John Locke argued that philosophy should use clear and distinct ideas and avoid figurative language.

ANALYZING A NEOCLASSICAL TEXT

Alexander Pope, *An Essay on Man* (1733–34)

Some of the features named above are worth bearing in mind as we look at a major neoclassical text, Pope's *Essay on Man*. The declared purpose of this philosophical poem, echoing that of Milton's *Paradise Lost*, is to "vindicate the ways of God to man" (1.16). Pope was writing at a time when, in his view, humanity relied excessively on its own intellect, on reason, on science, instead of acknowledging its place in the order of God's universe. Pope sees this exaltation of reason and science as evidence of the theological sin of "pride," defined by Augustine as a commitment to self-love rather than to the love of God. Ironically, though Pope adheres to the medieval hierarchy of nature—a "great chain of being" extending from God and the angels through human beings to lesser forms—he describes the cosmos in Newtonian terms, stating that it obeys mechanical laws. Crucially, Pope redefines the virtues of classicism in terms of Nature and Wit—the latter defined by Pope and his contemporaries as the capacity for seeing unexpected connections among things. The following passage appears near the beginning of *An Essay on Man*.

> Say first, of God above, or man below,
> What can we reason, but from what we know?
> Of man what see we, but his station here,
> From which to reason, or to which refer?
> Through worlds unnumbered though the God be known,
> 'Tis ours to trace him only in our own.
> He, who through vast immensity can pierce,
> See worlds on worlds compose one universe,
> Observe how system into system runs,
> What other planets circle other suns,
> What varied being peoples every star,
> May tell why Heaven has made us as we are.
> But of this frame the bearings, and the ties,
> The strong connections, nice dependencies,

> Gradations just, has thy pervading soul
> Looked through? or can a part contain the whole?
>   Is the great chain, that draws all to agree,
>   And drawn supports, upheld by God, or thee?

(1.17–34)

How does the passage express a **neoclassical worldview**?

- It stresses the limitations of human reason (mentioned twice), which can operate only in the sphere of actual human experience.
- It situates humanity within a much larger context, one that contains innumerable other planets and beings.
- It refers to the great chain of being, in which humanity represents just one link.

What **stylistic features** reinforce the passage's neoclassical vision, particularly its representation of the difference between God and humanity?

- **Antithesis.** The phrase "of God above, or man below" indicates the subordinate position of "man."
- **Parallelism.** The repetition of the word "what" in "What can we reason, but from what we know?" and "What other planets . . . ," "What varied beings . . ." indicates an entire range of things that lie beyond human knowledge.
- **Irony.** One definition of irony is a disjunction between what something actually is and a person's limited perception of it. Here, Pope makes irony a structural component of the passage: in general, he sets the *partial* perspective of humankind against the *complete* perspective of God.
- **Satire.** Pope employs this device to great effect. Using a dramatic speaker, he directly questions humankind, asking whether the entire system of the universe is upheld by God or by humans, thereby satirizing human pride and presumption.

Moving from notes to thesis

On the basis of these notes, you could formulate several different theses. The most basic would be something like

> Pope's neoclassical vision is expressed in *An Essay on Man* through certain features of content and style.

You could then go on to talk about these features. Or, if you wanted to be more ambitious, you could argue that Pope uses "wit" in associating the theological concept of "pride" with excessive use of human reason ("In pride, in reasoning pride, our error lies," 1.123), which is institutionalized in "proud Science" (1.101). Or you could argue that Pope is fighting a losing battle in advocating a return to a cosmological order that is rapidly eroding (Pope himself uses terms that refer to Newtonian mechanics).

THE ENLIGHTENMENT

The Enlightenment was an intellectual movement that roughly spanned the eighteenth century, often called the "age of reason." Enlightenment thinkers believed that knowledge is based on reason and experience rather than custom or authority; that human society is progressing intellectually, morally, and politically; and that human beings are free rational agents. Here are a few important features of the Enlightenment:

- **The influence of the new science.** Whereas medieval cosmology viewed the universe as directed by God, Newton and other scientists saw the universe as ordered by laws of motion and gravitation. The rapid rise of scientific perspectives toward the world undermined religious authority.

- **Rationalism.** Inspired by the French philosopher René Descartes, rationalism holds that all knowledge is derived from reasoning. Sometimes called the father of modern philosophy, Descartes rejected the authority of tradition. Finding that the only thing he could not doubt was his own mind, he issued his famous declaration: "I think, therefore I am" (*cogito ergo sum*). Hence, he created a dualism between mind, whose essence is thinking, and body, which, like other objects in the world, is characterized by extension in space and duration in time.

- **Empiricism.** Inspired by the English thinker Francis Bacon, modern empiricism asserts that knowledge is based on experience and observation. According to Bacon's "inductive" method, we can generalize only on the basis of repeated observations. Other empiricists included John Locke (in the seventeenth century) and the Scottish philosopher David Hume. Locke argued that the mind is a *tabula rasa* (blank slate). Our ideas come from experience, and we can know the world only through our ideas. Hume's skepticism went even further, holding that we can never know the world itself, only our ideas of it.

- **Political turmoil.** Enlightenment thinkers profoundly influenced the French Revolution of 1789, a massive upheaval that transferred political power from the monarchy and nobility to the bourgeoisie (the business classes), whose values of efficiency, pragmatism, individualism, and economic competition still dominate the globe. Locke was the central philosopher of modern liberalism. Voltaire and Montesquieu were also influential liberal thinkers. Jean-Jacques Rousseau set forth a theory of democracy and drew attention to the corrupting effects of private property. American Enlightenment thinkers include Thomas Jefferson, who drafted the Declaration of Independence, and James Madison, one of the architects of the U.S. Constitution.

- **Basic worldview.** The enlightenment worldview is characterized by the beliefs that (1) the world is pluralistic, consisting of distinct objects without any intrinsic unity; (2) there exists an external world somehow independent of our minds; and (3) general ideas (such as blackness or whiteness) are formed by our minds operating on the particular ideas and impressions they receive from the external world. These assumptions underlie not only much literary criticism from the eighteenth century until our times but the way in which many people still think about the world.

Enlightenment rationalism and empiricism influenced discussions of language, wit and judgment, and the connection between reason and imagination. They also inspired attention to empirical detail and realism and stimulated debates about human psychology. Enlightenment skepticism, which denied the notion of essence, fostered a new relativism that viewed literature as a product of the era in which it was created. An enduring debate was inspired by Locke's condemnation of the figurative language found in most literature, which—unlike the denotative language of philosophical discourse—misleads the judgment and conveys wrong ideas.

ANALYZING AN ENLIGHTENMENT TEXT

Mary Wollstonecraft, *A Vindication of the Rights of Woman* (1792)

Recognized since the 1960s as one of the first feminists, Mary Wollstonecraft was an ardent supporter of the French Revolution, which was about abolishing irrational feudal privilege and power. She urged that the principles of the Enlightenment as embodied in the revolution—reason, freedom, equality—should be extended to women. But she realized that such change would require additional social upheaval. The following passage from chapter 2 of her *Vindication* captures the essential argument of her great work:

> Consequently, the most perfect education, in my opinion, is such an exercise of the understanding as is best calculated to strengthen the body and form the heart. Or, in other words, to enable the individual to attain such habits of virtue as will render it independent. In fact, it is a farce to call any being virtuous whose virtues do not result from the exercise of its own reason. This was Rousseau's opinion respecting men: I extend it to women, and confidently assert that they have been drawn out of their sphere by false refinement, and not by an endeavour to acquire masculine qualities. Still the regal homage which they receive is so intoxicating, that till the manners of the times are changed, and formed on more reasonable principles, it may be

impossible to convince them that the illegitimate power, which they obtain by degrading themselves, is a curse, and that they must return to nature and equality if they wish to secure the placid satisfaction that unsophisticated affections impart.

Our questions might situate this argument in its historical context. As always, there's nothing wrong with answering questions with more questions.

What **arguments** are advanced in this passage?

- Women are currently degraded. As Wollstonecraft writes in subsequent passages, they receive a "disorderly" education that prevents them from learning how to reason, to generalize.

- What is meant by "false refinement"? Perhaps, that women's education has encouraged them to cultivate only their manners, their dress, and their appearance. True refinement would involve the mind and the moral faculty.

- What is "the most perfect education"? According to Wollstonecraft, it is one that enables an individual to use reason to make her own decisions, rather than "blindly" (a word she uses in several passages) submitting to authority.

- What are the obstacles to women's education? According to Wollstonecraft, women have been trained to enjoy the "regal homage" they receive for their appearance and manners. Thus the "manners of the times"—the prevailing opinions and customs—must change before women can acquire a better image of themselves.

How does the passage reflect **Enlightenment principles**?

- Perhaps the most basic premise of the passage is that a person must be free and independent, responsible for her own decisions.

- But in order to be free, we must be able to reason for ourselves.

- So freedom and reason presuppose each other; they must accompany each other.

On the basis of such notes, you might decide that Wollstonecraft's *main* argument runs something like this:

> According to Wollstonecraft, the main vehicle for the suppression of women is inadequate education, which encourages them to value their physical qualities at the expense of their minds, and therefore keeps them submissive. In order for women to progress, they must be made morally independent by being given an education that promotes their use of reason.

And you could add a sentence about historical context:

> This argument is based on Wollstonecraft's Enlightenment convictions that every human being should be a free rational agent, and that freedom and reason go hand in hand.

Once you've reached this point, you could write a paper expanding on and illustrating these ideas. Or you could discuss how modern feminists might disagree with Wollstonecraft's reliance on "reason," which some regard as permeated with male ways of looking at the world. Or, from a Marxist perspective, you could discuss how Wollstonecraft is aware of the workings of ideology, as she argues that women's image of themselves is essentially imposed by male traditions.

ROMANTICISM (ca. 1780–1830)

Romanticism was a literary and intellectual movement that reacted against both the Enlightenment and neoclassicism. Instead of emphasizing reason and objectivity, the Romantics championed the expression of the human self, of human subjectivity, and viewed imagination as a higher power than reason. They also exalted the state of childhood and innocence, seeing it as a time when the world could be viewed in a fresh way, unclouded by convention. And they extolled the status of the poet, with many of them insisting that poetry be free from the demands of morality and usefulness. Among the major Romantics were Schiller and Goethe in

Germany; Blake, Coleridge, Wordsworth, Byron, Shelley, and Keats in England; Rousseau and de Staël in France; and Emerson, Hawthorne, Fuller, Thoreau, and Melville in America. Crucial features of Romanticism include the following:

- **Ambivalent relation to the Enlightenment.** Romanticism reacted against the rationalist, mechanistic, and utilitarian strain of the Enlightenment as well as against neoclassical thought, which insisted on the classical values of decorum, moderation, and strict distinctions between literary genres. However, Romanticism did share some Enlightenment values, such as individualism, an emphasis on experience, and advocacy of freedom. The Romantics also shared Enlightenment beliefs in progress and the infinite potential of humanity. Indeed, many Romantics were inspired by the early stages of the French Revolution, which they saw as the first move toward a new world of egalitarianism and freedom from tradition.

- **Characteristic view of nature.** Whereas neoclassical writers viewed nature as a vast hierarchy, spanning cosmic and social levels, the Romantics saw nature as infused with a divine spirit and as a refuge from an industrialized and commercialized world torn apart by dualisms: individual and society, past and present, sensation and intellect. Their aim was to arrive at some vision of unity or totality by means of the poetic imagination.

- **Emphasis on individualism.** Where classical thought saw human beings as essentially social, Romanticism, with its emphasis on subjectivity, valued what was individual, unique, and novel. It also viewed human perception, centered on imagination, as active in its construction of the world, not passively receiving sensations from some objective world "already" there. Unlike the abstract economic individualism of Enlightenment bourgeois thought, which saw human society as an aggregate of individual units, individualism for the Romantics was founded on a deeper and more authentic "self." This self exercised imagination and irony in its attempt to make sense of a fragmented and senseless world.

- **Exaltation of imagination.** The Romantics exalted the imagination, viewing it as a faculty that can perceive the underlying truths and patterns of the world, which are inaccessible to reason alone. Coleridge and Shelley saw the poetic imagination as a unifying power that can overcome the divisive operations of reason, whose primary function is to separate and classify things.

- **Irony.** Romantic irony was a reaction against the Enlightenment reduction of the world to a utilitarian place governed by pragmatic interests. In the hands of the Romantics, irony came to embody an entire way of looking at the world, an ability to accommodate several differing and even conflicting perspectives while acknowledging that any unity imposed on them is ultimately subjective.

The literature and thinking of our own time owe much to Romanticism: our insistence that what we call reality cannot be confined to the material world; our sense that we have a deeper, more authentic self than what we display in our public and professional roles; our awareness that reason is not infallible; our fondness for pursuing experience as an end in itself; and perhaps above all, our acknowledgment that human subjectivity is inexhaustibly rich and contributes on many levels to the construction of the world around us.

ANALYZING A ROMANTIC TEXT

Percy Bysshe Shelley, "Ode to the West Wind" (1819)

It may be in the works of the English poet Shelley that the ideals of Romanticism find their most passionate voice. Shelley, who was only twenty-nine when he drowned, expresses a youthful enthusiasm and idealism, deeply committed to personal and political freedom, that often rejects compromise with traditional religious and social norms. Here is the first section of one of his most famous poems, "Ode to the West Wind":

O wild West Wind, thou breath of Autumn's being,
Thou, from whose unseen presence the leaves dead
Are driven, like ghosts from an enchanter fleeing,

Yellow, and black, and pale, and hectic red,
5   Pestilence-stricken multitudes: O Thou,
Who chariotest to their dark wintry bed

The winged seeds, where they lie cold and low,
Each like a corpse within its grave, until
Thine azure sister of the Spring shall blow

10   Her clarion o'er the dreaming earth, and fill
(Driving sweet buds like flocks to feed in air)
With living hues and odours plain and hill:

Wild Spirit, which art moving everywhere;
Destroyer and Preserver; hear, O hear!

In the first three sections (of five) the poet describes the effects of the wind on the earth, the sky, and the sea. The fourth section asks the wind (whatever it represents) to rejuvenate the poet himself. By the last section, the poet is actually identifying himself with the wind. With that larger context in mind, let's explore how this poem expresses a Romantic outlook.

What are the Romantic features of the poem's **content**?

- Nature (in this case, the wind) is viewed as a "spirit" that is "everywhere." This is a typical Romantic view: it sees the divine as a spirit expressed through nature.
- The wind's ability to profoundly affect earth, sky, and sea suggests that nature is not just a collection of physical phenomena but a living unity with a spiritual core.
- The poet views nature as a source of sustenance and rejuvenation ("Oh! lift me as a wave, a leaf, a cloud!" [line 53]).

- The poet identifies his own spirit with that of nature ("Be thou, Spirit fierce, / My spirit!" [lines 61–62]).

What are the Romantic features of the poem's **form**?

- The poem is an apostrophe, or direct address, to the wind, to which the poet even appears to be praying ("O hear!").
- Its form is highly original; each section integrates terza rima (used by Dante in *The Divine Comedy*) into the form of a sonnet.
- The elements of nature are seen as symbols of human or divine qualities. The wind is a "destroyer and preserver," and the leaves are likened in the last section to the poet's own thoughts.
- At first glance, the poem appears to be about the wind and its effects on the rest of nature. But, by the time we reach the last two sections, we realize that it's really about the poet himself, his own developing subjectivity, and the power of his poetry.
- The last section proclaims the power of poetry to show the world that from death comes life. This affirmation can be interpreted in many ways: for example, from the death of one social order (such as feudalism) comes a new one.

A thesis about this poem could take a number of forms. You might write something like this:

> Shelley's "Ode" is Romantic in its treatment of nature, its formal innovations, and its focus on human subjectivity.

You could then go on to talk about each of these features. Or you could explore in detail how each part is structured as a sonnet. Or you could examine the complex symbolism of the wind, or how elements of nature correspond to aspects of the poet's subjectivity. And you could ask why the poem ends with a question ("If Winter comes, can Spring be far behind?"). Is the poet unsure of himself?

We find similar traits in the work of other Romantic poets. For example, in "Lines Composed a Few Miles above Tintern Abbey" (1798),

Wordsworth describes how his view of nature has changed since he was a boy. Whereas nature once appealed only to his senses, he now views it as pervaded by "a spirit, that . . . rolls through all things." He also tells us that nature is a moral refuge for him from "the din / Of towns and cities."

THE LATER NINETEENTH CENTURY

Following the Romantic period, the nineteenth century continued to be a time of change and turmoil. Throughout Europe, the years 1830 and 1848 saw largely unsuccessful rebellions against conservative kings and governments. A related development was the growth of nationalism, with most nations in Europe attaining political unity by 1870. Imperialism reached its peak at the end of the century, with much of the world under the control of Britain, France, Germany, and Italy. Some of the tendencies lamented by the Romantics intensified: as industrialization increased, populations grew, and advances in technology and transportation spread; many moved from the countryside to the cities, leading to the growth of an urban workforce that eventually became conscious of itself as a political class.

The **Victorian period** (1837–1901), named for the long reign of Queen Victoria, was an era of progress for Britain, which was the first industrialized country and the world's major imperial power. Political developments in Britain included the Reform Bills of 1832 and 1867, which enfranchised and established the dominance of the middle class, as well as extending the vote to sections of the working class. Economic progress was also fueled by the policy of laissez-faire (freedom of trade; literally, "allow to do"), as advocated by figures such as Adam Smith and David Ricardo. There was some progress regarding the rights of women: a series of Married Women's Property Acts (1870–1907) expanded women's ability to own and control property. The first women's college opened in 1848, and by the century's end, women could attend twelve universities (though not necessarily receive degrees). But women did not receive the right to vote until 1918. And, as a result of educational reforms, basic literacy was almost universal in Britain by 1900.

Despite the Victorian ideals of progress, conquest, and civilization, this was also an era of doubt and self-questioning. Industrialization produced not only prosperity but poverty and squalor, with widespread unemployment, appalling working conditions, and the use of child labor. These conditions led to Britain's Chartist movement (1838–48), which fought for, among other things, universal manhood suffrage and voting by secret ballot. As an urban working class emerged, its outlook was shaped by contemporary socialist thinkers, most importantly Karl Marx and Friedrich Engels. Moreover, a number of developments precipitated a crisis of religious faith. David Strauss's *The Life of Jesus* (1835–36, translated from the German by George Eliot in 1846) saw the Gospels as "myth" rather than fact. Charles Darwin's *On the Origin of Species* (1859) was held by some to undermine the biblical accounts of creation. Many saw theology as having been displaced by science as the supreme archetype of knowledge. The forces of industrialization only sped up this process of secularization.

All these phenomena were reflected in a number of nineteenth-century literary developments.

- **Prominence of the novel.** The middle class greatly expanded the readership of literature, as reflected in the rise of the periodical press. Literature increasingly reflected the rationalist, empirical, and scientific values of the middle class. **The novel**, which had its beginnings in the early eighteenth century, was by the late nineteenth century the dominant literary form.

- **Growth of realism.** The nineteenth-century novel rested on a scientific or "realistic" (rather than religious) understanding of the world. **Realism** attempted to depict human behavior and events truthfully. Realist fiction adhered to the classical principle of portraying actions and events that were "probable"; but it also used detailed description, included characters from the lower social orders, used more colloquial language, and focused on contemporary issues. In England, realism was employed in the novels of William Makepeace Thackeray and Charles Dickens. But it was in the novels of George Eliot, Anthony Trollope, George Meredith, and Thomas Hardy that realism came into its own.

- **Naturalism** was a more extreme form of realism. Its proponents—notably Émile Zola, in France—tried to extend the observational and experimental methods of the natural sciences to the study of human behavior. Doing so meant portraying human beings as determined by their circumstances, family backgrounds, and lineages; some literary naturalism expressed a Darwinian struggle of individuals for survival within hostile surroundings. Both realism and naturalism reacted against the idealistic and mythical elements in Romanticism.

- **Symbolism** and **aestheticism** developed in reaction to Enlightenment notions of reason. Although these movements arose in the late nineteenth century, they had their roots in Romanticism; they too turned away from the sordid reality of the present world to the depiction of ideal worlds and psychological states. Influenced by Plato's theory of Forms and by Charles Baudelaire, the French symbolists (such as Stéphane Mallarmé and Arthur Rimbaud) saw the present world as a flawed manifestation of a higher realm. They rejected the descriptive and referential language of realism for suggestive and symbolic language that could evoke states of mind and experiences. Aestheticism focused on "art for art's sake," rather than on moral or political concerns; among its major proponents were Walter Pater and Oscar Wilde.

- **Reactions against commercial society.** Numerous thinkers critiqued middle-class values and institutions. These ranged from the socialists Marx and Engels to humanists such as Matthew Arnold.

ANALYZING A LATER NINETEENTH-CENTURY TEXT

Walt Whitman, Preface to *Leaves of Grass* (1855)

It was Walt Whitman who responded to Ralph Waldo Emerson's call in "The Poet" (1844) for someone to write the poem of America. Whitman saw himself as composing in a new, democratic vein, expressing what was distinctive about the physical, ideological, intellectual, and spiritual landscape of America. He rebelled against the artifice of European verse forms, meters, and diction. The foremost pioneer of modern American poetry, he anticipated the use of free verse by modernist writers; his vocabulary and sensibility were expansive; and his long poetic lines were well-suited to exploring both interior and exterior worlds. In the preface to *Leaves of Grass*, he lays out the vision underlying his poetic agenda:

> There will soon be no more priests. Their work is done. They may wait awhile . . perhaps a generation or two . . dropping off by degrees. A superior breed shall take their place . . . . the gangs of kosmos and prophets en masse shall take their place. A new order shall arise and they shall be the priests of man, and every man shall be his own priest. The churches built under their umbrage shall be the churches of men and women. Through the divinity of themselves shall the kosmos and the new breed of poets be interpreters of men and women and of all events and things. They shall find their inspiration in real objects today, symptoms of the past and future . . . . They shall not deign to defend immortality or God or the perfection of things or liberty or the exquisite beauty and reality of the soul. They shall arise in America and be responded to from the remainder of the earth.
>
> [*Whitman's ellipses*]

Once we've done our preliminary reading—asking, for example, what "priest" and "gangs of kosmos" mean—we can move on to broader questions.

What is the **basic argument** of this passage?

- Perhaps that the priest will be replaced by the common person. Presumably, by "priest" Whitman means not just church leaders but all forms of authority and tradition that are imposed upon people from above.

- Perhaps that men and women will build their own churches. In other words, people will choose for themselves how they want to live.

- Thus "divinity" is no longer viewed as something beyond us; it is within us.

- What, then, is the role of the "new breed of poets"? Perhaps they will deal not with abstract spiritual issues but with real people in the real world. This will be first an American phenomenon and then spread to the rest of the world.

What **stylistic elements** do we see at work?

- The first thing we might notice about this passage is its clarity. Elsewhere in the preface, Whitman states that "the glory of expression . . . is simplicity." So we see in this piece no complex turns of phrase or figures of speech.

- We also find fairly short, assertive sentences. Moreover, certain words—"priest," "breed," "churches"—are repeated, perhaps to ensure that readers will remember them.

How are the **theme and form** of the passage characteristic of later nineteenth-century writing?

- Like Matthew Arnold (and other writers in this period), Whitman believed that poets would supplant priests as "interpreters of men and women." He locates divinity within humanity itself; hence his vision is humanist and realist.

- Whitman believes that literature, as an agent of moral influence, must become "the justification and reliance" of American democracy.

- In his other writings, Whitman sees democracy as intrinsically imperial in its nature: it will be "the empire of empires," eventually dominating humankind, to create "a New Earth and a New Man."

Again, on the basis of these notes, we could develop several theses. We could argue that the content and form of Whitman's passage display not only a commitment to realism but also a later nineteenth-century desire to replace religion with literature. We could compare Whitman's realism with that of writers like fellow Americans William Dean Howells and Henry James. Or we could question whether his notion of democracy is actually imperialistic.

CHAPTER 12

MODERNISM AND POSTMODERNISM

odern literature was shaped by a number of transformative events, including the following:

The First World War (1914–18). The unprecedented devastation of this war (in which Germany, Austria-Hungary, Turkey, and Bulgaria fought against France, Russia, and Britain, allied with Japan, Italy, and the United States) led people to question the foundations of Western civilization. Enlightenment assumptions about reason, progress, and morality were plunged into doubt, leading to a spiritual and intellectual crisis.

- **The Russian Revolution of 1917.** Russia was already experiencing political turmoil before the war, but the effects of the war—disastrous losses, economic disruption, and food scarcity—led to the overthrow of Tsar Nicholas II. The faction that triumphed in the revolutionary struggle was led by the socialist thinker and activist Vladimir Ilich Ulyanov (known as Lenin), who drew on the theories of Marx and Engels to establish the first communist state.

- **The Second World War (1939–45).** Coming after the worldwide economic depression of the 1930s, this war was waged by Britain, the United States, and France to contain the expansionist ambitions of Nazi Germany (aided by the fascist regimes of Italy and Japan). It caused even more widespread and catastrophic destruction than the First World War and led to the disintegration of the colonial empires of Britain, France, Belgium, and the Netherlands, which had previously ruled over one-third of the world's population. Among the war's most horrific events were the Holocaust in Europe and the use of nuclear weapons on Japan.

- **The Cold War (1945–91).** This marked a period of hostility between the capitalist world (the "first world") and the various countries of the communist bloc (the "second world"), as well as the emergence into independence of the poorer countries of the "third world." In the West, the years from 1947 to 1973 exhibited the fastest economic and cultural transformations in recorded history.

- **Political and social upheavals.** These included revolutions against colonialism in many parts of the world, the U.S. civil rights movement of the 1950s and 1960s, and student and worker uprisings across the globe in 1968.

MODERNISM

Modernism arose in different places at slightly different times, fundamentally as a reaction both against the ideals of the Enlightenment, such as reason and historical progress, and against the legacy of literary realism. Realism assumes that there is a real world "out there" that can somehow be reflected in literature. The modernists rejected this view of human experience. They saw the world as created by the human self—not individual but collective human subjectivity. And they saw language as essential in this construction.

We are born into a world of language—a world shaped by language—that already contains many concepts. Love, to take one concept, seems real. But the modernists realized that if we want to convey a precise meaning of "love," we cannot assume that the word refers to an objective reality or universally agreed-upon meaning. We will have to use language in a special way to convey a precise meaning. This applies also to the notion of the human self: the self is not constituted by a preexisting fixed identity but is a continual exploration through language, often fragmented. The major exponents of modernism included Marcel Proust, T. S. Eliot, Ezra Pound, James Joyce, William Carlos Williams, William Faulkner, Virginia Woolf, and Franz Kafka. Here are some basic features of modernism:

- An awareness of the problematic nature of language and, more particularly, how we use it; also, an awareness of our connection to the literary traditions that precede us.

- A realization that language does not represent or reflect a pre-existing objective reality or self but is used by humans to construct both reality and self.

- The consequent recognition that experience and time are complex phenomena. Experience isn't linear; rather than having one experience after another, we have numerous experiences at the same time. Likewise, there is no pure "present" that is somehow separate from past and future.

- A rejection of the view that literature should be linear, with a beginning, middle, and end. Instead, modernists tend to use more indirect methods of expression, such as suggestion, symbolism, and allusions to other texts. In other words, language is not used in a "literal" sense: it is intrinsically metaphorical.

ANALYZING A MODERNIST TEXT

T. S. Eliot, "The Love Song of J. Alfred Prufrock" (1915)

Eliot began writing "Prufrock" in 1910, when he was a graduate student at Harvard. This poem, along with longer poem *The Waste Land* (1922), changed the nature of poetry written in English, and Eliot's influence eventually extended to most parts of the world. "Prufrock" begins:

> Let us go then, you and I,
> When the evening is spread out against the sky
> Like a patient etherised upon a table;
> Let us go, through certain half-deserted streets,
> The muttering retreats
> Of restless nights in one-night cheap hotels
> And sawdust restaurants with oyster-shells:
> Streets that follow like a tedious argument
> Of insidious intent
> To lead you to an overwhelming question . . .
> Oh, do not ask, 'What is it?'
> Let us go and make our visit.
>
> In the room the women come and go
> Talking of Michelangelo.

(lines 1–14)

As always, a good way to grapple with a challenging text like "Prufrock" is to ask questions. Here are some that you might ask about the poem as a whole, not just about the passage quoted above.

- What is the setting or situation of the poem? Who are the "you" and "I"?
- Is there logic to the progression of images?
- What is the effect of the rhyme in the couplet about Michelangelo?
- What is the significance of the "yellow fog" introduced in line 15?
- How can we explain the speaker's focus on time in lines 23–34 and 37–48?
- What fears preoccupy the speaker in lines 38–69?
- What is the significance of the speaker's focus on body parts such as eyes and arms?
- Why does the speaker compare himself with Hamlet in lines 111–19?
- Who are the mermaids at the end? Why won't they sing to him?

- Why does the poem use numerous allusions to the Bible and to Dante, Shakespeare, and other writers?

- Why is the poem called a "love song"?

What is the **setting or rhetorical situation**? Starting with this question might help us to answer some of the others.

- The couplet that mentions Michelangelo gives us a clue: the speaker is going to a social gathering (he later mentions cups, marmalade, and tea). That the women are talking about art tells us that it's probably an upper-middle-class affair.

- The "you" and "I" could be two different people. But as we progress through the poem, we realize that the speaker is probably talking to himself—perhaps not even talking but thinking. So, could the "you" and "I" refer to two aspects of the speaker's self?

- It seems that the speaker, in a roundabout way, is thinking of propositioning some woman at this gathering ("an overwhelming question"). But he is extremely self-conscious, worried about his "bald spot" (line 40), his thin arms and legs, and how he might be stereotyped or "formulated" (line 57). So perhaps the "you" and "I" represent two aspects of himself engaged in an inner struggle.

What are the **modernist stylistic features** of the poem? How can the evening be "like" a "patient etherized upon a table"? And how can streets and hotels "lead" to a question? And why the sudden shift to the women talking about Michelangelo? What is happening?

- Clearly, these lines are not intended to be taken literally. How, then, can we puzzle out their meaning? Perhaps we should just read the poem aloud and let it affect us. Perhaps that is how it conveys its meaning. We don't need to understand every single word or phrase. The first three lines—which the meter forces us to read slowly—convey a sense of lethargy and resignation. Reading in this mode, we can infer that the "half-deserted streets" are not physical but represent a journey in the speaker's mind. And the sudden transition to the Michelangelo couplet reflects the speaker's thinking about his destination—the gathering, where he will ask a woman his question.

- Hence the "logic" of the poem so far is one of image and suggestion, not literal denotation. This is a modernist feature, as are the abrupt transitions to different "scenes."

- Similarly, later in the poem the "fog" might represent the speaker's confusion or troubled sexuality; and his language is full of allusions to the Bible and various literary works. When he says "I am not Prince Hamlet," he may be comparing his own indecisiveness to Hamlet's. But the difference is that Hamlet was a prince, and his decision—whether to kill Claudius and avenge his father—had great consequences, whereas Prufrock's decision is relatively trivial.

What are the **modernistic features** of the poem's content?

- We could say that the theme of the poem is Prufrock's (or anyone's) attempt to find love in the modern world. But why is this poem modernist? Well, most love poetry before the early twentieth century portrayed an idealized vision of love, even if it was unattainable. This poem represents love in all its actual entanglement with feelings of confusion and inadequacy, fear of rejection, and fear of being misunderstood.

- The speaker's subjectivity is fragmented and occupies a fragmented world. This subjectivity is created and explored through the language of the poem itself. It exists in relative isolation, showing the barriers between human beings. As for the world, nothing in it is described as a whole; we get only images—fog, smoke, time, tea, fingers, mermaids—that appear in isolation, dragging with them the history of their previous meanings. Tellingly, Prufrock never describes a complete woman: all he talks of is arms, eyes, bracelets, shawls, dresses, and perfumes.

Moving from notes to thesis

Clearly, we could formulate many theses about "The Love Song of J. Alfred Prufrock." We could examine the devices with which it rejects literal language. We could show how it refuses a conventional narrative structure or how, as an internal monologue, it expresses the isolation of consciousness. Or we could analyze the poem's treatment of women. Any of these topics could lead to an interesting thesis dealing with the poem's modernist form and content.

POSTMODERNISM

Postmodernism is, broadly speaking, a late-twentieth-century movement that challenges all totalizing, or all-encompassing, explanations of society and the self. It rejects the "grand narratives" of modernity, especially the Enlightenment narrative of the rationality and progress of Western civilization. Instead of stressing the universal, postmodernism focuses on the local, the regional, and the particular—in a word, on difference. The postmodern vision doesn't try to find any "true" reality or meaning beneath the world of appearances. It accepts the surfaces that the world presents. And it acknowledges that reality is no more than the world of language or signs.

Like modernism, postmodernism recognizes that the human self and the world are constructions and that language is integral to this construction. And it relies on similar literary techniques: the breakdown of narrative and the use of allusion, collage, and imitation, as well as a rejection of the idea of "literal" meaning. But there are key differences between modernism and postmodernism.

- **Recognition of diversity.** Whereas modernism was largely focused on the West, postmodernism insists on acknowledging various kinds of diversity—religious, cultural, sexual, ethnic, and aesthetic. Although Joseph Conrad claimed that *Heart of Darkness* (1899) was a critique of colonialism, postmodernists may view it as racist because it does not grant any subjectivity to Africans, merely describing them as objects. Postmodernist works tend to show that the world can be viewed from various cultural perspectives.

- **Populism.** Whereas most modernist works were addressed to a highly educated audience that could grasp their often obscure allusions, postmodernism engages popular culture and often analyzes systems of domination and control. For example, T. S. Eliot's "Prufrock" draws on Western conventions of love poetry to challenge them, but the twentieth-century Urdu poets Miraji and Fahmidah Riaz show how the nature of love is deeply conditioned by political circumstances.

- **Rejection of identity and totality.** Whereas modernist writing—like Joyce's *Ulysses* (1922) or Eliot's *The Waste Land*—often alludes nostalgically to the lost unity of traditional societies or previous literary forms, postmodernism accepts a world that is fragmented, incoherent, and full of difference, a world without clear identity or unity or purpose. It is the reader herself who will bring coherence to the text as it interacts with her own perspective.

ANALYZING A POSTMODERN TEXT

Samuel Beckett, *Endgame* (1957)

Postmodernism doesn't shy away from exploring the meaninglessness of human existence. The twentieth-century philosophy of existentialism was founded on the view that "God is dead" and the consequent lack of meaning or purpose could produce human anguish. Existentialism applied the label "absurd" to a situation in which life lacks meaning and yet individuals are committed to finding it. Beckett's *Waiting for Godot* (1952) and *Endgame* (1957) are masterful expressions of this dilemma. Both plays take place on a bare stage, and both lack any coherent plot, or development of character, or conflict or resolution or unity of action—the conventional qualities of drama.

The action in these postmodern plays is repetitive, underlining the empty passage of time, which moves toward nothing but death. The setting is abstract and unnameable, and the characters exist in isolation. Though their situation is dire, their attempts to find meaning and to occupy themselves are also comical—when viewed from a distance. The only meaning they can find must be self-created, through a perpetual performance; ultimately, what is being performed is not a play but life itself. Consider the following passage:

CLOV: Why this farce, day after day?

HAMM: Routine. One never knows. *(Pause.)* Last night I saw inside my breast. There was a big sore.

CLOV: Pah! You saw your heart.

HAMM: No, it was living. *(Pause. Anguished.)* Clov!

CLOV: Yes.

HAMM: What's happening?

CLOV: Something is taking its course. *(Pause.)*

HAMM: Clov!

CLOV *(impatiently)*: What is it?

HAMM: We're not beginning to . . . to . . . mean something?

CLOV: Mean something! You and I, mean something! *(Brief laugh.)* Ah that's a good one!

HAMM: I wonder. *(Pause.)* Imagine if a rational being came back to earth, wouldn't he be liable to get ideas into his head if he observed us long enough. *(Voice of rational being.)* Ah, good, now I see what it is, yes, now I understand what they're at! *(Clov starts, drops the telescope and begins to scratch his belly with both hands. Normal voice.)* And without going so far as that, we ourselves . . . *(with emotion)* . . . we ourselves . . . at certain moments . . . *(Vehemently.)* To think perhaps it won't all have been for nothing!

CLOV *(anguished, scratching himself)*: I have a flea!

HAMM: A flea! Are there still fleas?

CLOV: On me there's one. *(Scratching.)* Unless it's a crablouse.

HAMM *(very perturbed)*: But humanity might start from there all over again! Catch him, for the love of God!

CLOV: I'll go and get the powder. *(Exit Clov.)*

Despite the apparent aimlessness of the dialogue here and throughout the play, focusing on certain points will help us begin to decipher meaning. Let's start by asking some questions.

What **absurdist themes** appear in this passage (and persist throughout the text)?

- **Time.** "Why this farce, day after day?" The subject of time comes up repeatedly; and in this context, time is little more than repetition of the same routine, the empty passing of moments. We often hear the phrase, "it's time it ended" and "it's a day like any other day." Clov repeatedly claims that he has "things to do" and then does nothing. At one point he mutters, "All life long the same inanities."

- **Life.** "What's happening?" and "Something is taking its course" imply that "life" is simply happening *to* these characters in a way they don't understand. Hamm repeatedly says he has had enough of "this thing" and affirms that "the thing is impossible." But he also recognizes the comedy in this situation: "it's the most comical thing in the world."

- **Meaning.** "We're not beginning to . . . to . . . mean something?" The idea that their lives could have meaning recurs throughout the play, but it never becomes more than an abstract possibility. Hamm talks of "infinite emptiness . . . all around you." Perhaps the play hints that there was once meaning, a time when humanity was at the center of things. Hamm remarks (sitting in a chair): "I was right in the center."

- **Self-conscious performance.** These characters have an ironic vision, looking at themselves from the outside. In the passage above, Hamm imagines a rational being from outside looking at their situation and stages his imaginary remarks. Later, he insinuates that *this very play* is being directed by him, saying "I'll soon have finished with this story . . . unless I bring in other characters." The idea here is that human existence is itself a performance, always temporary or ready to change, always shifting between various possible outcomes.

Moving from notes to thesis

These are just a few of the themes we could explore. A basic thesis might be something like the following:

> Beckett's *Endgame* exhibits postmodern characteristics in its treatment of time, meaning, and the notion of life as a performance.

Of course, you might write about a different theme. Beckett acknowledged that the "meaning" of his plays was open and that the audience had much to fill in. Thus the structure of the play relies in part on its being not only read (or watched) but *written* by the audience. You could take a statement such as Clov's "There is nothing to say" and analyze it in relation to the play as a whole. Does Clov mean that there *is* something to say, namely nothing, the nothingness or void of existence? But, as is true of all great literature, you need to immerse yourself in the play and, especially, see it performed. Why does *Endgame* matter to *you*? What dimensions of contemporary life does it illuminate? What does it tell viewers about themselves? Attempting to answer such questions will give you a better sense of your own points of entry into the text.

CHAPTER 13

CONTEMPORARY LITERATURE

"ontemporary literature" refers broadly to works produced by authors who are still living and writing. Much contemporary literature shares features of modernism and postmodernism. These include an awareness (as in modernism) that language doesn't necessarily represent a reality, that reality itself, and the human self along with it, is a construction. Like postmodernism, contemporary literature values heterogeneity and diversity; it is often pluralistic in its outlook—that is, it acknowledges that there are numerous ways of looking at the world and various ways of living within it.

But unlike modernism and postmodernism, which were both to a large degree reactions against realism, much literature today attempts to engage with the actual circumstances of the world in which we live. Hence it employs a kind of self-conscious realism, which it acknowledges to be a literary strategy rather than the actual description of any "real" world. This realism is often combined with modernist techniques such as symbolism, allusion, and nonlinear narrative. In addition, contemporary works often mix genres to create hybrids such as magical realism and creative nonfiction, which merges elements of fiction, autobiography, memoir, and reflective essay.

Groups such as Native Americans, African Americans, Chinese Americans, and Latinos and Latinas have been a powerful force in shaping contemporary literature. These writers have explored race, class, the hybrid nature of cultural identity, and the problems of immigration or exile, experimenting with language and using a mixture of realist and modernist techniques as they analyze actual cultural and ethnic conflicts. A powerful example of such writing is Toni Morrison's short story "Recitatif."

ANALYZING CONTEMPORARY LITERATURE

Toni Morrison, "Recitatif" (1983)

Toni Morrison is a central figure in contemporary American fiction. Her short story "Recitatif" explores race, class, identity, and time, showing how all of these are both cultural and psychological constructs. The story follows the friendship of—and antagonism between—two girls, Twyla and Roberta, as they become adults. One is black, the other white, but we are never told which is which. The following passage, in which Twyla reflects back on a conversation with Roberta about an incident at a youth shelter and school, recapitulates many of the story's themes and literary devices:

> I couldn't help looking for Roberta when Joseph graduated from high school, but I didn't see her. It didn't trouble me much what she had said to me in the car. I mean the kicking part. I know I didn't do that. But I was puzzled by her telling me Maggie was black. When I thought about it I actually couldn't be certain. She wasn't pitch-black, I knew, or I would have remembered that. What I remember was the kiddie hat, and the semicircle legs. I tried to reassure myself about the race thing for a long time until it dawned on me that the truth was already there, and Roberta knew it. I didn't kick her; I didn't join in with the gar girls and kick the lady, but I sure did want to. We watched and never tried to help her and never called for help. Maggie was my dancing mother. Deaf, I thought, and dumb. Nobody inside. Nobody

who would hear you if you cried in the night. Nobody who could tell you anything important that you could use. Rocking, dancing, swaying as she walked. And when the gar girls pushed her down, and started roughhousing, I knew she wouldn't scream, couldn't—just like me—and I was glad about that.

Let's start by establishing the context of the passage and considering its literary techniques. Then we'll be in a better position to identify its themes.

What is the **context** of this passage within the story?

- **Description of Maggie.** Earlier in the story, a kitchen worker named Maggie is described as "old and sandy-colored," as wearing a "stupid little hat," and as having "legs like parentheses" on which "she rocked when she walked." On one occasion, Twyla remarked that Maggie had fallen down and that the older girls (whom they nicknamed the "gar girls") had laughed at her and kicked her. Later, Twyla felt bad that she and Roberta had not helped Maggie. In fact, they had called her names, assuming that she could not hear them because she was deaf. In retrospect, Twyla sees those incidents differently: "it shames me even now to think there was somebody in there after all who heard us call her those names and couldn't tell on us."

- **Memory of Maggie.** The last time they met, Twyla and Roberta argued about Maggie. Roberta accused Twyla of kicking Maggie— of kicking "a poor old black lady when she was down on the ground." In the passage above, Twyla is reacting to that accusation.

What **literary devices** are used in the passage?

- **Narrator.** Is Twyla a reliable narrator? How can we decide? Twyla describes her feelings in detail, acknowledging her own doubts and the possibility that she might be wrong; moreover, the author allows Roberta to speak in her own words, thereby giving us insight into the girls' conflict from both points of view. Precisely because the narrator (Twyla) appears to be reliable, her doubts about her memory are all the more convincing—and disturbing.

- **Symbolism.** Since it is on Maggie that the protagonist (Twyla) and the antagonist (Roberta) focus their recollections, could she be a symbol of time and the ways in which the past relates to the present? At one point Twyla thinks, "Roberta had messed up my past somehow with that business about Maggie," suggesting that we manufacture and alter the past to suit our present needs and interests.

What are the **themes** of the story?

- **Construction of self.** We might view Maggie's symbolism as underlying the major themes of the story. To begin, we see in the passage above that the past influences how we construct our present identity. Twyla's assumptions about the past and how she behaved have been challenged. Not only does she doubt her memory of what happened but she now understands that Maggie has become a kind of symbol and substitute for her "dancing mother." Can we see dancing in this story as a symbol not just of freedom and escape but also of irresponsibility? The big girls in the orphanage—who had their own histories of abuse—dance regularly, and it is because her own mother "dances all night" that Twyla is in the shelter. Perhaps she projects onto Maggie her mother's irresponsibility, which leaves her to fend for herself. Her mother cannot hear her crying in the night. Her mother is effectively mute like Maggie, unable to speak or give advice.

- **Racial codes.** Morrison remarked that she left all racial codes out of this story, even though race was a central theme. We are unable to determine who is black, Roberta or Twyla, and African American characteristics are attributed to both. This strategy challenges us to question our own assumptions as we read and forces us to search for the racial codes ourselves.

- **Construction of reality as temporal.** What does it mean that in the end neither Twyla nor Roberta can remember Maggie's color with any certainty? Is color both a cultural and a psychological construction? But the symbolism of Maggie shows us that a deeper process underlies the construction of racial codes. If Maggie is a symbol of time, she shows that we construct all reality and our selves through the process of memory, which is imbued with and shaped by our deepest psychological needs.

Moving from notes to thesis

Morrison's story can be explored from a number of angles. It would be interesting to go beyond the theme of race as a construction to consider how the underlying theme might be "time" or "experience" and how we manipulate these in order to create our identities. Perhaps Morrison is showing that such strategies are an integral part of how we construct our own identities as well as those of the people around us. Of course, other issues, such as characterization, conflict between characters, and setting, could be discussed. Much could be said about the political circumstances in which part of the story is set: the attempt to desegregate schools by busing children far from their homes. How do these conditions affect and shape—and distort—personal relationships? How might Twyla and Roberta have had different views of each other? And to what extent have we, as readers, participated in their constructions of each other?

ANALYZING CONTEMPORARY LITERATURE

Zadie Smith, "The Waiter's Wife" (1999)

Postcolonial theorists often use terms such as "hybridity," "marginality," "exile," and "migration" (see chapter 16). All of these themes are present in the work of Zadie Smith, herself a daughter of an interracial marriage (a Jamaican mother and an English father). Smith's family was part of the influx of immigrants to England from its former colonies in the 1950s and 1960s, and her fiction records the emergence of a racially diverse, multicultural Britain. She portrays the emerging and sometimes problematic hybrid identities that arise in the midst of racism and poverty. Here is a passage from her short story "The Waiter's Wife," whose themes and characters anticipate those of her first novel, *White Teeth* (2000). It is a pointed exchange between the main character, Alsana, who recently migrated from Bangladesh with her older husband, and her Anglicized and irreverent niece.

> [I]n response Niece-of-Shame bats her voluminous eyelashes, wraps her college scarf round her head like purdah, and says, "Oh yes, Auntie, yes, the little submissive Indian woman. You don't talk to him, he talks at you. You scream and shout at each other, but there's no communication. And in the end he wins anyway because he does whatever he likes when he likes. You don't even know where he is, what he does, what he *feels*, half the time. It's 1975, Alsi. You can't conduct relationships like that any more. It's not like back home. There has to be communication between men and women in the West, they've got to listen to each other, otherwise . . ." Neena mimes a small mushroom cloud going off in her hand.
>
> "What a load of the codswallop," says Alsana sonorously, closing her eyes, shaking her head. "It is you who do not listen. By Allah, I will always give as good as I get. But you presume I *care* what he does. You presume I want to *know*. The truth is, for a marriage to survive you don't need all this talk, talk, talk; all this 'I am this' and 'I am really like this' like on the television, all this *revelation*—especially when your husband is old, when he is wrinkly and falling apart—you do not *want* to know what is slimy underneath the bed and rattling in the wardrobe."

In examining this story, we might look at the literary devices and themes Smith uses to re-create and shed light on the immigrant experience in Britain.

What **literary devices** help to convey the immigrant experience?

- **Dialogue.** Dialogue plays an important part in "The Waiter's Wife." It communicates the conflict of generations and the conflict of worldviews. While dialogue highlights the personalities of the two women, we see that they share certain traits: both are assertive, and both are committed to their positions. Are you surprised that the aunt, Alsana, is more cynical—and perhaps more sarcastic—than her Westernized niece?

- **Staging of a debate.** It's somewhat unusual that we see in fiction an explicit debate between two characters. Often, the conflict between characters stems from a clash of personalities or aims. But here, it is the beliefs—and indeed the worldviews—of the characters that are at stake, just as in the classical Greek drama *Antigone*. Perhaps this embedded debate gives the story a dramatic character and ensures that we picture the antagonists as if they are actors. For example, Neena "bats her voluminous eyelashes" as she speaks, and Alsana is described as "closing her eyes, shaking her head."

- **Metaphor.** What is the effect of Alsana's nickname for Neena ("Niece-of-Shame")? The nickname is a metaphor because it is a deliberate *displacement* of Neena's name by Alsana. It has no literal meaning and implies many things, including Alsana's narrow-minded attitude and the gap between generations. But Neena is never described as having done anything shameful. Is she simply too liberal for her aunt?

- **Humor.** Comedy can be a powerful weapon when used to expose people's follies or hypocrisy. In this story humor is sometimes created by the immigrants' misuse of English colloquialisms. At one point, Alsana exclaims: "Getting anything out of my husband is like trying to squeeze water out when you're stoned." Neena laughs and corrects her. This kind of humor can have various effects, perhaps encouraging the stereotype of the language-mangling immigrant or making the immigrant more likable. Also, hilariously, according to the narrator, Alsana is "very religious, lacking nothing except the faith."

What **themes** portray the experience of immigrants?

- **Hybridity.** This term could refer to the merging of cultures, religions, belief systems, and social customs. But we might also talk about degrees of hybridity. Though Neena is apparently more liberal and Westernized than her aunt, they both have assimilated elements of British culture, not least the language. While Neena is self-consciously feminist and has helped educate Alsana's friend Clara about feminist texts, Alsana has also changed since her arrival in Britain She has reflected on her marriage and has adopted a pragmatic attitude toward it. For her, a key word—which represents an entire attitude toward life—is "survival." Such internal conflict is a component of hybridity.

- **Marginality.** Both Alsana and her husband are marginal; they live at the edge of a culture and are regarded as outside the mainstream. Samad sees himself as trapped in a meaningless routine of work (as a waiter) and sleep, subject to condescension even from his own people. Samad always feels the need to tell others the story of what he used to be. Is this a way for him to reassert something of his old identity?

- **Race.** In this multicultural Britain, various groups live alongside one another. Smith's story challenges the stereotype of racism as a black–white issue: some Indians, too, have racist stereotypes. Having met Clara, the Jamaican wife of her husband's friend Archie, Alsana thinks to herself: "So some black people *are* friendly." And we are told that "it was her habit to single one shining exception out of every minority she disliked." Later, Alsana complains to her husband that their child will grow up in an area inhabited by children who are "half blacky-white." Racism is portrayed here as a complex phenomenon that permeates all cultures and people.

Moving from notes to thesis

Many themes could be discussed in terms of "The Waiter's Wife." There is the issue of a generation gap among immigrants, with the younger being more assimilated into English culture. Another is that of mental illness (Alsana, for example, is prone to "rage") and psychoanalysis: Neena believes in communication, but Alsana doubts the value of "talk, talk, talk" and endless "revelation." As always, you need to find *your* point of entry into the text and determine what *you* think the story is concerned with. On the basis of the notes above, you could formulate a thesis along the lines of the following:

> In her short story "The Waiter's Wife," Zadie Smith conveys the experience of immigrants through the themes of hybridity, marginality, and race. She foregrounds these themes through her use of dialogue and humor and other literary devices such as metaphor.

Alternatively, you could come up with a thesis about the depiction of marriage in this story or the treatment of race, or the conflict of generations. Finally, it might be worth investigating Alsana's religious perspective, which is highly practical and leaves her wishing to have the "whole bloody universe made clear—in a little nutshell."

CHAPTER 14

WORLD LITERATURE

The term **world literature** was coined by the German writer Johann Wolfgang von Goethe, who wrote in the 1830s that while literature does have national characteristics, it also expresses universal qualities. In 1899 the Danish writer Georg Brandes argued that many scientific and literary works should be regarded as world literature since they have risen above their national contexts to give us universal insights into the human condition. However, it wasn't until the 1990s that a significant number of teachers and critics started to broaden the curriculum to include texts from cultures outside the Western canon—from Asia, the Middle East, Africa, and Latin America.

Recently, the literary critic David Damrosch defined world literature as a way of reading that situates a text within a context broader than its culture of origin. The text thereby gains new levels of significance as it is translated into various languages. For example, the Qur'an—originally composed in what is now seen as classical Arabic—can be translated as prose, as poetry, in archaic and elevated language, in a more colloquial idiom, or even from a feminist perspective. So a text can become something quite different when it is translated into another language and received into another culture.

Other critics have defined world literature in more political terms, seeing it as a symptom of economic imperialism that destroys the values of traditional cultures. In this view, world literature is an ideological construct that, far from encouraging cultural and literary equality, privileges certain literatures and views others as marginal or exotic. Chinua Achebe's controversial decision to write in English rather than his native Nigerian language, Igbo, on the grounds that doing so would give him a global audience, touched on many of the issues raised here. Many argued that his writing in the "imperial" language of English forfeits the authenticity of native experience.

Clearly these matters are complicated. But however we view them, we live in an era when globalization is a fact, and we can't view literature as merely a regional or national phenomenon. Many great authors and texts are translated, read, and taught across the world—including Shakespeare, Dante, the Bible, the Qur'an, Confucius, the Hindu scriptures, Rumi, Jane Austen, George Eliot—and this interchange can only enrich our understanding of what "literature" means. It could also play a significant role in enhancing understanding between cultures.

GENERAL STRATEGIES

We've already looked at how we might approach texts of world literature, such as those of Homer, Virgil, Christine de Pizan, and Dante. When we look at texts from outside the Western tradition (and even those inside it), written originally in a language other than English, we should keep a few things in mind.

- **Translation.** It's always worth remembering when we're dealing with a translated text that we need to be careful when we analyze form or style. A translator may use certain literary devices (such as rhyme or assonance) not present in the original in order to compensate for effects in the original that she feels unable to reproduce. And remember too that any translation is an *interpretation* of the original. On the positive side, translations of the "same" text can vary widely; this shows us that there is no "pure" original with a fixed meaning. Comparing various translations of one text can show the range of its possible meanings and help us to understand the "original" better.

- **Historical and cultural context.** Reading a "foreign" text without any historical or cultural context can be misleading, and even dangerous—think of how passages from the Bible have been used to justify slavery and the oppression of women. So try to make sure that (a) you read the introduction to the text, if one is provided; (b) you do a little research into the background of the text and its author; and (c) you have some sense of what motivated the author to write the text. For example, to grasp how humanism and religious mysticism coexist in the Urdu poetry of Ghalib (1797–1869), we must know that he is reacting against *both* British rule *and* Islamic fundamentalism as he calls for a "common faith" among humankind.

- **Comparison across cultures.** We can't assume that literary modes such as "realism" or "symbolism" will have the same significance across cultures. A poem of T. S. Eliot's will seem different when approached in its native tradition and when placed in the context of international modernism. In its own culture (American and British), Eliot's work is often seen as a "symbolist" reaction against realism. But Eliot's influence on Indian poetry was in the direction of realism: because much Indian poetry belonged to a tradition that was symbolic and highly stylized, modernism represented a move *away* from symbolism toward a more realistic description of character and social problems.

- **Worldview and underlying assumptions.** Finally, bear in mind that the religious, social, and aesthetic assumptions underlying a text may vary vastly across different cultures. For example, in the Hindu scripture the *Bhagavad Gita*, the god Krishna advises the charioteer Arjuna that it is his "duty" to go into battle to kill his relatives. It is useful to recall here that human life in the Hindu scriptures is viewed as continuing beyond physical death. Also, whereas in the West "action" is viewed typically as an expression of the self or as a means to an end, in Hinduism it's viewed as a selfless expression of duty. Although we're not obliged to accept the ethical or religious assumptions in texts from various cultures, it pays to know what those assumptions are and how they are expressed in and influence the structure of a text.

ANALYZING WORLD LITERATURE

Confucius, *Analects*

The title of the *Lunyu* (*Conversations*) of the Chinese philosopher Confucius (Kongfuzi, or "Master Kong," 551–479 B.C.E.) is usually rendered in English as "analects" (from the Greek word for "table scraps" or, by extension, "literary gleanings"). Like Socrates (who was born just ten years after he died), Confucius did not write down his ideas. What we have is the record of his conversations with his disciples. In the second century B.C.E. the doctrines of Confucius became the basis of Chinese state ideology and of the training of civil servants, retaining those functions for more than two thousand years. In general, these doctrines suggest that we should learn from the wisdom of the past and that we should revere our parents, an attitude that will be the basis for honoring tradition, rituals, social roles or duties, and the state. This wisdom is embodied in great literature, and our overall goal should be to harmonize our individual desires with our social and political obligations. The following gem from the *Analects* is especially pertinent, since it concerns the significance of poetry:

> The Master said: "Little ones, why don't you study the *Poems*? The *Poems* can provide you with stimulation and with observation, with a capacity for communion, and with a vehicle for grief. At home, they enable you to serve your father, and abroad, to serve your lord. Also, you will learn there the names of many birds, animals, plants, and trees."
>
> *(17.9; trans. Simon Leys)*

From the translator's introduction, we learn that by "the Poems" Confucius means the *Classics of Poetry*, compiled around 600 B.C.E., which was the first Chinese anthology of verse. Now let's ask a few crucial questions.

What Confucian **values** are expressed in this passage?

- **Moral values.** Clearly, "serving" one's father and serving one's lord are important objectives, embodying reverence for parents and superiors, as well as loyalty to the state. This is evidently a hierarchical society that allows little social mobility—like feudal society in premodern Europe.

- **Pragmatic and scientific values.** This passage underscores the importance of observation of and empirical learning about nature. To grasp how "modern" and secular this outlook is, keep in mind that Christian Europe was "otherworldly" for many centuries. Clearly, Confucius is interested in *this* world, not in an afterlife.

- **Empathetic values.** Confucius stresses the value of "a capacity for communion," as well as the ability to display grief. An important part of his philosophy is reciprocal goodness between human beings.

What are the **stylistic features** of the passage?

- **Invoking the authority of tradition.** We can tell from this passage not only that Confucius valued poetry but also that, as in ancient Greek society, poetry had important social, political, and moral functions. Indeed, poetry was viewed in ancient China as a tool for self-expression and the release of emotion (similar to the catharsis that Aristotle associated with tragedy). But it also had moral and political functions, enabling rulers to justify their actions and to control people, as well as helping to encourage proper relations between husband and wife, parents and children. Poetry was regarded as containing all the wisdom of the past. Confucius's strategy here is to invoke the authority of this tradition.

- **Literary devices.** Instead of trying to force things on his listeners, Confucius addresses them affectionately as "little ones" and asks a rhetorical question: "why don't you . . . ?" There's also parallelism in "At home . . . abroad," underlining the parallel obligations to parents and to masters.

Moving from notes to thesis

The passage above is fairly short. To write a paper about Confucian values, it would be good to refer to other parts of the text, such as 2.4, where Confucius spells out the stages of his own spiritual development;

4.15, where the "thread" of his philosophy is described as "loyalty and reciprocity"; 6.18, where he states that a "gentleman" achieves a balance of "nature" and "culture"; 7.16, where he describes the poverty of riches and honor if these are not accompanied by justice; and 12.11, where he exhorts: "Let the lord be a lord; the subject a subject; the father a father; the son a son." These statements, in a way, summarize his philosophy. On the basis of notes and observations, you could formulate a thesis something like this:

> Confucius's *Analects* embody a range of moral and pragmatic values, all centered on the need to achieve harmony between oneself and one's social obligations to family, lord, and state. Confucius uses a number of literary techniques to underline these values.

You could also examine the importance of tradition, or how the parent–child relationship seems to be the foundation of other proper relationships. And you could compare the values expressed in *The Analects* with those in other scriptures. The important thing is to base your analysis on a close reading of one or two parts of the text, and then to cite other parts in support of your argument.

ANALYZING WORLD LITERATURE

Bhavakadevi, Classical Sanskrit Lyric

During the classical period in Sanskrit literature (ca. 400–1100 C.E.), the main goals of literature were *rasa*, or the capturing of a pure emotional state; *alamkara*, or embellishment by means of figures of speech (such as alliteration and rhyme) and figures of thought (such as metaphor and metonymy); and *dhvani*, or suggestion (rather than mere description). Poets aspired to achieve one or some combination of these in their work, and their language included both precise observation of nature and the use of literary devices. By definition, the Sanskrit lyric, called *subhasita*, was short, self-contained, and expressive of a precise emotional state. Here is a rare lyric by a female poet, Bhavakadevi:

> At first our bodies knew a perfect oneness,
> but then grew two with you as lover
> and I, unhappy I, the loved.
> Now you are husband, I the wife,
> 5   what's left except of this my life,
> too hard to break, to reap the bitter fruit,
> our broken faith.

(trans. D. H. H. Ingalls)

Despite its apparent simplicity, the poem isn't easy to understand. So let's start with some basic questions, which we can then relate to the specific form of the Sanskrit lyric.

What is the **theme** of the poem?

- There seems to be a decline in the relationship between the woman and her partner, changing from being one to being two lovers to being merely husband and wife.
- The poet mentions "broken faith," suggesting perhaps infidelity.
- Perhaps the actual theme is the poet's own state of mind or emotions.

Are there any striking **stylistic features**?

- **Antithesis.** The poem is structured as a contrast between two situations, "At first" and "Now." There is also a sharp antithesis between "you," as both "lover" and "husband," and "I," as both "loved" (that is, the passive object of love) and "wife."
- **Rhyme.** The translator creates rhyme between "knew" and "grew two," which emphasizes the loss of their oneness, especially as the stress on both these words (as in a spondee) breaks the natural iambic rhythm of English. The rhyming of "wife" and "life" underlines an imprisonment within the marital role.
- **Repetition.** The phrase "I, unhappy I," is powerful since it places great emphasis on "I" and slows down the movement of the line, as if to pay special attention to the poet's sorrow.

- **Parallelism.** A parallelism of meaning is implied in "to break, to reap . . ." What is it that is "too hard to break"? Her life? her marriage? And what is it that is left? The broken faith?

What **emotional state** is created by these lines? What *rasa,* or pure emotional state, do they re-create?

- **Emotions.** Perhaps sadness, regret, disappointment, resignation.
- **Rhetorical situation.** The speaker is not addressing anyone. The poem is an internal meditation or monologue, and her emotions are expressed by the contrast between past and present.
- **Universal element.** As is typical in Sanskrit lyrics, the speaker doesn't describe herself or her lover in personal terms. The poem represents a "pure" emotional state, freed from association with the conditions of actual life.

Moving from notes to thesis

A thesis could involve content/theme, form/style, and context. If we want to show *how* the Sanskrit lyric conveys a pure emotional state, the thesis could be something like this:

> This lyric conveys the speaker's sadness, disappointment, and resignation over how her bond with her lover has deteriorated in marriage. It achieves this through its performative situation and a number of literary techniques such as antithesis, rhyme, and parallelism.

Alternatively, you could write a paper on the meaning of the challenging last four lines. Or you could discuss what the poem implies about marriage at that time in India. Perhaps you could compare this lyric with a poem from the Western tradition, such as a Metaphysical poem or French symbolist poem, which often use similar compressed techniques.

ANALYZING WORLD LITERATURE

The Qur'an

Muslims believe that the Qur'an was revealed to the prophet Muhammad by the archangel Gabriel over a period of twenty-three years, starting in 610. In other words, it was originally an oral composition, like the Homeric epics. If we read chapters from the Qur'an, we can see that most don't have a clear narrative structure. Rather, the "voices" of the Qur'an span a number of situations: God addressing various people, the recounting of stories along with their moral lessons, exhortations to obey God, dialogues between historical figures such as Moses and Pharaoh, and arguments for God's existence. In general, the Qur'an seems highly aware of its audience and its own historical situation. Some of these attributes occur in Sura 1, "The Opening":

> [1] In the Name of God,
>   the All-Merciful, Ever-Merciful:
> [2] All praise to God, Lord of all worlds;
> [3]   the All-Merciful, Ever-Merciful;
> [4] Ruler on the Day of Reckoning.
> [5] You alone we worship; and You alone
>   we implore for help.
> [6] Guide us to the straight path,
> [7] the path of those whom You have favored, not
>   of those who have incurred Your wrath, nor
>   of those who have gone astray.

> *(trans. M. A. R. Habib and Bruce Lawrence)*

If you're analyzing a translated text, it's a good idea to read any footnotes in which the translator explains a word's meaning and the contexts of various words or phrases. Having done that, you might ask some basic questions about this passage.

What **image** of God is expressed in this text?

- God's first quality is mercy. But this mercy seems to have two aspects, as indicated by "all" and "ever." Perhaps "all" refers to the infinite range of God's mercy, while "ever" refers to its unending nature.

- God is also given the title "Lord," which implies that he has power (over "all worlds," or all kinds of creation). In addition, he is a judge and a guide. Finally, like the Old Testament God, he displays favor and wrath.

What is the **dramatic or rhetorical situation** of this passage?

- The Qur'an is meant to be the word of God, but clearly, it's not God who is speaking here. Instead, it seems to be a believer in God— not just one believer, but perhaps a community of believers, as indicated by "we."

- So the dramatic situation is complex: the words are not literally being spoken by any person or group of people. Rather, God is urging a community of people to recite these words—much as Jesus urged his followers to recite the Lord's Prayer (Matthew 6:9–13).

What are the **literary characteristics** of the passage? Even in translation, literary qualities and techniques are at work to make the Qur'an's theological message clearer and more appealing.

- **The use of refrains.** "All-Merciful, Ever Merciful." Such refrains are common throughout the Qur'an. As in the Homeric epics, they are rooted in the oral nature of the text, which was initially spoken aloud, in situations where there is a need for repetition and emphasis.

- **Parallelism.** "We alone . . . we alone," "Of those . . . of those." The Qur'an uses parallelism to establish a duality or contrast—between good and bad, between the just and unjust, and between those who obey God and those who don't.

- **Sound patterns.** If you listen to a recitation of the Qur'an in Arabic (YouTube has many examples), you'll notice that it has a melodious and rhythmic quality and that it uses much rhyme and assonance.

Rhyme isn't always easy to reproduce in English translations. But the translated passage above uses assonance (as in "name," "praise," "straight," "favored," "astray") as well as consonance (the repetition of the *r* sound in "Ruler" and "reckoning").

- **Divine epithets.** Just as Homer uses epithets such as "wine-dark" or "swift-footed," so in the Qur'an we find the "ninety-nine names" of God, such as "Merciful," "Powerful," and "Wise." These epithets not only announce the characteristics of God but also distinguish the divinity from humankind.

On the basis of these notes, you could formulate a thesis such as

> As expressed in this passage, the image of God in the Qur'an is of a being who has absolute power over all creation, is merciful, and is a guide to humankind, but is also capable of wrath and will be in command on the day of judgment. These qualities are expressed through a number of literary devices, including refrains, epithets, repetition, and parallelism.

There are, of course, many other possibilities. You could compare the image of God in the Qur'an with the God of the Old or New Testaments. You could write a paper on the dramatic situation of the passage. For a larger project, you could compare the image of Jesus in the Bible and the Qur'an, or you could compare the narrations of the story of Joseph in the Bible and in the Qur'an.

ANALYZING WORLD LITERATURE

Yehuda Amichai, "An Arab Shepherd Is Searching for His Goat on Mount Zion" (1980)

We now move to a modern text that draws on religious tradition. The Israeli poet Yehuda Amichai is known for his masterful exploitation of the Hebrew language and for evoking the war-torn Israeli landscape. Like English Metaphysical poetry, his verse often presents surprising juxtapositions, as it does in "An Arab Shepherd . . . ":

An Arab shepherd is searching for his goat on Mount Zion
and on the opposite mountain I am searching
for my little boy.
An Arab shepherd and a Jewish father
both in their temporary failure.
Our voices meet above the Sultan's Pool
in the valley between us. Neither of us wants
the child or the goat to get caught in the wheels
of the terrible *Had Gadya* machine.

Afterward we found them among the bushes
and our voices came back inside us, laughing and crying.
Searching for a goat or a son
has always been the beginning
of a new religion in these mountains.

(lines 1–14; trans. Chana Bloch)

The surprising juxtaposition is between the speaker himself and the Arab shepherd, or arguably between the child and the goat. But in order to appreciate this strategy, we need to grasp the poem's broader situation. So we might ask some of the following questions.

What is the **context** of the poem?

- Briefly, we know that in modern times there is a history of conflict between Israel and its Arab neighbors. This conflict is often characterized—perhaps wrongly—as one between Jews and Arabs, or even between Judaism and Islam.
- Arab and Israeli politicians often speak in extremely negative terms about each other.

What are the **themes** of the poem?

- One possible theme is that of "searching." The speaker and his Arab counterpart are both searching: the one for his boy, the other for his goat.

- Another theme is the possibility of *unity* between the two. Or is it the *search* for unity? or the searching after a "new religion"?

What **elements of style or form** help express or develop this theme?

- **Structure.** Parallelism is at work throughout the poem, since both men are "searching." At the beginning, they are on "opposite" mountains. But the word "both" in line 5 indicates that they are sharing something—here, a "temporary failure." And the rest of the poem unites the two figures: "Our voices meet . . . Neither of us . . . we found them."

- **Rhetorical situation.** Clearly, the speaker doesn't know what the Arab shepherd is thinking; he is empathetically re-creating the other's thoughts, in harmony with his own. He describes both himself and the shepherd as relieved—for a moment, at least, common humanity overrides political and religious differences.

- **Evocation of tradition.** *Had Gadya* is a traditional song in Aramaic and Hebrew about a kid (a baby goat) who is eaten by a cat, who is bitten by a dog, who is beaten by a stick, and so on, until the "Holy One" comes to slay the Angel of Death. This song has many interpretations, and researching it might be useful before analyzing the poem. For now, though, we can view the song simply as representing an endless cycle—perhaps a cycle of violence?

Moving from notes to thesis

What is Amichai's poem trying to do? Is it showing us that beneath their surface differences, Arab and Jew are the same? That they are both actually searching for a "new religion," one that they will share? Or should we read the poem as an allegory of the Arab–Israeli conflict, in which the peace process is bogged down in "temporary failure"? We could formulate a general thesis along these lines:

> This poem intervenes in a political situation characterized by heated conflict and deep misunderstanding. It attempts to show that individuals on both sides share the same needs of livelihood and family, and the same aspirations for unity and peace. The structure of the poem enacts this movement from opposition to unity.

Many other approaches are possible. You could analyze the poem's symbolism, asking why searching for a "goat or a son" initiates a new religion. What is the significance of "mountain" and "bushes"? All have biblical connotations. Does the poem suggest that poets are able to get a better perspective on current events than politicians or those involved more deeply in the difficulties?

ANALYZING WORLD LITERATURE

Bessie Head, "The Deep River" (1977)

The system of racial segregation known as apartheid existed in South Africa during Bessie Head's youth. Head campaigned against it and other forms of social injustice. She was particularly interested in the dilemmas of contemporary Africa, and her work "The Deep River: A Story of Ancient Tribal Migration" is a mythic account of how modern individualism emerged from the dissolution of an ancient tribal structure. Here are two passages that indicate this transition:

> On the day on which thanksgiving was to be held, the women all followed one another in single file to the chief's place. Large vessels had been prepared at the chief's place, so that when the women came they poured the beer into them. Then there was a gathering of all the people to celebrate thanksgiving for the harvest time. All the people lived this way, like one face, under their chief. They accepted this regimental levelling down of their individual souls, but on the day of dispute or when strife and conflict and greed blew stormy winds over their deep river, the people awoke and showed their individual faces.

> There was at first no direct challenge to the chieftaincy which Sebembele occupied. But the nature of the surprising dispute, that of his love for a woman and child, caused it to drag on longer than time would allow. Many evils began to rear their heads like impatient hissing snakes, while Sebembele argued with his own heart ... torn between the demands of his position and the strain of a love affair which had been conducted in deep secrecy for many, many months.

In a note to this story, Head acknowledges that it is a "fictionalized version" of the history of the Botalaote tribe. That information might influence the kinds of questions we ask.

Why does the author **fictionalize** history? What light can such a story throw on African society?

- Sometimes literary accounts of history are more powerful than factual ones. Literary narratives can give us insights into particular personalities, their psychologies, and what makes them unique.

- Head examines individualism in modern Africa, with all its accompanying features of internal conflict, conflict with community, and conflict with tradition. We know that in the West many factors were responsible for individualism—the Protestant Reformation, the Enlightenment, and the growth of the bourgeois class. But none of this happened in Africa. Hence, Head points to the breakdown of the tribal structure as the main cause of individualism.

How does the story's **form** help to convey the transition from tribal unity to individualism?

- The first passage conveys the image of an orderly society. The women follow one another "in single file" and do everything together, at appointed times. Head even describes the "regimental levelling down of their individual souls."

- The passage uses at least two metaphors. The first is that all the people have only "one face," which is the face of their chief. The second is the metaphor of the title, used in the first paragraph: "the people lived together like a deep river"—here, clearly, the river of tradition.

- But "strife and conflict and greed" are said—in a third metaphor—to blow "stormy winds" over this river. We know from elsewhere in the story that the tribe is disturbed by the love of Sebembele, the son of his father's first wife, for his father's junior wife Rankwana. The second passage uses a powerful simile to evoke the disastrous consequences of this love: evils appeared "like impatient hissing snakes," and all the symptoms of individualism arise: Sebembele's inner turmoil, the division of the tribe into factions, and its rapid dissolution.

Moving from notes to thesis

Your approach will depend on how you see the story. Do you see it as a mythical account of the emergence of modern African society? Or as a condemnation of modern individualism and a nostalgic recollection of a time of unity? Or as an allegory underscoring the fact that it takes bold people—such as Sebembele and Rankwana—to break the hold of tradition? Combining some of these alternatives might lead to something like this:

> In "The Deep River," Bessie Head offers an imaginative re-creation of the emergence of modern African society from tribal culture. While she seems to mourn the loss of communal unity, she also sees some positive traits in individualism, such as attachment to genuine emotions and the courage to defy traditional values and customs. In expressing this perspective, she uses a number of literary techniques, such as metaphor and simile.

Of course, you may be interested in something completely different. For example, you might focus on the symbolism of the "deep river." Or you could discuss the effectiveness of giving a mythical account of history, or examine the status and role of women in the story.

ANALYZING WORLD LITERATURE

Hanan al-Shaykh, "The Women's Swimming Pool" (1994)

The Lebanese writer Hanan al-Shaykh deals candidly in her fiction with the entire range of sexuality, including prostitution, homosexuality, and transvestism. In the process, she offers a powerful feminist critique of the religious and social customs of her native Arab society. Her short story "The

Women's Swimming Pool" is narrated by a girl who dreams of escaping from the hot tobacco fields of southern Lebanon to the sea. Here is part of the story's final paragraph, which describes her arrival, after much searching, at the women's swimming pool:

> I saw my grandmother standing and looking up at the sky. I called to her, but she was reciting to herself under her breath as she continued to look upward: she was praying right there in the street, praying on the pavement at the door of the swimming pool. . . . I would have liked to persuade myself that she had nothing to do with me, that I didn't know her. How, though? She's my grandmother whom I've dragged with my entreaties from the tobacco-threading tent, from the jagged slab of stone, from the winds of the South; I have crammed her into the bus and been lost with her in the streets. . . . And now here were the two of us standing at the door of the swimming pool, and she, having heard the call to prayers, had prostrated herself in prayer. She was destroying what lay in my bag, blocking the road between me and the sea.
>
> (trans. Denys Johnson-Davies)

The contrast between the grandmother and the young narrator is sharply drawn, in what for many readers may be an unfamiliar cultural setting. Those factors might offer a good starting point for our questions.

What are the most prominent **elements** of the cultural setting?

- Early in the story we learn that the girl comes from a part of Lebanese society steeped in religious customs, including the requirement that women cover their bodies completely. She complains that even in the heat, she must wear a long dress and a head shawl. Her grandmother even warns her against wearing a swimming costume: "If any man were to see you, you'd be done for."

- But when the girl gets to the city, Beirut, she sees a different world: she sees women with "bared arms" and "tight trousers," their hair visible.

What do the grandmother and the narrator represent? Is there a **central conflict** in the story?

- We first see the grandmother in "her black dress," and we know that her husband was a "celebrated religious scholar." The grandmother is superstitious: she thinks that "the sea puts a spell on people" and that seeking the swimming pool is a "devilish idea." In the passage above, she insists on answering the call to prayer just as the two arrive, finally, at the swimming pool, even though she is blocking the narrator's way to the sea. Her eyes are turned up and she ignores her granddaughter. The grandmother seems to embody religion, tradition, superstition, rigidity, and the past.

- At first, the narrator was close to her grandmother, "like an orange and its navel." But by the time of the final passage, set in a city whose atmosphere is liberal and "modern," she feels like disowning this person who is not only preventing her from reaching the sea but is destroying "what lay in my bag"—which we know to be a bathing costume, a sleeveless dress, and her headscarf (hijab).

What **stylistic features** contribute most to the story's meaning?

- Perhaps the most obvious device is the use of a young, innocent female narrator, who candidly tells us what she thinks, describes her physical condition, and expresses her emotions or desires without attention to social etiquette or taboos.

- Whereas the grandmother is inflexible in her views, the narrator changes during the story as she engages in an exploration of her developing identity or subjectivity.

- Is the sea used as a symbol—of freedom, of escape from "heat" (perhaps representing the oppression of tradition), of the possibility of new adventures and horizons?

Moving from notes to thesis

There are many possible topics here. You could write about the emerging conflict between narrator and grandmother. You could focus on the use of a young female narrator and the perspectives this allows. And you could relate either of these topics to the style of the story, its images, and its symbols. All of these elements could be shown to support the author's vision. A thesis paragraph might look like this:

> "The Women's Swimming Pool" offers a powerful feminist critique of Arab culture and religious customs by presenting them through the eyes of a young narrator who is not afraid to criticize them or to find them illogical. In the increasing estrangement between grandmother and narrator, the latter's feminist perspective and independent identity begin to emerge, a process that is underlined by the author's use of symbols such as the contrast between the sea and the oppressive heat of the South.

An even more ambitious paper might compare the feminism of Hanan al-Shaykh, as expressed in this story, with that of a Western feminist writer; does it rest on similar assumptions? Must feminism be the same in every culture, regardless of differences in religion, manners, and social customs? Or you could compare this story with other stories by Hanan al-Shaykh, such as "A Season of Madness," which also uses the sea as a symbol of escape or freedom.

ANALYZING WORLD LITERATURE

Isabel Allende, "And of Clay Are We Created" (1989)

The Chilean writer Isabel Allende is one of the first major women novelists from Latin America. Much of her work adopts the conventions of magical realism, a form of realist fiction that incorporates imaginative and fantastic elements. Her novels explore political situations in South America, represent the experiences of women, and exhibit a commitment to social justice. Some of her work takes the form of memoir. Her short story "And of Clay Are We Created" combines elements of fact and fiction. Published in *The Stories of Eva Luna* (1989), the story is based on a real event: the 1985 eruption of a volcano in Chile that left more than 23,000 people dead in mudslides. The media focused obsessively on a teenage girl, named Azucena in the story, who was trapped in the mud, making her the symbol of the entire tragedy.

Eva Luna narrates how her lover, the photojournalist Rolf Carlé, deals with the story of Azucena. Usually able to distance himself from the events he "covers," he finds himself emotionally engaged in the girl's plight, which plunges him into confrontation with his traumatic past—his own imprisonment in a closet by his abusive father and his guilt at having abandoned his sister.

> Katharina materialized before him, floating on the air like a flag, clothed in the white tablecloth, now a winding sheet, and at last he could weep for her death and for the guilt of having abandoned her. He understood then that all his exploits as a reporter, the feats that had won him such recognition and fame, were merely an attempt to keep his most ancient fears at bay, a stratagem for taking refuge behind a lens to test whether reality was more tolerable from that perspective. He took excessive risks as an exercise of courage, training by day to conquer the monsters that tormented him by night! But he had come face to face with the moment of truth; he could not continue to escape his past. He *was* Azucena; he was buried in the clayey mud; his terror was not the distant emotion of an almost forgotten childhood, it was a claw sunk in his throat.
>
> (trans. Margaret Sayers Peden)

This passage seems to display most of the themes of this text. Let's start by identifying the most obvious ones.

What are the **themes** of the story?

- **Critique of the media and voyeurism.** Are we shocked that the media focuses relentlessly on Azucena, but doesn't do anything to help her? A pump is needed to drain the mud pit so that the girl might be freed. The story seems to be criticizing the media's disengagement from the events it covers. Distanced behind a "lens," the media may actually desensitize its audience to the reality of tragedy.

- **Critique of the government.** The "President of the Republic" visits the site, which he declares "holy ground," and personally speaks to Azucena, telling her that her courage is "an example to the nation." He promises that he will "personally" secure a pump but, predictably, he doesn't. Perhaps the story is criticizing the incompetence of Latin American leaders, or even of the culture itself (a priest passes by and blesses Azucena, hanging a medal of the Virgin around her neck).

- **Discovery of self.** As a prominent member of the media, Rolf Carlé has usually succeeded in remaining disengaged. But in this case, so close to the trapped girl, he is forced to confront reality without a "lens." This also means confronting his own past. In the process, he recognizes the true motivations for his wanting to be a reporter and to see everything through a camera at a "fictive distance."

These and other themes are undoubtedly worth analyzing. But perhaps even more striking is this story's blurring of fact and fiction, as it questions the line between them and shows that fiction can have a factual basis and that fact itself is a form of fiction. "And of Clay Are We Created" is an imaginative re-creation of a real event; it draws on the power of literature to tell a story in the most vivid terms. No mere historical account, no mere news reportage, could possibly convey these real happenings with such depth and force. In turn, the "real happenings" themselves are shown to be fictions, literary constructions. In other words, there's no "original" event that literature somehow "copies." The "event" itself is already a kind of fiction, created by language and reflecting human interests and desires. We might, then, consider how the form of the story contributes to its force.

What **formal elements** underlie the story's imaginative re-creation of a "real" event?

- **Omniscient narrator.** Perhaps the most fundamental feature is that the narrator, Eva Luna, knows "everything." She can take us inside the mind of Rolf, and into her relationship with him, and into the thoughts of Azucena (which a reporter's camera or even a historian's account cannot do). In fact, the narrator is a kind of self-conscious meta-reporter who is watching and reporting on the reporter himself.

- **Dialogue.** Sometimes reporters do talk with the people they are covering, but this story presents the entire dialogue, with the reporter Rolf himself being part of the story.

- **Description of emotions.** At one point, as Rolf is talking to the girl and his voice breaks down, the narrator remarks, "I loved him more than ever." In describing the girl's death, she says: "She sank slowly, a flower in the mud." This is a far cry from so-called objective reporting—which, in any case, is a pretense since even the work of the camera is guided by subjective interests and agendas.

- **Literary devices.** Throughout the text, the author uses similes (the young girl's head "budding like a black squash from the clay"), metaphors ("the mountain had awakened again"), and symbols ("lens" becomes a symbol for maintaining fictive distance, for presumed objectivity, and even for fear of reality or oneself).

Moving from notes to thesis

This story can be approached from numerous angles. Is it a political commentary? a social critique? an exploration of love? If you focus on how it undermines the distinction between fact and fiction, the following thesis would be appropriate:

> "And of Clay Are We Created" unsettles the distinction between fact and fiction. It takes a real event, a horrifying tragedy, and re-creates it in order to bring out its emotional power and appeal. It does this by using a number of literary devices, notably an omniscient narrator who serves as a kind of "meta-reporter" as well as techniques of metaphor, simile, and symbolism. This process of re-creation helps us understand that there is no "original" event and that all reporting is interpretation from a subjective perspective.

Alternatively, we could focus on how the story offers a critique of the media, which, with all its sophisticated technology, is more concerned with sensational coverage than with saving the girl. Another angle might be to look at both the process whereby the girl accepts her imminent death and what she teaches the journalist about himself. There are many appealing points of entry into this text.

PART FIVE

LITERARY CRITICISM AND THEORY

CHAPTER 15

LITERARY CRITICISM AND THEORY, PART I

HUMANISM, FORMALISM, NEW CRITICISM, PSYCHOANALYSIS, MARXISM, FEMINISM, AND GENDER STUDIES

Literary criticism, in the simplest terms, refers to the practice of interpreting and evaluating literary texts. Literary theory examines the foundations and assumptions behind that practice, situating it within broader historical, social, intellectual, and ideological contexts and relating it to issues of language, identity, psychology, power, gender, race, economics, and colonialism.

Literary criticism and theory are more than two and a half thousand years old. Over that time, they have addressed a number of recurring themes, concepts, and questions.

- **Imitation.** Does literature "imitate," or represent, reality?

- **Beauty.** How do we define "beauty," and how does it relate to "truth" and "goodness"?

- **The function of literature.** Is it educational, moral, political, or aesthetic?

- **The connection of literature to other disciplines.** How does literature relate to philosophy, rhetoric, and the other liberal arts?

- **The cultural and social contexts of literature.** How is literature affected by economic developments and prevailing religious or cultural assumptions?

- **Language and literary techniques.** Does language represent or mirror reality? How is language modified by figures of speech such as metaphor and metonymy?

- **Audience.** How does literature relate to its audience intellectually, emotionally, and sensually? Does an audience contribute to the meaning of a text?

- **Genres.** How do we define genres such as tragedy and epic, and what are the distinctions between them?

HISTORICAL PERIODS

Not all kinds of criticism and theory address the issues listed above in the same way. Each period has its distinctive emphases.

- **Classical criticism** (Aristotle, Horace) saw literature as a realistic representation of objective human actions and events and assigned it a moral and educational purpose. It stressed moderation, balance, and decorum (the harmony of form and content).

- **Neoplatonic criticism** (Plotinus, Proclus) saw literature as giving us access to the higher spiritual realms from which we came and to which we will return. Ironically, this contrasted sharply with the views of Plato—the source of Neoplatonism—who urged that poetry be banished from the ideal state on account of its "falseness" and its evocation of emotions that might overcome reason.

- **Medieval criticism** (Augustine, Aquinas, Dante) emphasized the notion of allegory, the idea that language has meaning on several levels—literal, moral, and mystical. Things in this world refer beyond their "literal" existence to a deeper significance in a spiritual realm.

- **Renaissance criticism** (Philip Sidney, Giambattista Giraldi, Joachim du Bellay) was secular and humanistic (centered on the human rather than the divine) and returned in part to classical values, though it also stressed individual creativity.

- **Neoclassical criticism** (Alexander Pope, John Dryden, Samuel Johnson, Jean Racine) returned even more strictly to classical values such as rationality, moderation, balance, and decorum. It stressed the notion of "wit," which referred to conceptual ingenuity and creativity, as well as the notion of "nature" as an ordered hierarchy ranging from God through angels to humans, animals, and inanimate objects.

- **Enlightenment philosophy** (John Locke, David Hume) disapproved of wit, which it saw as vague and metaphorical. Instead, it advocated using language that is clear, concise, and distinct.

- **Romantic criticism** (Goethe, Friedrich Schlegel, Friedrich Schiller, Wordsworth, Coleridge) rebelled against literalism, moderation, and the neoclassical emphasis on reason and objectivity. It saw imagination as a higher and more inclusive faculty than reason and saw literature as expressing not an objective world but human subjectivity.

- **Nineteenth-century movements:**

  Realism: literature should portray human character and events as accurately as possible. **Naturalism:** literature should draw on "scientific" observation of human psychology and the outside world. **Symbolism:** literature does not describe any particular world but evokes a higher realm through suggestion. **Aestheticism:** the aesthetic qualities of literature are most important; they are autonomous, independent of morality or religion. **Marxism:** literature must be viewed in relation to its economic and social conditions.

CRITICISM AND THEORY IN THE TWENTIETH CENTURY

Since the early twentieth century, there have been a number of significant developments in literary criticism and theory. The first movements were Russian formalism and the so-called New Criticism, which, reacting against historical and biographical criticism as well as the ethical emphasis of liberal humanism, sought to identify the aesthetic properties of literature. The formalists and New Critics focused on the text as a verbal construct, analyzing only the "words on the page," isolated from other considerations. In some respects, the theoretical approaches that followed were all reactions against this alleged autonomy of literature. Marxist criticism located literature within economic and ideological contexts. Structuralism saw literature as simply one sign system among others. Feminism and gender studies placed literature in the larger context of women's struggles and the understanding of sexuality. Deconstruction examined literature's connections to philosophy and its intellectual foundations. Reader-response theory saw the text as a function of its audience. New Historicism placed literature among broader intellectual discourses and viewed history itself as a construct. Postcolonial and global studies examined literature within the global contexts of colonial and imperial history.

Many of these approaches overlap in several areas: for example, most reject the Aristotelian notion of fixed identity (of the human being or any aspect of the world; see chapter 9); some see the world and the self as constructions enabled by language; and some are committed to empowering the voices of minorities and colonized peoples and rejecting the grand narratives of the past concerning historical progress. Below we'll examine the most important features of these theories.

Liberal Humanism

Modern liberal humanism developed out of the work of nineteenth- and early-twentieth-century writers such as Matthew Arnold and Irving Babbitt. In general, it was a reaction against the perceived excesses of modern industrial society, such as rampant individualism, social fragmentation, and mechanization of human behavior. Liberal humanism continued in the work of F. R. Leavis, and some of its concerns have been visited more recently by writers such as Elaine Scarry and Martha Nussbaum. Features attributed to liberal humanism include

- An emphasis on **empirical method**, on textual analysis, rather than theory or large conceptual frameworks

- A belief in a **stable "human nature"** and an objective, independent world

- A belief that **truth is "timeless"** and that language basically represents reality

- A nostalgia for the past or **"tradition,"** looking back to premodern societies that enjoyed organic unity

- A belief that the modern **worship of science** has produced a mechanical mentality

- A stress on the moral, ethical, and **civilizing functions of literature**, which prepare citizens for a richer role in society

To many of us, the liberal humanist analysis of a literary text is almost second nature—it seems to be a common-sense approach. In looking at a text, we tend to emphasize its moral conflicts and ethical insights, what it tells us about human nature, and any truths it offers about our world. In general, our assessment of the text rests on our direct experience of it—which is difficult for us as individuals to paraphrase or fully describe.

Russian Formalism

As its name suggests, this movement focuses on the formal properties of literature, its specifically *literary* qualities. The approach has a long history, but in modern times it was advanced by the Russian formalists around the time of the Russian Revolution (1917) and then from the 1930s on by the New Critics. Its major proponents included Boris Eichenbaum, Mikhail Bakhtin, and Roman Jakobson. Some important emphases of Russian formalism were

- **Literature as independent object.** The Russian formalists focused on the formal or aesthetic properties of literature, viewing it as an object in its own right, as autonomous (with its own laws) and independent of truth or morality.

- **Literariness.** The Russian formalists, especially Viktor Shklovsky, saw literature as a unique kind of language that was not paraphrasable.

- **Defamiliarization.** A central concept of Russian formalism was that literature defamiliarizes ordinary things, making us see them in a new light.

The New Criticism

Though the New Criticism is generally viewed as an American movement, two of its central influences were works by English critics; both emphasized the "close reading" of a text: I. A. Richards's *Practical Criticism* (1929) and William Empson's *Seven Types of Ambiguity* (1930). The American New Critics included John Crowe Ransom and Allen Tate. There were three important manifestos of New Criticism:

- *Criticism, Inc.* (Ransom, 1938) argues that literary criticism must become a scientific discipline and that its proper domain is literature *as* literature. Hence, literary criticism must exclude personal impressions, considerations of the author's biography, historical studies, or moral content.

- *The Intentional Fallacy* (William K. Wimsatt and Monroe C. Beardsley, 1946) argues that the author's intention is irrelevant to our reading of a text since if the intention is successful, it is already realized in the text.

- *The Affective Fallacy* (Wimsatt and Beardsley, 1946) argues that we should not judge a literary text by its effect on us. We need instead to use objective aesthetic criteria.

A New Critical analysis looks at the text as an independent verbal structure. It focuses on the formal techniques used in the text, such as irony, ambiguity, metaphor, and paradox. It acknowledges that what the text "says" is unique and cannot be paraphrased.

In a sense, many of the theories considered below are reactions to New Criticism. Whereas New Criticism wanted to look at literature in isolation from its context, other theories sought to reestablish literature's connections with its social context. It's worth stressing that some of these theories arose *before* the New Criticism. But it was only later that they were widely disseminated and used in the teaching and analysis of literature. It's also worth remembering that in practice it may be necessary to use hybrid approaches that combine, say, elements of gender studies and deconstruction. Three especially foundational approaches are psychoanalysis, Marxism, and feminism.

Psychoanalysis

Psychoanalysis highlights the irrational behavior of human beings, stressing how our thoughts and actions are governed less by reason than by instinct. The application of psychoanalytic principles to the study of literature was initiated in the late nineteenth century by the father of psychoanalysis, Sigmund Freud. During the twentieth century, psychoanalytic criticism broadened to include analysis of the psychology of the author, of the audience, and of characters, as well as of the process of literary composition, of symbols, and of the conscious and unconscious functioning of language. Freud's most influential themes and concepts include

- **Infantile sexuality.** Children are sexual from an early age. Freud believed that sexuality is initially polymorphous (that is, it has many forms) and becomes gendered through the pressure of social conventions.

- **The Oedipus complex.** The infant boy directs his sexual wishes toward his mother and develops hostility toward his father. Only with the perceived threat of castration does the child repress this desire and come to obey the father. Freud believed that this scenario was the foundation for all subsequent development of sexuality.

- **Repression.** Thoughts and feelings that are deemed embarrassing, painful, or shameful are driven out of the conscious mind but remain in the unconscious.

- **The interpretation of dreams.** What a patient remembers of her dreams is the "manifest" content, a series of associations. From these the psychoanalyst weaves together the "latent" content, which has been repressed or distorted.

- **The talking cure.** In psychoanalysis, the analyst attempts to construct an explanatory narrative that contextualizes the patient's disjointed memories and associations, thereby finding the causes of his symptoms.

- **Lacan's rereading of Freud.** The French poststructuralist psychoanalyst Jacques Lacan (1901–1981) famously declared that "the unconscious is structured like a language" and rewrote Freud's Oedipal process. In Lacan's account, the child passes from the "imaginary order" (where it feels unified with its surroundings, seeing no distinction between itself and its mother's body or other objects) to the "symbolic order," the world of distinct objects, differences, and gender roles, as marked by language. This passage is marked by the "mirror phase," the point at which the child recognizes itself in the mirror as a separate, coherent entity.

A psychoanalytic analysis of literature could proceed in several different ways. It could consider a text in light of an author's psychology. This approach might be fruitful for the stories of Edgar Allan Poe, many of which depict macabre situations that we can better understand by learning about his life. Or, we could look at the psychology of characters themselves in order to explain their behavior. For example, we could analyze the psychology of the kings Shahrayar and Shahzaman in *The Thousand and One Nights*, showing how their actions result from profound insecurity about their masculinity and their fear of women. Alternatively, we could show how in *Antigone* the "symbolic order"—represented by Creon—is disrupted by Antigone's quest to delve back into an "imaginary order." Indeed, we could analyze the whole play, as well as *Oedipus the King*, in terms of a breakdown of the Oedipal process.

Marxist Literary Criticism

Marxism originated in the nineteenth century as a critique of capitalism by the German thinker Karl Marx and his collaborator Friedrich Engels. Though Marx saw capitalism's ideals of reason and freedom as an improvement on feudalism, he believed they would actually be realized only in a communist society, where the wealth of a nation was communally owned. Until the collapse of the Soviet Union in 1991, communist regimes (influenced by but distorting Marx's ideas) governed one-third of the globe. Some of Marx's predictions proved false, but he did accurately predict that there would be an increasing and intolerable gap between the rich and poor—across the entire world. The main elements of the Marxist critique of capitalism include the following:

- **Exploitation.** Capitalism is a system of exploitation, with society divided into two broad classes. One, the bourgeoisie or business owners, controls society's wealth or means of production. The other class, the proletariat or workers, receives insufficient compensation for its labor.

- **Private property** in a capitalistic society is concentrated in the hands of a very few people.

- **Imperialistic.** Capitalism is by nature imperialistic, always needing to expand its markets over the globe and to revolutionize and modernize its instruments of production.

- **Ideology.** The ideology (or collective beliefs and values) of the ruling class or bourgeoisie represents its private interests as the universal interests of the people or nation as a whole.

- **Class struggle** is the driving force of history, waged between slaves and freedmen, between serfs and nobles, and between the proletariat and the bourgeoisie. Eventually, Marxists believe, capitalism will be overthrown and replaced by a communist society, which will have no class distinctions and no private property.

- **Base and superstructure.** The nature of both human beings and society is determined neither by divine agency nor by abstract ideas but by material, economic conditions. This economic base shapes the entire realm of ideas, the "superstructure" of religion, politics, culture, and art. For example, feudal economic relations gave rise to values such as courage, honor, loyalty, and obedience. But capitalist economics requires different values, such as freedom, rationality, pragmatism, competitiveness, and individualism.

Though Marx and Engels did not produce a systematic literary theory, a long tradition has accommodated Marxist approaches to literature. Influential Marxist critics include György Lukács, Antonio Gramsci, Raymond Williams, Fredric Jameson, and Terry Eagleton. Their works suggest a number of key strategies.

- **Author's biography.** We can research the author's life to see what her basic worldview was, what circles she moved in, and what intellectual and social currents influenced her.

- **Historical context.** We can place literature in its historical, economic, and social context. For example, what circumstances led the eighteenth-century French American author Hector Saint John de Crèvecoeur to define an "American" as an individual committed to religious tolerance, pluralism, industry, and freedom?

- **Literary production and audience.** We can consider the material conditions of literary production and the nature of the audience. For example, the proliferation of periodicals in the nineteenth century catered to a rapidly growing middle class.

- **Ideology.** We can relate the literary work to the prevailing ideologies of its time. Is the text itself an instrument of some ideology? For example, how does Benjamin Franklin's "The Way to Wealth" (1758) relate to capitalist economics?

- **Social relations.** We can explore how a text portrays social relations, especially those pertaining to class. For example, in Kate Chopin's "At the 'Cadian Ball" (1892), how do marriage conventions dictated by class create further conventions of insincerity?

Chapter 17 includes a Marxist analysis of a story by Katherine Mansfield.

Feminist Criticism and Gender Studies

Strains of feminism—belief in the social, political, and economic equality of men and women—appear early in literature. Aristophanes' comic play *Lysistrata* (411 B.C.E.), for example, shows a group of women taking control of the Athenian state via a sex strike. We see traces of feminism in Chaucer's Wife of Bath, who points out that stories written by men do not give a fair account of the relations between the sexes, and in the medieval writer Christine de Pizan, who redefines "reason" as a feminine virtue (see chapter 10). In the late eighteenth and the nineteenth centuries, Mary Wollstonecraft and Margaret Fuller were powerful feminist voices. The first wave of feminism, from Wollstonecraft through the British and American suffragists, focused on women's legal rights, such as owning property and voting. Second-wave feminism, an outgrowth of the civil rights and student protest movements of the 1960s through the 1970s (expressed by figures such as Betty Friedan and Kate Millett), was concerned with all aspects of women's experience, including sexuality, domestic life, employment, and language. So-called French feminism—especially the writings of Julia Kristeva, Hélène Cixous, and Luce Irigaray—began to be published in the 1960s, but only started to appear in English in the 1980s. At about this time arose gender studies, which was grounded partly in feminism but also grew out of a sense that gay, lesbian, and queer studies had been marginalized. It addresses the constructed nature of gender categories, as well as the intersections of gender with color, race, and class. Among its major theorists are Gayle Rubin, Eve Kosofsky Sedgwick, and Judith Butler. Major concerns of feminism and gender studies include

- **Equality.** The fundamental aim is to achieve economic, social, and political equality for women and people of all sexual orientations, with full recognition of their rights in all spheres of life.

- **Gender as an ideological construction.** Recent feminists have rejected the idea that there is a natural "essence" of "woman" or the feminine. Male traditions have perpetuated the myth of woman as angel, whore, goddess, obedient wife, and mother figure.

- **Rejection of "masculine" modes of thought.** Western logic, going back to Aristotle, has rested on fixed notions of "identity" that divide the world into binary opposites such as man and woman, master and slave, black and white. Feminists tend to stress the continuities between these terms and to seek unity rather than opposition. Many gender theorists have rejected any stable categories such as "gender" or "woman" or any absolute distinction between hetero- and homosexuality.

- **Language.** Language as we have inherited it embodies male ways of thinking about the world and cannot adequately convey the experiences of women. Some feminists have urged the creation of a "female" language, or at least significant modifications of conventional language.

- **The body.** Whereas much of the male philosophical tradition has viewed the process of thinking as objective and "disembodied" (free of the constraints of the body), feminists and gender theorists have pointed out that how we think and feel depends on the body we inhabit: its color, its class, its gender, its location. So the body becomes a metaphor for historical specificity and uniqueness, as well as the impossibility of objectivity.

A feminist or gender studies analysis of literature will usually be based on some combination of these elements. In addition to looking at the portrayal of gender, or male–female relations, or simply the portrayal of women, we could examine gendered language in a text, or the connection between gender and literary form (for example, the epic usually engages conventional male virtues pertaining to fighting, heroism, and conquest). We could analyze how considerations of gender inform a text's relation to its audience. We can explore how African American writers have articulated a feminism that reflects their cultural circumstances. And we might consider texts from other cultures and examine differences between Western and Eastern modes of feminism.

CHAPTER 16

LITERARY CRITICISM AND THEORY, PART II

STRUCTURALISM; POSTSTRUCTURALISM
(DECONSTRUCTION, NEW HISTORICISM,
READER-RESPONSE THEORY); CULTURAL,
FILM, POSTCOLONIAL, AND GLOBAL STUDIES

STRUCTURALISM

Whereas Marxism and feminism were explicitly political in orientation, a less activist but deeply influential approach to literature and culture was structuralism, which became prominent in the 1950s. The proponents of structuralism were linguists such as Ferdinand de Saussure, anthropologists such as Claude Lévi-Strauss, and literary theorists such as Roland Barthes. Advocates of this approach viewed the human mind, society, and language as "structures" that could be analyzed at a given point in time. They also downplayed the role of human agency, instead viewing the self as a position within a linguistic and cultural structure. The foundations of structuralism were laid by Saussure in his lectures, posthumously reconstructed by his students as *Course in General Linguistics* (1916). Saussure formulated a conception of language that has influenced nearly all subsequent literary theory. Here are its most important features.

- **Language is a system of signs.** No word alone can mean anything. For example, "red" has meaning only in relation to "green" and the other colors. Meaning is *relational* and is produced by the interaction of words.

- **The connection between words and things is arbitrary.** There is no natural connection between the word "table" and an actual table; the connection is determined by social convention, by collective agreement. Language does not somehow "represent" reality. Rather, we look at reality *through* language. When we look into the sky, we see the object that we call the "moon" *through* the concept "moon."

- **Nature of the linguistic sign.** The sign has three terms:

  The signifier is the *sound* of a word as we register it in our minds— for example, the word "table."

  The signified is the *concept* to which the sound or word refers—for example, "a flat surface with legs."

  The sign refers to the *entire construct*, signifier + signified. Together, these refer to the actual object in the world, the actual table. The overall structure is

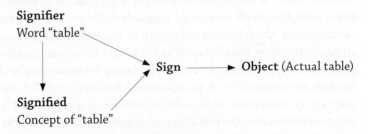

A structuralist analysis examines a literary text as a set of interacting elements, often a series of binary oppositions. For example, we might look at Chinua Achebe's *Things Fall Apart* (1958) in terms of binaries

such as colonizer and colonized, tradition and novelty. Or we might see Achebe's text as enabled by its participation in broader registers of meaning involving both imperialism and tribalism, and his characters as themselves created by their positions within the system of language. For example, Okonkwo, unlike his father Unoka, is driven by a preexisting narrative of "manliness" to which he strives to mold himself. We could examine the signifier "manliness" and explore its subversion in this story.

POSTSTRUCTURALISM

Poststructuralism is a broad term that covers several critical approaches, three of which we'll consider below: deconstruction, New Historicism, and reader-response theory. In general, poststructuralism reacts against the binary oppositions of structuralism, as well as its emphasis on the concept of structure. However, poststructuralism retains the idea that human identity and the world are structured and conceived through language, and above all the idea that language is a system of signs. Nonetheless, poststructuralists see language and human identity and institutions as more fluid and indeterminate than do structuralists. These characteristics of poststructuralism are most clearly exhibited in deconstruction.

Deconstruction

Deconstruction is not easy to define. Let's start at the simplest level. When applied to anything, including a literary text, deconstruction effectively *reverses* the process of *construction*. Let's use the analogy of a house. When we see a house as a finished product, we think of it as a unified entity, a stable object. What we don't see is how it was constructed, the materials that went into its making, the labor, the kinds of expertise that were required. To see these things, we cannot simply demolish the house. We must deconstruct it—take it apart—until we arrive at its foundations.

If we start with the roof, we will find that there is an entire industry devoted to the making of shingles. Indeed, as we unpeel the house layer by layer, we will see that the paint, the shingles, the bricks, the mortar, the drywall, and the concrete are not independent objects but spread their connections through vast industries, each with its own social status and its own ethics and business practices. And these industries have been brought together by a contractor whose own economic and social connections spread far and wide. The purchaser of the house will have her own points of entry into the economic system, as well as into ideological systems in which the values of independence, the work ethic, and economic foresight have been promoted, and perhaps packaged into a formula such as the "American dream." And let's not forget the function of advertising in all of this.

So, what we originally saw as one entity—a house—we now see as composed of numerous relations, ethical, ideological, economic. The true foundations of the house—the unquestioned assumptions on which it was built—are not stones and concrete but business relations governed by a broader market, in which certain personal and ideological goals and assumptions have played a large role. Hence the term "house" might now be seen as a metaphor for this entire complex of relations, which itself has a long history. And if the house is under foreclosure, economic conditions themselves will have facilitated its "deconstruction" on all of these levels.

This analysis of "house" has employed a number of deconstructive strategies.

- We've unearthed its foundations in business practices, work ethics, ideology, and personal identity. When such foundations are viewed as "natural" or inevitable and appear to be beyond questioning, Derrida calls them **transcendental signifieds**.

- We've displayed its **relations** with a host of industries.

- We've identified the **binary oppositions** governing its marketing (buyer/seller, lender/borrower). Such oppositions often represent not equivalence between two terms but rather a "violent hierarchy" (such as master/slave, man/woman).

- We've exposed the **contradictions** in its fluctuating status (owner/mortgage, dream/foreclosure).

- We've shown that "house" is not an object or an isolated entity. Rather, it's a signifier, an element of **discourse**, which brings together several registers of meaning.

Deconstruction and language

The basic goal of deconstruction, then, is to expose and challenge the authority of the transcendental signifieds—the unquestioned foundations or assumptions behind a text, the foundations that give the text stability, unity, and definite meaning. Deconstruction tries to show that these signifieds *can* be questioned and that they are in fact not independent concepts but are related to other concepts. Hence a deconstructive analysis tends to prioritize language and linguistic operations. Here are a few ideas stressed by deconstruction.

- **Logocentrism.** Jacques Derrida coined the term "logocentrism" to denote the use of such unquestioned foundations. In Western thought, the Logos is the ultimate foundation that stabilizes our concepts and the meanings of words in language. Sometimes this Logos or ultimate authority has been identified with God, but modern equivalents might be concepts such as "freedom" or "democracy." All of these terms function as transcendental signifieds.

- **Metaphysics of presence.** Like Saussure, Derrida views language as a system of relations: no word has meaning in isolation but depends on its connections with other words. This is true of even the simplest thing, such as the word "chalk." Such a view belongs to what Derrida calls the "metaphysics of presence," which sees the meaning of objects as contained in their immediate presence. Deconstruction would argue that the meaning of the word "chalk" actually lies in relations (with a blackboard, classrooms, etc.) that extend far beyond its immediate existence.

- **Arbitrariness of the sign.** Following Saussure, deconstruction views the sign as arbitrary and conventional. There is no natural connection between the sign "table" and an actual table in the world. Equally conventional is the connection between the signifier "table" and the concept of a table to which it points.

- **Aporias (impasses).** Deconstruction tries to identify any conceptual aporias, or unresolvable contradictions, in a text.

- **Reality as language or discourse.** No "truth" or "reality" stands outside or behind language: truth is a relation of linguistic terms, and reality is a construct that a human community builds up through concepts. For example, a "university" doesn't have any absolute reality; it is a human construct. Even the identity of the human self has no pregiven essence or stability but is rather a linguistic construct or narrative.

Reading as a deconstructive critic

A deconstructive reading of a text is a multifaceted project: in general, it will attempt to display **logocentric** operations in the text, by focusing on a close reading of the text's language, its use of unquestioned assumptions or **transcendental signifieds**, its reliance on **binary oppositions**, its **self-contradictions**, its **aporias**, and the ways in which it effects **closure** and resists **free play** (the possibility of numerous other meanings). Hence deconstruction will examine all the features that went into the *construction* of a text. In chapter 17 we will conduct a deconstructive analysis of Blake's "The Tyger" (1794).

New Historicism

Historicism, which goes back to nineteenth-century German thinkers such as Johann Herder and G. W. F. Hegel, sees all phenomena as the result of specific historical circumstances and emphasizes that history operates according to certain laws. New Historicism, which emerged in the 1980s, exhibited a number of different features, some of which are traceable to its founding figures, Michel Foucault and Stephen Greenblatt.

- It sees "history" itself as a discourse, with no unity or homogeneity.

- It views "power" not as wielded by specific agents but as something operating more diffusely and subtly, conditioning people's very subjectivity.

- Like Marxist criticism, New Historicism seeks to situate literature within a social context; but it differs from Marxism in its lack of a specific political commitment and its refusal to give priority to the economic dimension, which it views as just one among many discourses.

- It sees literature, too, as a discourse that interacts with other discourses—political, economic, religious, and aesthetic.

A New Historical analysis situates a literary text within the context of other discourses. For example, some of Foucault's work analyzes sexuality as it is expressed not just in literature but also in medical discourses. In Britain, where a more political form of historicism known as "cultural materialism" arose, critics challenged the idea that Shakespeare's work was "timeless" and showed how it must be placed against political and religious discourses of his time. They allowed us to see how Shakespeare subverted specific forms of authority (such as kingship) and how he exhibits the conflict of larger forces, such as those between feudal ethics and an emerging commercial mentality.

Reader-Response Theory

Reader-response theory, which emerged in the 1970s and 1980s, has its roots not only in the "reception theory" of German thinkers but also in a long tradition of rhetoric that recognized the importance of using strategies to affect an audience. In brief, reader-response theory argues that the text is not an independent object that is "consumed" passively by the reader. Rather, meaning is produced through a *dialogue*, or interaction, between text and reader. The major proponents of reader-response theory include Wolfgang Iser and Stanley Fish. Here are some of its basic principles:

- While authors use certain techniques to "guide" the response of a reader, the reader plays a creative role, filling in "**gaps**" in the text and bringing her own assumptions into play.

- Reader-response critics often draw a distinction between the real author and an "**implied**" **author**, as well as between a real reader and a "postulated" or "ideal" reader.

- The tradition of a text's "**reception**" by readers over generations plays a crucial role in the text's aesthetic status.

- What shapes a text's interpretation is not any fixed meaning but the assumptions of an **interpretive community**. The shared codes of such communities explain why readers often have similar interpretations of a text.

A reader-response analysis can take many forms. We could analyze what features of a Shakespeare play audiences might have found comic or how they might have reacted to a word like "ambitious," which for Elizabethans had negative connotations. Or we could discuss the relationship between a text and audience in a given historical period. But the simplest way to conduct a reader-response analysis is to analyze our own responses to a text. For example, if we read Robert Browning's dramatic monologue "My Last Duchess" (1842)—about a duke who has had his young wife killed—we could (a) consider what moral assumptions we are bringing to the poem; (b) explore how our reactions to the words and images of the poem develop from start to finish, moving perhaps from a sense of exploration to a judgment of the duke; and (c) work out what devices of the poem (such as its use of dramatic monologue) shape our reactions both to the duke and to the poem as an aesthetic construct.

CULTURAL STUDIES

Looking at literature in a broad cultural context flourished in the nineteenth century in the work of Matthew Arnold, Thomas Carlyle, and others. But the main impetus for modern cultural studies came in 1964 with the founding of the Centre for Contemporary Cultural Studies at the University of Birmingham in Britain; the scholars most closely associated with cultural studies are Stuart Hall and Raymond Williams. Its distinctive traits and concerns include

- **Interdisciplinarity.** Cultural studies embraces inquiries in a broad range of disciplines, such as sociology, anthropology, literature, and the arts.

- **Broad definition of literature.** It extends the meaning of "literature" to include not only poetry, drama, and fiction but also popular print genres such as romance novels and thrillers, as well as television, mass media, music, and film. A TV program or a political speech or an advertisement has equal claim to be treated as a "text" that can be analyzed, often by using the same techniques that we use in examining literature.

- **Use of a cultural framework.** Influenced by Marxism, feminism, and other modes of literary theory, cultural studies situates literature in the contexts of ideology, power, class, and gender. Influenced by structuralism, it sees literature as a set of codes within a larger network of cultural codes.

- **"Culture" as the site of ideological struggle.** It sees mass culture as an instrument of oppression that molds people's subjectivities to meet the requirements of the market. But it also sees culture as the site of possible resistance—emphasizing, for example, the subversive potential of various subcultures.

Reading as cultural studies critics, we could analyze an advertisement in a magazine or on TV, showing how it portrays women and the demands it imposes on women's self-image. We could examine a television comedy such as *The Office* or *Modern Family*, discussing its intended audience, its presentation of characters and situations, its comic techniques, and its satire of prevailing beliefs and ideologies. Or we could compare the ways in which TV channels around the world present the news, analyzing each program as a rhetorical structure. In all these cases, we would draw on our skills in literary analysis and extend them to address other elements such as images, sound, gesture, and performance.

FILM THEORY

Film theory began in the 1910s and 1920s as a series of reflections by directors concerned with the technical and artistic aspects of film. Early major theorists include Rudolf Arnheim and Siegfried Kracauer, who each analyzed the connection of film to the real world. The idea of realist cinema was advanced by André Bazin and Kracauer; in contrast, Jean Mitry argued that a film expresses the director's subjective vision. The theory that the director is the author (*auteur*) of a film was advocated first in France in the 1950s by Bazin, François Truffaut, and others and then in the United States in the early 1960s, most influentially by Andrew Sarris. In the 1960s and 1970s, film theory became an academic discipline. Under the influence of structuralism, Marxism, and feminism, the field has extended its scope to address issues of audience, genre, ideology, gender, and the cultural and economic contexts of film, as well as its relation to reality.

Major themes and concerns of film theory are

- **Realism.** Some theorists have argued that because of the techniques at its disposal, such as the close-up, and because of its ability to portray events, sounds, and images in time, film can capture reality in a way that words cannot. Others have argued that the value of film lies in its ability to defamiliarize the world and to present it in a new light. Indeed, films can help shape our perception of reality and our ability to produce meaning.

- **Semiotic systems.** Like other forms of expression, films are viewed as "texts"—as systems of signs operating within a larger cultural semiotic (signifying) system. Films have their own system of codes (see the terms below). Critics have analyzed the ideologies behind the construction of films and their reception by audiences.

- **Portrayal of gender and race.** Many critics have analyzed how women and sexuality have been portrayed in film. A central issue, raised first by the feminist film theorist Laura Mulvey, has been the "male gaze" directed at women, a gaze that is both controlling and objectifying; many movies have been made to accommodate this gaze, and many movies see the world through the eyes of male protagonists. Likewise, critics have analyzed the racial and ethnic stereotypes that have permeated much film construction.

- **Artistic form.** Some basic terms are useful in analyzing any film.
  - *Frame:* A single image on a strip of film; in a digital film, a single still.
  - *Shot:* A single run of the camera, which can occupy any number of frames. This is the basic unit of a film.
  - *Sequence:* The unified action presented by a number of shots.
  - *Cut:* The joining of two shots together so that one appears to replace the other immediately.
  - *Camera angle:* The level and height of the camera in relation to the subject being photographed. A high camera angle looks down on its object, a medium angle is on the same plane, and a low angle looks up.

- *Long shot:* A shot that shows the entire object of interest (often a human figure) and typically some of its surroundings. A *close-up*, in contrast, shows part of the body or other object.

- *Deep focus:* A shot that creates the illusion of depth within the frame.

- *Montage:* A sequence of shots that expresses an action or psychological state or event. Surprising juxtapositions can generate new ideas or effects. For example, in *The Godfather* (1972), scenes of the christening of a baby in a church alternate with scenes of various murders.

With a basic understanding of film and its terminology, we can produce an interesting analysis. Indeed, we can use much of our training and terminology from the study of literature, as long as we remember that we must also consider other factors, such as visual images, movement in time, gestures, and other aspects of performance. You could analyze a movie in terms of characterization and plot, or its portrayal of gender or race, or its artistic techniques and how these underline its content. You could also compare a movie adapted from a literary text—whether a novel, such as Jane Austen's *Sense and Sensibility* (1811), or a play, such as Shakespeare's *King Lear* (1605)—with the written work itself.

POSTCOLONIAL CRITICISM

The roots of postcolonial criticism go back through Edward Said's pioneering *Orientalism* (1978) to works by colonial activists such as Frantz Fanon and Aimé Césaire. It's worth recalling that imperialism reached its height in the later nineteenth century, which brought much of Africa, the Middle East, and Asia under the dominance of Britain, France, Germany, Italy, and Belgium. The Second World War weakened the major European powers, and after it ended, decolonization began around the world. In general, postcolonial criticism analyzes the cultural and economic dilemmas produced by imperialism, as well as the process of emancipation. Major postcolonial theorists include Gayatri Spivak, Homi K.

Bhabha, Dipesh Chakrabarty, and Aamir Mufti. Among the themes and concerns of postcolonial criticism are

- **Orientalism.** As many postcolonial critics have argued, imperialism rests on assumptions and stereotypes that have constructed the Orient (the East) as the Other—as barbaric, backward, stagnant, and religious, in contrast with the West, which has been seen as enlightened, rational, progressive, and secular.

- **Overcoming binary oppositions.** Postcolonial critics have sought to undermine outright oppositions between East and West, or colonizer and colonized. They argue that the relation between these terms is more complex and that the "West" is just as much a cultural and political construction as the "East."

- **Rewriting history.** Postcolonial critics reject the mainstream Western narrative of history as progressing toward civilization and progress. They draw attention to phenomena that the West has sought to ignore or repress such as slavery and its integral role in the growth of the modern world. In their view, history is a set of diverse and conflicting narratives.

- **Political liberation.** Many postcolonial theorists have been involved not only in the struggle for emancipation but also in the attempt to theorize these struggles. Decolonization has given rise to its own problems—such as an exploitative native class replacing the imperial rulers, or the choice between using native dialects and the more widely spoken imperial language.

- **A reevaluation of the status of English.** Postcolonial critics want to acknowledge and analyze the numerous varieties of English used throughout the world.

- **Terms** common in postcolonial studies include
  - *Race:* A classification of people based on shared inherited physical characteristics, such as skin color.
  - *Ethnicity:* A classification of people based on shared cultural and social backgrounds and experiences, such as religion, language, and nation.

- ○ *Diaspora:* The migration of peoples, either voluntary or under compulsion, in large numbers away from their native land.

- ○ *Hybridity:* A state of "in-betweenness" that creates intercultural forms of cultural identity.

- ○ *Mimicry:* The process whereby colonized people imitate (and adapt) the culture and language of the colonizer.

- ○ *Subalterns:* Colonized populations who remain voiceless in terms of cultural, political, or intellectual expression unless they adopt the language and assumptions of the colonizers.

A postcolonial analysis could place a literary text in the context of imperialist discourses (such as Enlightenment narratives of progress that attempt to prove the superiority of the European peoples). It could analyze the treatment of "race" or "hybridity" or any of the other terms listed above. Or it could consider the ways in which an "orientalist" image of Eastern cultures is created. For example, we might examine the differences between Conrad's descriptions of Europeans and of Africans in *Heart of Darkness* (1899).

GLOBAL STUDIES

Although the concept of globalization reaches back into the ancient and medieval worlds, modern discussions of it can be traced to Canadian philosopher Marshall McLuhan's idea of a "global village" in which time had "ceased" and space had "vanished" (see *The Medium is the Message* [1967]). McLuhan anticipated modern developments: that space and distance would be "annihilated" by the creation of virtual and digital worlds and that print technology, which had fostered an individualistic public, would be replaced by new media that would promote collaborative learning through "discovery."

The term "globalization" has had numerous, often conflicting, definitions. To be sure, a number of elements remain constant: global flows of capital and exchange, high-speed technologies, the increasingly available internet, and the global distribution of ideas, brands, ideologies, and identities. Beyond these, though, there is much disagreement. Some theorists view globalization as a welcome *process* that could create a single social and political space, transcending national and ethnic interests, where it might be meaningful to talk of "world citizenship." But others view globalization as *policy*, as a new form of imperial expansion through the "free" market supported by the World Trade Organization and World Bank, accompanied by the exportation of Western, and specifically American, ideologies and models of media, travel, fashion, and entertainment. Yet other critics see globalization as a myth, arguing that national, ethnic, linguistic, and religious differences have become even more intense.

Global studies is an emerging field that has its roots largely in economics and the social sciences, as well as in postcolonial studies. More recently, critics have started discussing its implications for the humanities and in particular for the study of literature. Many writers have entered the debates concerning global studies, among them Benedict Anderson, Benjamin R. Barber, Arjun Appadurai, Immanuel Wallerstein, and Francis Fukuyama. Their approaches and the issues they raise include the following:

- **Situating literature in a global context.** How do literatures from various traditions relate to one another? Theorists are struggling to free literary texts from their merely national traditions and to see them as part of a global network.

- **Decentering and pluralizing the world.** Critics are also struggling against the legacy of colonialism, in which all economic and cultural influence was seen as flowing from a European or Western "center" to the colonial peripheries. How do we reenvision the world so that we can learn from other modes of thought and education? Can we even do this while the West maintains economic and informational dominance?

- **Reevaluating Western historical and philosophical narratives.** Adopting a global perspective, critics have begun to situate conventional Western accounts of history in a broader framework that includes the histories of minorities and oppressed peoples. We can also revisit the ancient Greek philosophers or the Enlightenment thinkers to see how their pronouncements about race or non-Western cultures shape their overall thinking.

- **Undertaking global explorations of literary theory.** We still need to investigate other traditions of literary theory, such as Chinese and Indian and Arabic, to see how their assumptions differ from ours. For example, "organic unity" and "mimesis" are ideas that have dominated Western literary composition since Aristotle, but they are absent from other literary traditions, as is the tradition of "realism."

- **Examining the role of "literature" in globalization.** What part does literature play in narratives of globalization? What literary or rhetorical techniques are involved? How are these modified in digital media? How is literature affected by the globalized publishing industries that control its production and consumption?

A global studies analysis could address any combination of these issues. This is a new field and there is no right way of going about such a project. But there are plenty of things that anyone interested in this approach could research on their own. For example, you could look at the "English literature" curricula at various Indian or Chinese or Middle Eastern universities and analyze the Western influences found there. Or you could focus on a specific Western writer and compare his work with that of a writer from a different tradition, taking account of differences in their social and cultural contexts. Or you could look at how processes of globalization are represe-nted in a literary work. In chapter 17, we'll undertake a postcolonial or global studies analysis of Conrad's *Heart of Darkness*.

AFTER THEORY

The past three decades have witnessed several developments we should mention here. The first is what has been termed a "religious turn" or a "postsecular turn" in literary theory and other fields: major theorists have acknowledged that religion is an enduring institution and that secularization was merely a "thesis" or claim of mid-twentieth-century sociology and not a historical fact or phenomenon. Stanley Fish remarked in 2005 that the conventional "triumvirate of race, gender, and class" would be superseded by religion as the focus of literary study.

A second development might be called a "new aestheticism." Critics such as George Levine and Michael Bérubé have sought to protect the "relative autonomy" of the aesthetic properties of literature from what they see as the intrusion of theory's ideological interests. Such renewed attention to the aesthetic has also been called a "post-critical turn" by the critics Bruno Latour and Rita Felski. According to Felski, much theory is motivated by what philosopher Paul Ricoeur labeled a "hermeneutics of suspicion," a strategy of reading texts against the grain of conventional interpretation. This outlook should be complemented, she argues, with strategies of reading that accommodate aesthetic pleasure and the power of literature to affect and shape our entire being.

A third tendency is evident in a renewed liberalism, which has tried to restore attention to literature's concern with ethical issues and its potential to contribute to social justice, as well as to the formation of character. Thinkers and critics such as Martha Nussbaum, Elaine Scarry, and John Carey have intervened eloquently in the public and political spheres, showing how the skills of literary analysis are invaluable in examining the cultural dilemmas and narratives of our time.

In general, since the early twenty-first century, the grand narratives of theory—which sought to investigate history, philosophy, language, class, race, and gender—have given way to more empirical modes of inquiry, such as queer theory, trauma theory, ecocriticism, and animal studies. These have usually been hybrid approaches, drawing elements from various other theories. Indeed, in practice, when we analyze a literary text, it is usually fruitful, and even necessary, to integrate various approaches.

CHAPTER 17

USING THEORY

In this chapter, we'll look at how three modes of literary theory—deconstruction, Marxism, and postcolonialism/global studies—might be used in analyzing literary texts. First, let's review some basic points about studying and using theory.

- **Don't be intimidated.** A great deal of theory, for a variety of reasons, is hard to understand. In reading an essay or book of literary theory, focus on the parts you *can* understand, while being aware that some ideas might—just like a passage from Shakespeare—take two or three readings to grasp. A good strategy is to try to take at least five basic points from any text you read.

- **Read original texts.** Try not to rely on summaries of or reactions to a writer's work. It is more important to read Simone de Beauvoir herself than what the latest critic says about her. In this way, you can get a sense of the author's style and perspective, and you can speak with more authority about the text. If a writer is difficult, like Marx, start with something relatively simple, such as the *Communist Manifesto*. Still, working through difficult texts will gradually raise your intellectual level. If you read only things that are easy, your level of understanding will remain the same.

- **Focus on important thinkers.** Since you have limited time, both at college and in life, be selective in your reading and focus on the important thinkers, texts, and developments in whatever area you are studying.

- **View different theories as related.** Different modes of literary criticism don't necessarily exclude one another. For example, a Marxist or feminist approach might use insights from deconstruction. And deconstruction itself might use insights from a New Critical reading.

Now let's consider some specific modes of literary theory and how to use them. Though the following accounts treat each theory separately, remember that when we analyze literature, we may well use elements from various theories.

A DECONSTRUCTIVE ANALYSIS OF WILLIAM BLAKE'S "THE TYGER"

Let's apply the basic features of deconstruction outlined in the previous chapter to Blake's "The Tyger" (1794), a poem we also looked closely at in chapter 5. In deconstructing the poem, we can try to uncover its unspoken assumptions and foundations, its relationships with other poetic modes, and its own aporias, or impasses. And, in this case, we can show how the poem itself performs a deconstructive function.

Deconstructing the poem

- **Assumptions or transcendental signifieds.** Is the poem's critique of religion constrained within the terminology and assumptions of religion? In order to explain the existence of the tiger, the poem confines itself to the idea of some kind of divine being, even one whose qualities are mysterious or questionable. Does "The Tyger" consider the possibility that the so-called created world might be the product of cosmic chance with no ordering agency?

- **Binary oppositions.** The poem remains stranded at the level of traditional binary oppositions, such as "tyger" and "lamb," which it uses to represent opposing forces. Does the poem itself reduce all theological complexity to a simple and unquestioned opposition between good and evil?

- **Aporias.** As a Romantic poet at odds with the industrial world, Blake cannot offer any reconciliation of opposites, even in the sphere of imagination. While he does place good and evil in mutual relation, the concepts of good and evil are not thereby transformed. Does the entire poem, in fact, arrive at an aporia that it cannot overcome? Does it exhibit its own incapacity to understand the divine or the purpose or order of nature? Perhaps it shows the failure of Romantic imagination even as it asserts its power to reconcile opposites.

Viewing the poem as a deconstructive gesture

- **Contradiction between form and content.** The form mimics a nursery rhyme, fostering the illusion that a child is speaking. But the content is heavily theological, raising such questions as the existence of evil, the connection between good and evil, and the nature of the creator. By placing these questions apparently in the mouth of a child, does the poet lend an air of innocence to a kind of questioning that might otherwise be seen as irreverent or even blasphemous?

- **Use of language.** At the level of language, the poem forces the concepts "tyger" and "lamb" into mutual relation, which makes the questioning of the creator even sharper. The images "forests of the night" and "distant deeps or skies," as well as the portrayal of God as a blacksmith, give a sinister appearance to the process of creation.

- **Questioning the Bible.** Does the poem's account of creation offer itself as a substitute for the more serene biblical account?

- **Rhetorical devices.** While the poem uses the device of asking questions, it refrains from offering answers. Is the implication that its questions are unanswerable? Perhaps the poem thereby deconstructs the traditional images of God, nature, and the process of creation.

Moving from notes to thesis

The simplest thesis might incorporate both aspects explored above, deconstructing the poem and viewing the poem itself as deconstructive.

> This paper will offer a deconstructive analysis of Blake's "The Tyger," showing both how the poem itself is deconstructive and how its assumptions and binary ways of thinking lead to a conceptual impasse, miring the poem in the very theological assumptions it seeks to undermine.

You could also focus on the poem's binary oppositions or deconstruct its "Romantic" status or its use of language and rhetorical devices. Below are questions to help you work out your own perspective in a deconstructive analysis.

Overall significance of the deconstructive reading

- What is it about this text or its author's apparent intentions that makes you want to scrutinize it?
- What would you consider to be a "conventional" reading of this text, and what are its limitations?
- What is the kind of reading of this text that you wish to subvert or oppose?
- Is the text itself deconstructive in some way?

Basic foundations of the text

- What assumptions remain unspoken in the text?
- Does the text take any important terms or concepts for granted?

Contradictions and aporias

- Are there any contradictions in the text, or between its form and its content?
- At what points does the text arrive at an aporia, in either moral or intellectual terms?

- At what points does its explanatory power fail, or fall back on conventional assumptions?
- Is there a conflict between the apparent and deeper meanings?

Gaps and oversights

- What kinds of closure occur in the text? At what points does it close off the possibility of discussion?
- What are the values put forth by the text? What values are marginalized or suppressed?
- How is the text involved with or actually supportive of what it opposes?

Binary oppositions and use of language

- What binary oppositions structure the text?
- What are the figures of speech in this text and how are they used?
- How do formal devices support or subvert the text's content?

You don't have to consider all these questions; you might think of different, and possibly better, ones. But most questions will fall into these categories.

A MARXIST ANALYSIS OF KATHERINE MANSFIELD'S "THE GARDEN PARTY"

As suggested in chapter 15, Marxist analysis requires us to do a little research. So let's proceed according to some of the categories mentioned in that chapter.

- **Biography.** Mansfield grew up in a socially prominent family but experienced poverty as an adult. She depicts class relations in many of her stories; most were published in politically radical magazines such as *The New Age*, which was a forum for socialist and feminist ideas. She died early, of tuberculosis, in 1923. In fact, she wrote "The Garden Party" about a year before she died. Perhaps her failing health influenced her outlook, especially toward death.

- **Historical context.** Mansfield is usually categorized as a modern-ist, alongside figures such as Virginia Woolf and D. H. Lawrence. She was writing in the aftermath of the First World War, which had led to a profound sense of disillusionment with the values of West-ern civilization. In fact, a major economic depression was looming.
- **Literary production and audience.** Most of the readership of liter-ature during this time was middle class, and publishing houses catered primarily to this audience. Perhaps Mansfield was daring in attempting to elicit sympathy for the working classes and in exposing some of the vices of the upper classes.

Analyzing the story

Keeping all this in mind, let's turn to "The Garden Party" itself. Here is a description from early in the story of one of the workmen and Laura's reaction to him:

> Already the men had shouldered their staves and were making for the place. Only the tall fellow was left. He bent down, pinched a sprig of lavender, put his thumb and forefinger to his nose and snuffed up the smell. When Laura saw that gesture she forgot all about the karakas [New Zealand trees] in her wonder at him caring for things like that—caring for the smell of lavender. How many men that she knew would have done such a thing? Oh, how extraordinarily nice workmen were, she thought. Why couldn't she have workmen for her friends rather than the silly boys she danced with and who came to Sunday night supper? She would get on much better with men like these.
>
> It's all the fault, she decided . . . of these absurd class distinctions. Well, for her part, she didn't feel them. Not a bit, not an atom. . . . And now there came the chock-chock of wooden hammers. Someone whistled, someone sang out, "Are you right there, matey?" "Matey!" The friendliness of it, the—the—Just to prove how happy she was, just to show the tall fellow how at home she felt, and how she despised stupid conventions, Laura took a big bite of her bread-and-butter as she stared at the little drawing. She felt just like a work-girl.

A couple of themes emerge from this passage—and the text as a whole—namely, class relations and the nature of class ideology. We also see some self-exploration and growth on Laura's part. So we can make some notes under these headings.

Class relations

- For a few moments at least, Laura feels a common humanity with the workmen. Does this undermine class distinctions? She *feels* these distinctions to be "absurd"—a word used later by her mother to indicate Laura's lack of awareness of class etiquette.

- Laura favorably compares the sensitive workman to the "silly boys" she socializes with. She even likes his working-class language, which sounds friendly, and she *feels* herself to be like a "work-girl."

- More objectively, Laura is talking to the workmen in the garden because she likes "arranging" things. But what are those "things"? Can't we say that she, like her mother and all the women of the family, arranges merely an isolated fantasy world—of dress, furnishings, and parties—rather than anything in the real world? They have no idea what life is like for the poor, and their desires make sense only within their insulated, artificial world, as when Mrs. Sheridan exclaims that "for once in my life I shall have enough canna lilies."

- We don't know what Laura's father does, but we do know that he is the authority of the house and its connection to the outside world. The mother threatens her children: "[S]hall I have to tell your father when he comes home tonight?"

- The party continues after the workman's "horrible accident," and the Sheridan family (in their guilt?) sends a basket of food to his family. Does this gesture betray an unfamiliarity with the real condition of the working classes, attempting to address by an individual act of charity what is really a widespread structural problem?

Class ideology

- We get a glimpse of objective class ideology when the narrator intrudes to reinforce the idea that stopping the party, as Laura suggests, would be extravagant: "That really was extravagant, for the little cottages were in a lane to themselves at the very bottom of a steep rise." The cottages are described as "far too near" and "the greatest possible eyesore," with "no right to be in that neighbourhood at all." The Sheridan children were "forbidden to set foot there. . . . It was disgusting and sordid."

- Who speaks this passage? Given her working-class sympathies, perhaps the narrator is not inserting her own opinions but is giving us an overview of the ideology in which the Sheridans are immersed: a belief in the absolute separation of the classes, with no attempt to understand the Other.

- Despite her earlier sense of empathy with the working men, and her natural—human—sympathy for the dead man, Laura is easily drawn back into the mentality of her own class. For example, when she looks in the mirror and sees how charming she looks wearing a new hat, she resolves to repress temporarily the thought of the man's death.

Self-exploration

- Clearly, Laura has courage and independence. Despite the weight of class ideology, despite the warnings from her family about the working classes, she tries to see working men in the light of her own experience.

- The progression of this independent spirit comes to a climax when Laura sees the dead man's body and reflects that he was "wonderful" and "beautiful": "What did garden parties and baskets and lace frocks matter to him? He was far from all those things." Is there irony here? Did these things *ever* matter to him, or only to her? She is reflecting on how death will make all the accoutrements of her life meaningless. She is seeing the values of her class in a larger human context, which includes the passing of life. On the other hand, doesn't she remain unable to articulate what is "marvelous" about life?

Moving from notes to thesis

There is a lot of material here, and your thesis will depend on how you see the story. Do you see it as focusing on how identity can grow beyond class and upbringing? Or is the story about ideology and how it blinds people to the real world, encouraging them to live with convenient fictions? Or should we read the story in its social context, as revealing that a young girl, even though she has sympathies with other classes, has no language to express her feelings? Here's a general thesis:

> This paper will analyze the presentation of class relations in Katherine Mansfield's "The Garden Party." It will argue that there is a rift between classes, which are entirely different in their ways of life and views of the world. This rift is created not only by economic conditions but by ideology. Even the protagonist Laura, despite her relative independence, is unable to overcome her ideological conditioning and articulate her sense of a common humanity between classes.

If you want to take your analysis to another level, you could apply the insights of particular Marxist theorists. You could show, for example, how the story exemplifies György Lukács's critique of modernism as fragmented and unable to resolve the contradictions of commercial society. Or, using the work of a Marxist-feminist writer such as Michèle Barrett, you could discuss the intersection of class ideology and gender ideology, showing how the women in this story are doubly trapped in class and gender roles that prevent them from developing any true individuality.

A POSTCOLONIAL/GLOBAL STUDIES ANALYSIS OF JOSEPH CONRAD'S *HEART OF DARKNESS*

Conrad's novella *Heart of Darkness* (1899) sets out to expose racism and imperialism, yet the Nigerian writer Chinua Achebe saw its author as "a bloody racist" and deemed it unfit to be taught in schools. For all the demythologizing of imperial themes that we see in *Heart of Darkness*, the central myths of imperialism seem to haunt Conrad's worldview: work, service, nation, and above all, law. Before deciding how to analyze this text, let's review some background information (easily available with just a little research).

Conrad was born in Ukraine, the son of a Polish patriot who was exiled for his nationalist activities. This must have given Conrad an outsider's view of the enterprise of imperialism. After serving on various merchant ships, Conrad received his first command and took a steamboat up the river Congo in Africa. His diary of his experiences forms much of the background of *Heart of Darkness*.

Another point to consider is that Belgium established the so-called Congo Free State in 1885; in fact, the state was the personal property of King Leopold II of Belgium, who claimed to be spreading Christianity in the "darkness," but who was actually making a fortune by monopolizing first the ivory and then the rubber trade, committing innumerable atrocities in the process. Conrad witnessed some of these firsthand, and what he saw shook his views not only of race and imperialism but also of the entire fabric of civilization. Let's turn now to the text. We can make notes on its content and form in order to decide what to focus on for a postcolonial/global analysis.

General themes

The most obvious themes of *Heart of Darkness* include imperialism, race, and perhaps the nature of civilization itself.

Form or style of the text

The form of the book contributes to its critique of racism. The tale is told by a narrator who himself recounts the narration of Marlow, who is reflecting on his experiences and attempting to make sense of them. There's an ambivalence here: the Marlow who relates the story retrospectively is not the same Marlow who undergoes the events of the book. Marlow the adventurer is to some extent complicit with racist ideology; he betrays an uneasy affiliation with Kurtz. It is Marlow the narrator who undermines this ideology. There are also a number of oppositions that structure the book, such as Europe and Africa, light and darkness, speech and silence, civilization and nature, law and criminality.

Elements of a postcolonial/global studies analysis

Chapter 16 set out some of the features of a postcolonial and global studies analysis. Which of these might be useful for analyzing Conrad's text? The obvious ones include the treatment of imperialism, the presentation of Africans and Europeans, and the binary oppositions that structure the book.

- **The narrative of imperialism.** Many statements in *Heart of Darkness* criticize imperialism. Marlow states: "The conquest of the earth, which mostly means the taking it away from those who have a different complexion or slightly flatter noses than ourselves, is not a pretty thing when we look into it too much." He rejects the usual narrative that colonizers bring civilization or moral improvement: "To tear treasure out of the bowels of the land was their desire, with no more moral purpose at the back of it than there is in burglars breaking into a safe."

- **"Orientalism," or constructing the Other.** Does the discrepancy in Conrad's portrayal of Africans and Europeans undermine his critique of racism? Africans are usually spoken of in the plural, denied personality or voice. Marlow describes them as "ants," "dark things," "black shadows," "black shapes," "black figures," and "vague forms of men." The overall effect is to reduce these people to objects and to alienate them from the reader. In contrast, the Europeans are described individually and in detail—for example, the Company's chief accountant: "Yes; I respected his collars, his vast cuffs, his brushed hair. His appearance was certainly that of a hairdresser's dummy; but in the great demoralization of the land he kept up his appearance. That's backbone."

- **Binary oppositions.** As the book progresses, it undermines the oppositions on which imperialism is based.

  - *Europe and Africa, light and darkness.* At the beginning of the book, darkness is associated with Africa; Marlow speaks of "the profound darkness of its heart." However, darkness is increasingly associated with the European enterprise, especially with its paramount representative, Kurtz. By the end of the story, we see that the darkness is the darkness of his heart.

  - *Law and criminality.* On seeing a chain gang of African men, Marlow remarks that they "were called criminals, and the outraged law . . . had come to them, an insoluble mystery from the sea." In stressing the naming process (they "were *called* criminals"), Marlow expresses skepticism. By the end, it is the Europeans whom Marlow views as criminal, and Marlow describes Kurtz's very soul as "unlawful."

- ○ ***Speech and silence.*** Initially, Western civilization is associated with speech (the expression of reason) and Africa with "dumb" silence. But by the end, the Europeans' speech is viewed as empty, absurd, and meaningless. Marlow remembers Kurtz as nothing more than "a voice." Conrad progressively identifies the whole of Western civilization with language that loses its power to mean anything: "all of them were so little more than voices . . . one immense jabber . . . without any kind of sense."

Moving from notes to thesis

Despite Conrad's intention to offer a critique of imperialism and racism, there are some problems with his strategy. Africa is represented through the collapse of the law as embodied in a European, but it is never allowed to speak for itself. The natives are always remote, and the entire critique is expressed from the vantage point of Western narratives (of the Enlightenment, of imperialism) experiencing their own breakdown rather than being genuinely subverted by an informed presentation of a native's vision. Perhaps these problems are a function of the racial and imperial frameworks within which Conrad worked. At any rate, a possible thesis might read something like this:

> This paper will argue that despite the overt condemnation of imperialism and racism by the narrator Marlow in Conrad's *Heart of Darkness*, this critique is undermined by the book's own presentation of race, by the ambivalence toward Kurtz on the part of Marlow the protagonist, and by Conrad's inability to allow Africans to speak for themselves.

If you wanted to go a little deeper, you could discuss the various racial discourses that circulated during the late nineteenth century, attempting to prove the superiority of Europeans over Africans, and how such discourses might have shaped Conrad's vision. Or you could compare Conrad's text with, say, Achebe's *Things Fall Apart* (1958), showing how Achebe is in a position (culturally and historically) to imbue Africans with their own perspective and interiority, whereas Conrad can never progress beyond treating them from the outside, as objects. Or you could explore how Conrad reduces Kurtz to a mere signifier and how his developing symbolism during the story enacts the collapse of the signifiers "Europe" and "civilization." All these approaches attempt to place the text in a larger, more global context that invokes other possible narratives of history and race.

PART SIX

WRITING ABOUT LITERATURE

CHAPTER 18

THE WRITING PROCESS

When you are asked to write about literature, remember that there are many ways of approaching a text. We've already encountered some of them. And there are different levels of literary analysis. For convenience, I have divided these levels into *frames*, a term taken from photography and film. The early parts of this book introduced the idea of three broad frames: theme–form–context. Analysis often starts by focusing on *what* a text says, its central idea, then considers *how* the text conveys this theme through its formal or stylistic features. But it's not always necessary to proceed in that order, and analyzing content and form are not two entirely separate enterprises; they are distinguished here only for the purpose of highlighting some of their main features. Also, an analysis may need to be set within the framework of the author's life, the literary and intellectual contexts of the author and the text, and the larger historical context. Plus, it might engage with issues of aesthetics, philosophy and politics, gender, class, and history.

STAGES OF THE WRITING PROCESS

Let's use William Blake's "The Tyger" (guidelines for analyzing this work as a lyric poem and for examining its meter can be found in chapters 5 and 8; also, see a deconstructive analysis of it in chapter 17). Here are three broad stages that a literary analysis should move through—although, again, they may overlap and not proceed in chronological order.

Understanding and defining your purpose

Why are you writing this essay? What kind of assignment have you been given? There are many ways of writing about literature, even at this initial level, which focuses primarily on the text. Your general purpose should determine what kinds of notes you make. If you make notes in categories relevant to your purpose, you are already on the way to writing an effective thesis that will provide the basis for organizing the rest of your paper.

Some of the most common assignments for writing about literary texts are listed below. If, as often happens, you are given an open assignment, you might decide, after initial exploration and reflection, that one of these formats would be the most appropriate for expressing your ideas.

- **Exposition** (discussion of the main themes of a text, the ways they are developed, and the form of the text). You might say that Blake's poem questions the justice of God through a series of questions voiced by a childlike narrator.

- **Comparison and contrast.** You could compare this poem with another one by Blake or a different author, perhaps from a different era.

- **Argument.** You could argue that the tiger represents the frightening conditions created by the industrial revolution, or that there is a contradiction between the poem's near-childish questioning and the theological importance of the issues it raises.

Later, we will examine how these different kinds of papers might be organized. But for now, you need to be clear about what you are trying to accomplish. And that purpose needs eventually to be expressed in a clear thesis statement.

Finding something to say

During the reading process you arrived at a sense of the poem's overall structure and development, as well as of the formal devices it uses. But you may still not have an opinion about the poem. If you are still unsure about what to say, here are some things to try:

- **Look for personal relevance.** Focus on some aspect of the poem that is relevant to your life. There may have been times when you thought the world was cruel, questioned God's justice, wondered why God allowed evil in the world. Or perhaps you think such thoughts are blasphemous and the poem makes you angry. Either way, you now have a strong motive to write.

- **Talk with friends.** Discuss the poem with a friend or relative. You might be surprised at how easily your ideas flow. Both Plato and Aristotle recognized that knowledge is "dialogic": it arises not in isolation but in dialogue or conversation, where we are exposed to other views and begin to see both the potential and the limitations of our own.

- **Read the critics.** Find and read a short essay on the poem by a literary critic. Inevitably, you'll find some things to disagree with, or at least to react to. Again, that is how our ideas take shape—in opposition to or interaction with someone else's views.

Organizing your notes and working out your perspective

Let's assume that after your conversations about and rereadings of the poem, you have worked out a **provisional thesis**, which could be something like this: "In this poem, the poet assumes the persona of a child to question the attributes of God and his creation." This is not yet detailed enough or precise enough to take you all the way through a paper, but it's an important starting point. It is a thesis because it is argumentative, taking a position or making a claim, so you can look back over your notes and find material to support it. You now need to refine it and create an outline for the paper. Here are some questions and observations that can help in that process:

1. How does "fearful symmetry" indicate the contradictory nature of God's creation?

2. How do the simple rhymes, repetitions, and diction create a childlike persona?

3. Why is the poem a series of questions, with no answers or explanations?

4. The process of creation is described mechanically, with God portrayed as a blacksmith. Is this a positive image of God, or a negative one? The images of "hammer," "chain," "furnace," and "anvil" don't seem particularly poetic or spiritual.

5. Perhaps the tiger's ferocity is used to project the even greater ferocity of its maker. The word "dare" is used several times, and "dread" is used of God's attributes three times.

6. Though it certainly seems as if a child is raising the questions, we might note that they are assertive and emphatic, as indicated by the rhythm.

7. The contrast of opposites—the lamb with the tiger—shows the paradox of God's creation. Does the poem thereby question the purpose of creation?

Depending on how you respond to these comments and questions, you could proceed in two ways. You could use your responses and notes to develop a thesis, which will provide the basis for organizing your paper. Or you could plan the entire paper first and then frame a thesis that reflects the paper's overall content. In either case, points 2, 3, and 6 could be grouped under a heading such as "persona and questioning," while points 1, 4, 5, and 7 could be grouped under a heading such as "the nature of God's creation." The points would then be arranged something like this:

Persona	God's Creation
Childlike: in content and form	Contradictory, contains opposites
Assertive, questioning	Mechanical
No answers given	Contains ferocity and evil
	Paradoxical

This very rough outline could structure the paper, which would be divided into two sections, according to the divisions above. But let's step back a bit to ask, What is the most basic point such a paper would be arguing? Perhaps it is that the entire poem is an implicit criticism of the nature of God. Taking this as the heart of our thesis, we can now add the other two dimensions, the attributes of the persona and the attributes of God's creation. The result might be something like this:

> In this paper, I will argue that William Blake's poem "The Tyger" offers an implicit criticism of the nature of God, questioning God's justice by (a) creating a childlike persona to ask very simple questions that are not answered, (b) describing the creative power of God in a mechanized way, and (c) highlighting the fact that God's creation is paradoxical, containing both good and evil.

One or two paragraphs could be devoted to each of the points made in this thesis. Again, it's worth stressing that there are many ways of looking at this poem.

GENERAL GUIDELINES

Once you have read the text carefully, following the steps listed below will help you to succeed in the writing process:

- Understanding the nature of the assignment
- Reading critically
- Organizing notes
- Working out a thesis
- Making an outline
- Writing a first draft
- Revising
- Editing
- Proofreading

Let's review these steps.

- **Understanding the nature of the assignment.** Are you required to compare and contrast, analyze an argument, or make an argument? Your answer to this question will govern the way in which you read the text and the kind of notes you'll make.

- **Reading critically.** As we saw in chapters 3 and 4, this involves

  ○ *Effective note-taking and gathering textual evidence.* First read the text quickly to gain an overview of the main themes and issues and the writer's style and approach. Before reading it again, be aware of what you are looking for. As you reread the text, underline or highlight what appear to be the most significant passages and words, making notes in the margins. Doing this will give you a firm grasp of the writer's main points and of the basic structure of the text.

  ○ *Using specific headings.* These provide the framework for taking notes. You can start with the headings "theme," "form," and "context." If you want to be more specific, you might use headings (for "The Tyger") like "Ways in which the narrator questions God" or "How does this poem use a persona?"

- **Organizing notes.** Using effective headings will take care of much of the work of organization. But the kind of assignment will determine how the notes should be ordered into a series of specific points. For example, a comparison-contrast paper demands a different kind of organization than an argumentative paper.

- **Working out a thesis.** After reviewing your notes, you need to work on your thesis. A good thesis will (a) give a clear statement of your **position** or **viewpoint** on the subject and (b) cite at least two or three **reasons** in support of your perspective. In general, a thesis statement need not be a single sentence; the more detailed and specific it is, the better the reader will be able to understand your position. It's hard to write a compelling, well-organized paper without a clear and detailed thesis.

- **Making an outline.** It's a good idea to make a one-page outline so that you can see the structure of your proposed paper at a glance. Below (in outline form!) are guidelines for creating an outline.

    I. **Introduction**
       A. Briefly introduce the topic of the paper. Avoid stating the obvious, such as "Dante was a writer of genius." Instead, use the introduction to provide **relevant** and **necessary** background for the topic under discussion.
       B. **Thesis statement.** State your overall **position**, citing reasons **A, B, C**, and so on in the order of their importance.

    II. **Argument and evidence to support reason A**
        A. Supporting statement 1.
        B. Supporting statement 2. (Each paragraph or set of related paragraphs should focus on **one** aspect of your argument. You can make this focus clear by including a **topic sentence** that indicates the **main theme or subject** of the paragraph.)

    III. **Argument and evidence to support reason B**
         A. Supporting statement 1.
         B. Supporting statement 2. (As you move from the first to second reason, you need a **transition** sentence, which helps the reader see the connection between them. This sentence might be incorporated into the topic sentence of the first paragraph about reason B, or it could be a separate sentence.)

    IV. **Argument and evidence to support reason C**
        A. Supporting statement 1.
        B. Supporting statement 2. (Again, you need a transition to introduce this section.)

    V. **Conclusion**
       A. Avoid simply restating your thesis.
       B. Highlight your most important point.
       C. Point to additional implications of the topic.
       D. End with a provocative question or with a striking general reflection.

Here's a somewhat fleshed-out outline for a paper on "The Tyger."

I. Introduction. Blake was writing in a period that was beginning to challenge traditional Christian conceptions of God. Blake was typical of the Romantics in having unorthodox religious beliefs, and we can see his questioning of God in "The Tyger."

Thesis Statement. Blake's poem offers an implicit criticism of the nature of God, questioning God's justice by (a) creating a childlike persona to ask simple questions that are not answered, (b) describing the creative power of God in a mechanized way, and (c) highlighting the fact that his creation is paradoxical, containing both good and evil.

II. First paragraph of body of paper [topic sentence]. Although "The Tyger" is written in a simple form and uses a childlike persona to ask apparently innocent questions, it raises troubling and unanswerable questions about the nature of God. It uses the tiger as an example of a ferocious creature. If the creature is so fierce, what must its creator be like? Adding to the narrator's innocence is the fact that his questions are addressed to the tiger, not to God.

III. Second paragraph [transition + topic sentence]. What reinforces the poet's unusual view of God is his description of him in mechanical terms. God is spoken of as a divine blacksmith who uses a "hammer," "chain," and "anvil." He is even said to have a "dread grasp," which dares to "clasp" the terrible tiger.

IV. Third paragraph [transition + topic sentence]. After offering these strange images of God, the narrator suggests that God is really a mystery, given that his creation is so paradoxical: "Did He who made the lamb make thee?" If the tiger represents ferocity or evil, while the lamb embodies goodness, how could the same God create both?

V. Conclusion. Though the poet uses an apparently naïve narrator, he raises some complex theological problems. What kind of God would allow violence in the world? If there is evil in the world, doesn't this cast doubt on the very existence of God?

- **Writing a first draft.** The outline on the opposite page shows how one paper might be organized. This outline would be expanded for the actual draft, which would use more examples from the poem. As you can see, if you have made thorough notes and organized them, writing your first draft will be much easier.

- **Revising.** Often, the difference between a good paper and a poor paper lies in the revision process. In revising your paper, you should consider the following elements:

  - *Thesis.* Is it clear? detailed? focused? Does it accurately reflect the content of your paper? If your answer to any of these questions is no, you need to revise the thesis.

  - *Paragraphs.* Does each paragraph focus on a single theme or point? Are the paragraphs in the right order (based on some logical criterion such as importance), or do they need to be rearranged?

  - *Paragraph structure.* Is the point of each paragraph clear? Is there a topic sentence, and is it adequately developed? Have you made adequate reference to the text being analyzed? Are any sentences unnecessary, irrelevant, or repetitive? Are there any that might be moved? Is any in need of clarification or amplification?

  - *Transitions.* Do these clearly show the connections between successive sections and paragraphs? Have you used the same transitions too often?

  - *Reasoning and evidence.* Do you offer clear reasons for the points you make? Are these reasons appropriately ordered, whether by importance or some other logical criterion? Do you also acknowledge that there may be other ways to interpret the evidence, but go on to show how your way is stronger? Is the basic point of each paragraph supported by reference to specific parts of the text? It's a good idea to use several brief quotations from the text, but you can also refer to specific passages without quoting them.

  - *Audience awareness.* Are your tone and language appropriate?

- **Editing.** Once you have revised your paper, you are ready to edit it. Here are a few guidelines:

    ○ *Sentence construction.* Is the meaning of every sentence clear? Are there any superfluous or repetitive words or phrases? Is the diction (word choice) appropriate?

    ○ *Mechanical problems.* Are there any common errors such as sentence fragments, comma splices, run-on sentences, dangling modifiers, or lack of agreement between subjects and verbs or between nouns and pronouns?

- **Proofreading.** You should read through your paper line by line to find and correct any errors. It's a good idea to read the paper backward, starting with the last sentence first. It's easy to miss typographical errors when focusing on a text's meaning.

BEYOND THE FIVE-PARAGRAPH ESSAY

The previous section describes a very basic and traditional way to organize a paper. Over the past few decades, however, teachers of writing—especially in colleges and universities—have moved beyond what is often called the "five-paragraph essay." They see this model as too restrictive, as pressuring students to fit their ideas into neat categories and thus to focus more on the organization of a paper rather than its content and the creative exploration of their ideas.

Remember, then, that the format given above is flexible and is only a starting point. In certain cases a thesis could make just one central assertion, and the rest of the paper might be devoted to justifying it. The body of the paper might then be divided according to the various reasons for that claim, with larger or smaller sections devoted to each reason as seems fit. Indeed, during the writing of your paper, you can continue to explore the ideas that you came up with during brainstorming, and can modify the format above accordingly. For example, you might find that one reason far outweighs the others; in this case, you would devote most of your paper to that reason and the evidence for it. Alternatively, you might begin by gathering evidence, which could then suggest to you a thesis. If you begin by making a claim and find that the evidence runs counter to it, you will need to modify your thesis or "stand" (a term favored by some writing instructors).

Sometimes a thesis could be an entire paragraph long. Perhaps you are trying to prove not one point but several points, as is true of many academic papers. In such instances, your organization will be more complex. For example, if your topic is, say, "The Nature of Rudyard Kipling's Imperialist Views," you will want to clarify how your paper differs from existing works on the topic, what the scope of your analysis is, and what methods you will use. Here, your thesis might be that, contrary to widespread belief, Kipling's imperialist views are inconsistent and that, despite his commitment to British imperialism, his writings display sympathy for Indian customs and characters. You might also want to set Kipling's views within the context of European ideas about India prevailing during his lifetime. So you might modify the basic principles of organization into a pattern such as the following:

Thesis. Claim 1 Kipling's views are often oversimplified + **Claim 2** He strongly supports the British imperialist cause, while showing affection for Indian life + **Claim 3** His views must be understood in a broader European context, since they were influenced by those of imperialists such as Cecil Rhodes, who, like many, believed in British supremacy + **Methods** I will focus on Kipling's novels and his poem "The White Man's Burden."

Body paragraphs. Analysis of **evidence** and **reasoning** for each claim.

Conclusion. Rather than merely restating your thesis, you might consider the further implications of your study or examine how your study contributes to a deeper understanding of Kipling.

CHAPTER 19

SPECIFIC ASSIGNMENTS

L et's consider the most common kinds of writing assignments given in literature courses.

Exposition. This assignment asks you to present and explain a writer's views or the features of a literary trend or genre. For example, you may be asked, "What, according to Mary Wollstonecraft, were the main obstacles facing women in the late eighteenth century?" or "What stylistic devices does Harriet Beecher Stowe use to portray the horrors of slavery in *Uncle Tom's Cabin*?"

- **Comparison and contrast.** For this assignment, you could be required to contrast the critiques of capitalism offered by Karl Marx or Annie Besant with those offered by a literary figure such as Percy Bysshe Shelley, Charles Dickens, or Matthew Arnold. Or you might be asked to compare and contrast two views of imperialism, such as those of Joseph Conrad and Rudyard Kipling.

- **Argumentation.** This assignment will ask you to construct an argument concerning some aspect of a text or group of texts. You might argue, for example, that Blake's "The Tyger" is a revolutionary poem, gathering evidence from the poem itself and about the contexts of both the poem and the poet. Alternatively, you may be asked to evaluate the argument(s) of one or more writers. You may be required, for example, to assess Edmund Burke's arguments against the French Revolution or Thomas Paine's arguments supporting it, or the respective arguments for and against evolution by T. H. Huxley and Bishop Samuel Wilberforce.

There are no firm boundaries between these assignments; a paper **contrasting** the views of Burke and Paine will also consider the nature of their **arguments**; and it will, of course, require **explanation** of their views. Also, bear in mind that no matter what the assignment is, you are dealing with literature and must take into account its style or formal properties.

EXPOSITION

If you are asked to **expound on** or **summarize** or **explain** a text, you need to

- Identify and paraphrase (in your own words) the author's **thesis** or central argument. If the text is not argumentative in nature, try to work out what the author's **central point** or **purpose** is: What factors or circumstances motivated the author to write this piece? What is it attempting to achieve? To whom is it addressed?

- Identify the **major points** the author uses to support the thesis. Also make a note of any **illustrations** or **examples** that figure substantially in the text.

- Arrange these major points in the **order** they follow in the text. Try to figure out why the author chose that order.

- Paraphrase the author's **conclusion.**

- An expository paper might have the following format:

  Brief **introduction**, giving the background of the author and the text

Statement of the work's **thesis**

Brief statement of the text's **main points** and how they are **organized**

A **more detailed description** of each of these points

Commentary on the use of **examples**, **evidence**, and/or **reasoning**

Statement of the author's **conclusion**

COMPARISON AND CONTRAST

Comparison and contrast can be used for a number of purposes:

- To define or put into context a person, place, or event
- To argue that something is preferable to something else
- To help the reader understand a difficult or unfamiliar subject by referring to a familiar one

There are two basic ways to organize a comparison-and-contrast paper. If you are analyzing, for example, the views of two authors on the French Revolution, you could choose four aspects of that conflict and consider in turn the views of both writers on each aspect (the **point-by-point model**). Or you could examine one writer's views on all four aspects and then consider the other writer's views on those aspects (the **block model**). Whichever approach you choose, the **basis** and **purpose** of the comparison need to be made clear. Here are the basic stages in writing a comparison and contrast paper:

- After a first reading of the texts, decide which **aspects** of them you are going to compare and contrast.
- **List** these aspects and **arrange** them in order of importance.
- Read the texts again, **making notes** on the aspects you have chosen.
- Under a heading for each aspect, list **specific points** (with examples where possible).

- Work out a **detailed thesis**, which will indicate
  - the **purpose** of comparing the two texts
  - the broad **aspects** on which your comparison/contrast will focus
- Make an **outline**, which might take the following form:

  Introduction

  Thesis

  Aspects 1–4: discussion of these aspects in first text

  Aspects 1–4: discussion of these aspects in second text

  Conclusion

Alternatively, the outline might look like this:

  Introduction

  Thesis

  Aspect 1: discussion of this aspect in both texts

  Aspect 2: discussion of this aspect in both texts

  Aspect 3: discussion of this aspect in both texts

  Aspect 4: discussion of this aspect in both texts

  Conclusion

Once you have made an outline, you can follow the guidelines in chapter 18 for drafting, revising, editing, and proofreading.

ARGUMENT

Of the types of papers you may be required to write, **argument** papers are the most common and perhaps the most difficult. An effective argument typically contains the following elements:

- **Audience awareness.** In every paper that you write, and especially in an argument paper, you should be aware of **who** is being addressed. The nature of the audience will determine at what level you pitch your writing, whether and how you define terms, what strategies you deploy, and what general tone you use. If you're writing, say, about the value of literature, you can take a lot for granted on the part of your classmates or professor in a literature class. But if you're addressing high school students, many more things will need to be spelled out.

- **Thesis.** It's always a good idea to make your thesis as specific as possible. You should indicate your **position** clearly and give the **reasons** for it, in order of either increasing or decreasing importance depending on the order in which you will discuss them in the body of the paper itself.

- **Definitions.** If your argument draws on any terms your audience may find difficult or controversial, you must offer clear definitions of them. One approach is to state the **essence** or **distinctive qualities** of a term. For example, you might define a triangle as a plane figure composed of three straight lines. But the notion of "essence" is problematic in literary studies. For example, how would you define "gender"? For some terms, you'll need to offer a **stipulative** definition, which specifies precisely how *you* are using the term: "For the purposes of this argument, I will define 'world literature' as . . ." You can always use examples to clarify your definitions.

- **Reasoning** is conventionally divided into two categories:

  ○ *Inductive reasoning* entails observation of a number of **particular** cases, from which you form a **general** conclusion. If the premise is true, then the conclusion is **probably** true. For example, you could argue that the narrator in any story by Edgar Allan Poe is likely to be unreliable, since many of his stories have unreliable narrators.

  ○ *Deductive reasoning* is a form of argumentation in which a general rule is applied to a particular case, so that if the statements of the rule and the case are true, it is certain that the conclusion is true. For example, you might argue, "Killing is justified only in self-defense. Self-defense means acting to protect oneself from immediate danger. Oedipus was not in immediate danger when he killed King Laius. Therefore, Oedipus committed murder." Such deductive reasoning is relatively rare in writing about literature.

- **Evidence.** There are various ways of providing evidence for an argument:

  - ○ *Using examples.* If you were arguing that T. S. Eliot's "The Love Song of J. Alfred Prufrock" disparages women, you could point to numerous examples from the poem, such as the viewing of women as body parts ("the eyes that fix us," "arms that lie along a table") or the equation of women with "mermaids."

  - ○ *Using statistics.* Statistics can also be offered as evidence, though they are open to various interpretations. If you were writing a paper on the reception of Shakespeare over the centuries or the increase in the reading public for literature in the nineteenth century, you could cite attendance figures for play performances or circulation figures for magazines and journals.

- **Refutation/accommodation of counterarguments.** You can't simply assume that your arguments will convince people who don't agree with your position. You need to look at the major arguments against that position and show their weaknesses. You might even make your case more credible by conceding the value of part of an opposing argument. For example, if you are arguing that Oedipus does not deserve his punishment and that he is a victim of a fate beyond his control, you still need to acknowledge that he is impulsive, headstrong, and responsible for his choices.

Evaluating the Arguments of Others

In literature courses, students may be asked to evaluate the argument of an author or a text, or a to compare and contrast two arguments. For such assignments, here are a few steps to take:

- Read through the text(s) once to get a sense of the author's overall thesis and the specific points he or she is making.

- Reread the text closely, looking for the author's **reasoning** and **evidence**. List, in order of importance, the reasons and evidence offered. Are there contradictions or inconsistencies in the reasoning? Is the evidence appropriate and substantial?

- Ask yourself whether the text overlooks any **counterarguments** or **evidence** that might weaken the author's case.

- Ask yourself what the author's **assumptions** are. Are they stated or unstated? Are they justified?

- Decide what your attitude is toward the author's argument. Use the information obtained in the steps above to make a list of its strengths and weaknesses.

- Organize these strengths and weaknesses according to the following categories: **assumptions, reasoning, use of evidence, refutation and accommodation of counterarguments, awareness of audience**.

- Draft a **thesis**, along the lines of "The author's argument for X is generally sound with respect to A, B, and C, but it is unpersuasive about D, E, and F."

- You are now in a position to make an **outline** for your paper, perhaps in the following format:

    Introduction: brief identification of the issues in question

    Thesis: a clear and detailed statement of your evaluation of the author's argument

    Part 1: evaluation of the author's **first point** in terms of the categories given above (assumptions, evidence, reasoning, treatment of counterarguments, awareness of audience)

    Part 2: evaluation of the author's **second point**

    Part 3: evaluation of the author's **third point**

    Conclusion: a statement of the general significance of the argument and the author's success or failure in presenting it

Alternatively, the outline could look like this:

Introduction

Thesis

Part 1: evaluation of the author's **assumptions**

Part 2: evaluation of the author's use of **reasoning**

Part 3: evaluation of the author's use of **evidence**

Part 4: evaluation of the author's treatment of **counterarguments**

Part 5: evaluation of the author's **audience awareness**

Conclusion

You can now follow the usual procedures for drafting, revising, and editing.

JOURNAL WRITING

Many instructors ask students to keep a journal in addition to doing formal writing assignments. Informal writing gives you a chance to experiment with your ideas and expressions and to develop ease in your work. But there are other good reasons for keeping a journal.

Reading is only the beginning of the learning process. We learn more and remember more when we express our thoughts in writing. Writing about an issue actively engages us in our own learning and enables us to reflect on the material covered, to clarify our thoughts about it, and to ask questions. If we merely read a text, we often will forget most of what we have read; writing about it reinforces and consolidates our learning.

It's a good idea to write your journal entry before coming to class. If you have tried to understand a text and have worked out your ideas about it through writing about it, you will benefit more from class discussion. There you'll be exposed to other perspectives, you'll see the limitations of your own views, and you'll be in a position to ask good questions about whatever you did not understand. If you write your entry after class, don't just repeat what was said in discussion but express your own views, supporting them with detailed references to the text.

If your instructor requires you to write on most of the texts you study, by the end of the course you'll have a journal of considerable length. This will be a significant achievement and a concrete manifestation of your learning throughout the semester. Many institutions ask students to prepare an electronic portfolio of their best work by the time they graduate. The result is a collection that students can use to impress a prospective employer, and a good journal can be an important part of the portfolio.

Requirements for what should be in the journal will vary according to the instructor and the class. Some instructors may require a one-page entry for each text you read. This is your chance to show the instructor that you have read the text carefully and have thought about it.

What should you write about?

First, here are some things that it would be better not to write in your journal (unless specifically instructed to do so):

- A summary of the text

- An entry that reproduces class discussion

- An entry that focuses on information about the author's life rather than on the text

Instead, keep these points in mind:

- Your journal entry will be more impressive if it is based primarily on the text and conducts a close analysis of it, citing page numbers to demonstrate that you have read it carefully.

- You don't need to use long quotations, but be sure to refer to several parts of the text.

- While a journal entry is not a formal essay, it is not a mere "response" either.

Here are some questions you can ask about **poetry**.

What is the basic theme of the poem? How is this articulated?

What oppositions or contrasts structure the poem?

What formal devices are used in the poem?

Does the poem depend on any central symbols, metaphors, or images?

Does the poem appeal primarily to the intellect, or to emotion?

And here are some for **fiction**.

What is the central theme of the story?

How is this theme developed through the plot?

Who are the central characters, and what are their attributes?

How do details contribute to the portrayal of a given character?

Is there a central conflict in the story, between characters or perspectives?

What is the basic structure of the story?

What kind of narrator tells the story? Who is the intended audience?

What is the setting of the story? Why might it be significant?

And for **drama**.

How do the setting and stage directions frame the play as a whole? How do they frame individual acts or scenes?

What are the themes of the play?

Who are the main characters? How are they developed?

Is there a central conflict between characters or worldviews?

What is the plot? How does it structure the play? Conventionally, drama has been divided into exposition, rising action, climax or turning point, falling action (which includes the denouement or resolution), and conclusion (terms defined in chapter 5).

If you are able to see the play performed, what features strike you? Does the performance (gestures, movements, intonation) modify your understanding of the written text?

How does the performance engage the audience? What is the effect of the stage sets or arrangements? Do they reinforce the theme and characters and conflict?

In any single journal entry, of course, you won't be able to write about all these issues. Simply choose one theme, or one character, or another element of the text that interests you, and write about that.

CHAPTER 20

DOCUMENTATION
AND RESEARCH

When you join an academic community, you begin to have a voice in a large network of knowledge in which many people, both past and present, participate. Academic knowledge is a communal and collective affair, with each of us contributing. One way in which we keep track of who has contributed what is by documenting the sources of information or insights or perspectives. It's fine for writers to use the thoughts of other people and to build upon them or to disagree with them. But it's vital that we acknowledge their work, whether we find it in books or journal articles or on websites.

USING AND DOCUMENTING SOURCES

Here is a very brief guide to documenting the kinds of sources that you'll frequently use. There are a number of documentation systems, laid out in publications such as *The Chicago Manual of Style* (CMS), the most widely used authority in humanities publications; *Publications Manual of the American Psychological Association* (APA), dominant in the social sciences; and *MLA Handbook* (MLA). English majors are typically asked to use the MLA system, so that is what we follow here.

The four basic aspects of documentation are in-text citations, the works-cited list, the use of quotations, and the use of endnotes or footnotes. Let's consider each in turn

IN-TEXT CITATIONS

There are a number of ways to refer to sources within the text of a paper. MLA uses the "author-page" method. At the end of the sentence where the source material appears, include in parentheses the author's last name and the page number(s) of your quotation or of the material that you are paraphrasing or summarizing. Then include a complete reference to the book in the works-cited list. If the author's name has already appeared in the sentence, use just the page number(s) in parentheses.

> The main object of poetry should be to use "incidents and situations from common life" (Wordsworth 13).

> Wordsworth argued that the main object of poetry should be to use "incidents and situations from common life" (13).

> Wordsworth insisted that poetry should depict everyday situations (13).

THE WORKS-CITED PAGE

Here, the sources should be listed alphabetically, by last name of the author or first major word of the title if no author is identified in the source. Of the many kinds of sources, here are a few of the most common.

Book

Author's Last Name, First Name. *Title*. Publisher, Year of publication.

> Ferber, Michael. *Romanticism: A Very Short Introduction*. Oxford UP, 2010.

Journal Article

Author's Last Name, First Name. "Title." *Journal name*, volume number, issue number, year of publication, page number(s).

> Lentricchia, Frank. "Four Types of Nineteenth-Century Poetic." *Journal of Aesthetics and Art Criticism*, vol. 26, no. 3, 1968, pp. 351–56.

Magazine Article

Author's Last Name, First Name. "Title." *Periodical name*, **day month year of publication, page number(s).**

Gopnik, Adam. "American Prophet: The Gifts of Frederick Douglass." *The New Yorker*, 15 Oct. 2018, pp. 76–82.

Electronic Sources

Incorporate as many of the following features as are available:

Author's Last Name, First Name. "Title of Article." *Source name,* **Publisher, date of publication, location (page numbers and URL, DOI, or permalink). Date of access.**

Loeffelholz, Mary. "International Women's Day: Spotlight on Emily Dickinson." *Fifteen EightyFour: Academic Perspectives from Cambridge University Press,* 10 Mar. 2017, www.cambridgeblog.org /2017/03/international-womens-day-spotlight-on-emily -dickinson. Accessed 31 Oct. 2018.

Rasch, Emily. *"Death as a Symbol of Feminism in the Works of Emily Dickinson."Medium*, 5 Dec. 2017, medium.com/@emilyrasch /death-as-a-symbol-of-feminism-in-the-works-of-emily -dickinson-c6f0959029bb. Accessed 31 Oct. 2018

Help in documenting the many other kinds of sources you may use can be found in the *MLA Handbook*, Eighth Edition, and on websites, including the Purdue Owl and the MLA Style Center. These sites contain sample works-cited pages and sample MLA-style papers.

QUOTATIONS

When using **short prose quotations** (four lines or fewer) in your paper, put double quotation marks around the quoted words and place punctuation after the parenthetical reference to the source.

The United States seems to be "the only country" where world literature is taught (D'haen 93).

According to some critics, "the only country" where world literature is taught is the United States (D'haen 93), though others disagree.

> According to Theo D'haen, the United States appears to be "the only country" where world literature is taught (93).

When quoting **more than four lines of prose**, set off the entire quotation as a freestanding block of text *without* quotation marks; indent the block a half-inch from the left margin; indent the first line of each subsequent paragraph if multiple paragraphs are quoted; and place end punctuation *before* the parenthetical documentation of the source.

> Here is an example, a powerful moment in Harriet Jacobs's slave narrative where her feelings toward her master crystallize:
>
> > For my master, whose restless, craving, vicious nature roved about day and night, seeking whom to devour, had just left me, with stinging, scorching words; words that scathed ear and brain like fire. O, how I despised him! I thought how glad I should be, if some day when he walked the earth, it would open and swallow him up, and disencumber the world of a plague.
> >
> > When he told me that I was made for his use, made to obey his command in *every* thing; that I was nothing but a slave, whose will must and should surrender to his, never before had my puny arm felt half so strong. (Jacobs 18)

When quoting **three lines or fewer of poetry**, run the quotation into the main text, and enclose it in double quotation marks; indicate line breaks with a forward slash (/), inserting a space before and after the slash; include line numbers in parentheses; and place punctuation *after* the parentheses.

> Audre Lorde's "Love Poem" concludes, "I swing out over the earth / over and over / again" (18–20).

When quoting **more than three lines of poetry**, set if off as a freestanding block of text and keep formatting as close to the original as possible.

> In her poem "The First Book," Rita Dove issues a powerful invitation to the act of reading:
>
> > Sure, it's hard to get started;
> > remember learning to use
> > knife and fork? Dig in:

You'll never reach bottom.
It's not like it's the end of the world—
just the world as you think
you know it. (8–14)

ENDNOTES AND FOOTNOTES

MLA discourages extensive use of explanotary notes, mainly because they can be distracting, but does allow endnotes or footnotes for **bibliographic purposes**—that is, to recommend other publications to the reader.

1. For a comprehensive treatment of music in the work of Kafka, see Hargraves (167–93).

2. For Arnold's views on the Incarnation, see *Literature and Dogma* (177–95).

3. For contrasting views on the question of racism, see Bernasconi (32–34) and McCarney (34–37).

Endnotes and footnotes are indicated by superscript arabic numbers, usually placed at the end of a clause or sentence. The notes are numbered consecutively throughout the text.

Several scholars have argued that Yeats was not strictly a modernist.[6]

Elaine Scarry ventured beyond the academic sphere to address political issues,[7] a gesture that was welcomed by many.

THE RESEARCH PAPER

One of the major ways that you can contribute to an academic community is by writing a research paper. In the process of doing research and composing your text, you find out what other people have said on a particular topic and then add your own voice or perspective to that broader conversation.

FINDING A TOPIC AND NARROWING IT DOWN

As is true whenever you analyze a text, you first need to find *your* connection with the literary text you're writing about, *your* point of entry into the conversation about it.

What is it about the text that interests you?

What do you find problematic or disturbing in it?

What unanswered questions do you have about it?

Let's say that one of the things that interests you is Shakespeare's portrayal of women. You might want to make your broad topic something like "Gender in Shakespeare."

Once you've settled on a broad topic, there are at least two ways of arriving at a focused topic: by narrowing the range of your inquiry—for example, by focusing on just one or two plays by Shakespeare, or even just a part of one play; or by formulating a particular question that you would like to address. Your answer to your question will develop into a specific position or thesis.

CONDUCTING LIBRARY RESEARCH

Although it may be tempting to begin your research on the internet, try to resist doing so. College and university libraries have electronic resources that are usually more reliable than what can be found on the web. Here are the essential steps you need to take:

- **Take an online library tutorial.** Nearly all libraries offer this service, which will provide an overview of the library's resources and where to find them. The library's main webpage has useful links to help you search for many kinds of information in many places, including books, journals, indexes, databases, audio and video resources, encyclopedias, dictionaries, research guides, and the library catalogue.

- **Take a library tour.** If a tour has not already been arranged for your class, ask your teacher to do so or ask a librarian to give you an individual tour. Librarians have the expertise to direct you to appropriate sources for your research.

- **Do some exploratory research.** You can start by consulting encyclopedias and handbooks to get an overview of your topic. General online encyclopedias like the *Britannica* and more specialized online reference works, such as those found in the Literature Online (LION) database, can provide background on Shakespeare and the characters in his plays.

- **Conduct research in depth.** Encyclopedias and bibliographies, whether printed or online, will help you narrow the focus of your research. For example, Wikipedia has a long entry on the history of Ophelia in stage productions of *Hamlet*. Such information could give you ideas for further, more specialized research.

  - You can now search the library catalogue for books and articles, by book title, by author, or by subject or keyword. Here, you could try search terms such as "Shakespeare and gender" or "women in Shakespeare."

  - You can also search the *MLA International Bibliography*, the *Annual Bibliography of English Language and Literature* (ABELL), the *World Shakespeare Bibliography*, and, more generally, the Humanities Index and Academic Search Premier. These resources contain listings and links for books and peer-reviewed articles (and, in the case of the MLA's database, book chapters).

  - Databases like LION and the Gale Literature Resource Center will also lead to articles, as well as other reference material.

  - Some databases allow searches by subject headings. Using "Shakespeare" or "Hamlet" or "Ophelia" as a subject heading rather than as a keyword narrows down the number of results considerably.

RESEARCHING ON THE INTERNET

Internet research can certainly complement the research you do in the library, especially since there are many online reference tools useful for literature papers. For example, numerous editions of classic texts, such as Freud's complete works or translations of the Bible, are available in searchable formats. Wikipedia (and the bibliographies it provides) can be helpful, but make sure that you use information that is supported by citations of reputable sources. Here are some tips for working on the internet:

- Stay focused and resist the many distractions—ads, links, irrelevant information.

- Try to assess the validity of any information you find. A number of scholars have come up with lists of criteria that can help in that assessment: Who is the author of the site? Who published it? Does it refer to other sources? Is the information verifiable? Is it up-to-date?*

Useful resources in addition to those already mentioned include

- **Google Scholar.** Using this search engine, you can locate scholarly resources through a keyword search; if you're logged in to your library's system, you'll have access to a larger number of complete texts.

- **Google Books.** The search engine for Google Books gives access to many books, in full or in part; in some cases, you can look over the table of contents, search for specific terms, and sample material.

- **Amazon.com.** often allows access to the contents and substantial portions of a book.

- **The Online Books Page.** This index of ebooks available on the internet, hosted by the University of Pennsylvania library, includes works in the Gutenberg Project—the oldest digital library, with a large collection of ebooks that can be read online or downloaded.

- **Bartleby.com.** A website that offers some fee-based services but also provides free access to a wide range of texts, including Shakespeare, the King James Bible, poetry anthologies, and classic works of fiction.

* See, for example, "The CRAP Test," developed by Molly Beestrum, at ccconline.libguides
.com/craptest, and "Five Criteria for Evaluating Web Pages," which can be accessed from
that page.

- **Archive.com.** A nonprofit digital library that contains millions of books not included in the Online Book Page listings.

WRITING THE PAPER

- **Organizing research findings.** Let's say that you've come up with about eight relevant sources, five books and three articles. Remember, at this stage you are only skimming resources, not reading in depth. The idea is to get a sense of what is out there and to find material that will help you develop your own perspective. To that end, make brief notes as you

  - Look at the *table of contents* of each book and see if any chapters are relevant to your project.

  - Look at the *abstract* of each article and see if it contains anything of interest.

  - Skim through each book's *preface*, which often gives an overview of what the book covers.

  - Look at the *bibliography* of each book, to see if there are additional important sources that you have missed.

- **Making an annotated bibliography.** Once you've got a list of material directly relevant to your project, you're ready to make an annotated bibliography, using either your computer or index cards. You can arrange the bibliography in a number of ways:

  - By author: simply summarize the perspective of each author and the material he or she deals with.

  - By perspective: if there is a conflict of opinion (some critics might defend Shakespeare's treatment of women, while others condemn it), make a list of the authors on either side of the conflict, stating what their perspectives are.

  - By chronology or school: organize the various sources by when they were produced or by the affiliation of their author (feminist, liberal-humanist, structuralist, etc.).

- **Determining the focus and thesis of your paper.** You have now reached the stage at which you can decide what the focus of your paper will be and what position you're going to take.

  - Reread your **primary sources** (the actual texts of Shakespeare you've selected) in light of what your **secondary sources** (the criticism written *about* the primary texts) say, as recorded in your notes.

  - Then decide what your basic thesis is going to be and how you are going to organize your paper.

Let's say your thesis is something like this:

In *Hamlet*, Shakespeare diminishes the female characters. By giving Gertrude and Ophelia less time onstage and minimal lines of dialogue, he does not allow their characters to be fully formed or represented, and he fails to articulate their perspectives. However, in this failure, he is effectively complying with the conventions of his age.

- **Organizing and drafting an outline of your paper.** There are several ways to organize a paper on the basis of the thesis above. Here's one way:

  - **Introduction.** Give a brief overview of what feminist criticism in general has said about *Hamlet*. Then introduce *your* main concern about Shakespeare's treatment of women, and state your **thesis**. Also state how you will organize your paper: "This paper will first consider . . . then examine . . . and will conclude with . . ." It will be useful to divide the paper into at least three sections, using a heading for each, such as

    Shakespeare's Presentation of Ophelia

    Shakespeare's Silencing of Ophelia

    Conditions of Women in Shakespeare's Time and How They Were Represented

All of this will give the reader a clear sense of what you're arguing and what to expect.

- **Body of paper, part 1.** Analyze Shakespeare's presentation of Ophelia, focusing on one or two scenes. You might also refer to one or two performances of these scenes on YouTube or elsewhere. At this point, you can include the insights of any critics—your secondary sources—that you think illuminate your argument.

- **Body of paper, part 2.** Examine the ways in which Shakespeare's presentation of Ophelia effectively silences her and fails to infuse her with any genuine subjectivity. Critics have talked at length about Hamlet's subjectivity and his "inner" nature. But what about Ophelia? We are denied access to her view of the world. Again, refer to your secondary sources. Do they support or contradict what you say?

- **Body of paper, part 3.** Explain the basic conditions of women's lives in Shakespeare's time and how women were represented in plays and other texts. Do those conditions and representations justify Shakespeare's treatment of women in his plays? The secondary sources will disagree on this issue, so here is the place to state the most influential opinions. There is a broad range of feminist criticism available on Shakespeare, but it may be useful to look at Marxist and New Historicist readings as well.

- **Conclusion.** Without simply repeating your thesis, you can situate your claim in a context of overall honest disagreement: "While I have argued that . . . , I acknowledge that . . . , and we need to consider certain aspects of Shakespeare's contemporary situation."

Of course, you could organize your paper differently. You could begin, for example, by outlining the conditions of women's lives in Shakespeare's time or by pointing to a central and enduring conflict in Shakespeare criticism. Or you could contrast the portrayal of Ophelia with that of Hamlet. What is important is that you (a) have a clear and detailed thesis, (b) indicate the organization of your paper, and (c) integrate secondary sources into your argument—as making points that either support your claims or need to be countered.

APPENDIX: JOINING AN ACADEMIC COMMUNITY

When you join any community, it's important to learn its conventions and etiquette. Here are a few simple—but important—reminders of what makes for positive behavior in most academic environments. You will always create a good impression by arriving early (or on time!) for class and a bad impression by arriving late. If you have to miss a class, be sure to let your instructor know in advance. When you email your instructor, be courteous (of course!) and always address her as she prefers (usually as Professor or Dr.).

It's a good idea to sit near the front of the classroom or lecture hall. During class, try to participate actively, by showing interest in what your teacher and classmates have to say, by asking questions, and by volunteering answers. If you're unclear about an assignment or any aspect of your coursework, ask your teacher for clarification. In a large lecture course, the leader of your discussion section should be able to help you. But try to have some contact with your instructor as well, so that she knows who you are and is aware of your interest in the subject.

Giving Effective Presentations

Classes today tend to be very interactive: instead of the instructor simply lecturing slide students take notes, students are encouraged to play an active role in their learning. Often they are required to give one or more class presentations, either alone or with a few peers. The assignment could be to offer an introduction to a certain poet or writer or to delve deeply into some aspect of a writer's work. Here are some tips for giving presentations:

- Avoid simply reading, whether from a printed text or from a Power-Point slide. You should know your subject well enough that you only need a list of bullet points on an index card or two to remind you of the topics you need to cover. If you use PowerPoint, don't make the slides too detailed—three or four points per slide is enough. Again, rather than reading these, talk a little about each point.

- Be sure to talk *to* the class, making eye contact with various people and addressing the audience directly. Doing so makes listeners feel engaged. And a little humor never hurts.

- Try to ask a few questions of your audience, *eliciting* rather than simply *stating* information.

- Ask questions about topics that genuinely puzzle you. Doing so gives you a good chance of having a stimulating discussion with your classmates.

Learning how to give good classroom presentations can help prepare you for professional life, where you may well have to present material to co-workers, to people from other companies, or to the general public.

Using Digital Media and YouTube

It's a good idea to remain aware of developments in digital media, as long as you recognize the need to evaluate your sources and their validity. It's also worth knowing about the vast array of resources on YouTube, including

- **Lectures.** Many reputable institutions have posted lectures on a huge variety of topics. For example, a Yale University series offers introductions to literary theory, modern poetry, ancient Greek history, the Old Testament, and deconstruction.

- **Dramas.** If you are studying a play, seeing it perfomed will enhance your understanding of it. YouTube even makes it possible to compare several enactments of an entire play or a particular scene.

- **Guides.** Help is available on many subjects, including how to use the Gale Literature Resource Center, how to write research papers, and how to conduct online research.

- **Materials on individual authors.** YouTube offerings include biographies, interviews, and readings of authors' works (by themselves or others). It's always worth listening to poems read aloud.

Online and Blended Courses

Online courses provide scheduling flexibility, do away with the need for travel, and often allow students to work at their own pace. Many instructors prefer to teach blended, or hybrid, courses, which supplement conventional classroom teaching with digital resources. In fact, most courses today are web-facilitated in some way.

Online and blended courses use course management systems such as Blackboard, Sakai, and Moodle—virtual spaces that let instructors post lectures, notes, videos, and links to other audio or visual resources. They also contain bulletin boards, chat rooms, discussion threads, wikis, and blogs—all of which make it possible for students to work collaboratively. The following tips can help if you're in an online or blended course:

- **Discipline.** To succeed in an online course, you will need good work habits and a commitment to studying independently. You must go online regularly and be alert for announcements by and emails from the instructor.

- **Syllabus.** Read the syllabus carefully and make sure that you understand not only the assignments but the overall timetable. Students in an online course need to be especially conscious of meeting deadlines for written work and of making contributions to chat rooms and blogs. If you have questions about due dates or requirements, email your instructor as soon as you can.

- **Construction of your online self.** Remember that just as your teacher will be constructing this course and her personality online, so too must you construct *your* online self. This will be your only identity, as far as your teacher and fellow students are concerned. Be sure that your online self is prompt, diligent, polite, responsive, and articulate.

- **Interaction with instructor and other students.** One of the most important factors in an online class is the creation of a cohesive online learning community. Try to participate fully in all class activities.

- **Collaboration.** Many online and blended courses require students to collaborate. Try to take a leadership role, reaching out to other students and encouraging them to offer their ideas in shared projects.

- **Responding to the work of other students.** In chat rooms and discussion threads, it's not helpful to merely tell other students that you "really like" their points. To advance the discussion, try to make more constructive comments. You could say, for example, "Could you please explain the basis of your opinion?"; or "While I see why you said this, I think one could also argue that . . ."; or "I think you're right, because . . ." (and provide a new piece of evidence). There is nothing wrong with disagreeing with someone else's point, as long as you are respectful. In fact, this is how we arrive at knowledge—through collaboration, sharing opinions, and discussing the strengths and limitations of any given perspective.

- **Listening to audio or visual lectures.** If your instructor posts a lecture, be sure to listen to or watch it carefully. It will likely be only several minutes long, and it will offer the instructor's insights into what is important in a text or advice about how you should study it.

As is true of any class, you'll take from an online course what you put into it. If you work hard and participate fully, you'll find it to be a rewarding experience.

SELECTED
BIBLIOGRAPHY

English Studies and Literary Theory

Bertens, Hans. *Literary Theory: The Basics*. Oxford: Routledge, 2014.
  A succinct and readable guide, with clear explanations.
Eagleton, Terry. *Literary Theory: An Introduction*. Anniversary [3rd] ed. U
  of Minnesota P, 2008.
  An accessible overview of the rise of English studies.
McComiskey, Bruce, ed. *English Studies: An Introduction to the Discipline(s)*.
  National Council of Teachers of English, 2006.
  Analysis by a number of scholars of the content and role of various
  fields of English studies, including literature, criticism, critical
  theory, creative writing, and cultural studies.

Writing about Literature

Brannon, Lil, Sally Griffin, Karen Hagg, Tony Iannone, Cynthia Urbanski,
  and Shana Woodward. *Thinking Out Loud on Paper: The Student Day-
  book as a Tool to Foster Learning*. Heinemann, 2008.
  A guide to the techniques and potential of informal writing.

Graff, Gerald, and Cathy Birkenstein. *"They Say / I Say": The Moves That Matter in Academic Writing.* 4th ed. W. W. Norton, 2018.
A best-selling work that demystifies academic writing and includes a chapter on writing about literature.

Genre

Bawarshi, Anis S., and Mary Jo Reiff. *Genre: An Introduction to History, Theory, Research, and Pedagogy.* Parlor, 2010.
A historical overview of genre in various fields and how it has changed.
Boland, Eavan, and Mark Strand, eds. *The Making of a Poem: A Norton Anthology of Poetic Forms.* W. W. Norton, 2001.
An introduction to the genres of poetry by two leading contemporary poets.
Dewdney, Andrew, and Peter Ride. *The Digital Media Handbook.* 2nd ed. Routledge, 2014.
A guide to the history and theory of digital media, with analyses of important debates.
Friedman, Lester, David Desser, Sarah Kozloff, Martha Nochimson, and Stephen Prince. *An Introduction to Film Genres.* W. W. Norton, 2013.
An extremely accessible overview.

Figures of Speech and Literary Terms

Cuddon, J. A. *Dictionary of Literary Terms and Literary Theory.* 5th ed. Rev. M. A. R. Habib. Wiley-Blackwell, 2013.
A comprehensive, updated resource.
Hamilton, Sharon. *Essential Literary Terms: A Brief Norton Guide with Exercises.* 2nd ed. W. W. Norton, 2016.
An easy-to-use guide, with helpful exercises.

Game Studies (Ludology)

Mäyrä, Frans. *An Introduction to Game Studies: Games in Culture.* Sage, 2008.
An overview of the history, definition, structure, and cultural significance of computer and video games.

Poole, Stephen. *Trigger Happy: Videogames and the Entertainment Revolution.* Arcade Publishing, 2000.
> An investigation into what video games share with other art forms such as film and literature.

———. *Trigger Happy 2.0: The Art and Politics of Videogames.* Amazon Digital Services, 2013.
> On the cultural and political assumptions encoded in video games.

Prosody

Fussell, Paul. *Poetic Meter and Poetic Form.* Rev. ed. McGraw-Hill, 1979.
> An excellent introduction to traditional forms.

Pinsky, Robert. *The Sounds of Poetry: A Brief Guide.* Farrar, Straus and Giroux, 1998.
> On the hearing of poetry as an act that engages the entire body.

Histories of Literature and Criticism

Habib, M. A. R. *Literary Criticism from Plato to the Present: An Introduction.* Wiley-Blackwell, 2011.
> An overview of the various periods of literary criticism and theory.

Lees, Clare A., et al. *The New Cambridge History of English Literature.* 7 vols. Cambridge UP, 2013.
> From the end of the Roman Empire through the twentieth century.

Nisbet, H. B., and Claude Rawson, general eds. *The Cambridge History of Literary Criticism.* 9 vols. Cambridge UP, 1989–2013.
> From the classical period through the twentieth century.

Ruland, Richard, and Malcolm Bradbury. *From Puritanism to Postmodernism: A History of American Literature.* Routledge, 1991.
> A readable account, with attention to religious and cultural contexts.

World Literature

Casanova, Pascale. *The World Republic of Letters.* Trans. M. B. DeBevoise. Harvard UP, 2004.
> An examination of the notion of world literature in economic and ideological contexts.

Damrosch, David. *What Is World Literature?* Princeton UP, 2003.
A pioneering attempt to define world literature.

Research Papers and Documentation

Lester, James D. *Writing Research Papers: A Complete Guide.* Pearson, 2014.
A more detailed guide than the MLA publications cited below.
MLA Handbook. 8th ed. Modern Language Association, 2016.
The standard text for guidelines on documentation in MLA style.
MLA Handbook for Writers of Research Papers. 7th ed. Modern Language Association, 2009.
A guide to both research and MLA documentation.
Turabian, Kate L. *A Manual for Writers of Research Papers, Theses, and Dissertations: Chicago Style for Students and Researchers*. 9th ed. U of Chicago P, 2018.
A guide to the style (Chicago) used by most scholars and students in the humanities.

Online Courses

Van Ness, Richard J., and Steven B. McIntosh. *How to Succeed with Online Learning: Techniques That Work.* BookSurge.com, 2009.
A thorough guide to coping in an online learning environment.

CREDITS

Amichai, Yehuda: "An Arab Shepherd Is Searching for His Goat on Mount Zion" from THE SELECTED POETRY OF YEHUDA AMICHAI, NEWLY REVISED AND EXPANDED EDITION, edited and translated by Chana Bloch and Stephen Mitchell. © 1986, 1996 by Chana Bloch and Stephen Mitchell. Reprinted by permission of University of California Press.

Bishop, Elizabeth: "One Art" from POEMS by Elizabeth Bishop. Published by Chatto & Windus. Copyright © 2011 by The Alice H. Methfessel Trust. Publisher's Note and compilation copyright © 2011 by Farrar, Straus and Giroux. Reprinted by permission of The Random House Group Limited and Farrar, Straus and Giroux.

Brooks, Gwendolyn: "We Real Cool" from THE BEAN EATERS by Gwendolyn Brooks. Reprinted by consent of Brooks Permissions.

Dove, Rita: Excerpt from "The First Book," originally published in THE LANGUAGE OF LIFE, ed. Bill Moyers. Doubleday and "Open it," bookmark and poster, commissioned by the American Library Association. © 1995 by Rita Dove. Reprinted by permission of the author.

Ingalls, Daniel H. H.: "At First Our Bodies Knew a Perfect Oneness," from AN ANTHOLOGY OF SANSKRIT COURT POETRY: VIDYĀKARA'S "SUBHĀṢITARATNAKOṢA," translated by Daniel H. H. Ingalls (Harvard

INDEX OF AUTHORS
AND WORKS

NOTE: This index includes most of the authors and works discussed in *Literary Studies*. For literary critics and theorists, see the subject index on pages 317–31.

INDEX